The SOUTH AFRICANS in ENGLAND
1894-1965

Compiled by
William A. Powell

Foreword by
H. E. Kent Durr

LIMLOW BOOKS

First published in Great Britain by
Limlow Books Limited
St Peter's Hill, Litlington, Royston SG8 0QF
1994

British Library Cataloguing-in-Publication Data.
A catalogue record for this book is available from the British Library.

ISBN 1 874524 10 6

Printed by Peartree Printers, Derby

Dedicated
to the following
who assisted greatly with the author's visit to South Africa

Dr. Ali Bacher
Margie and Denzil Bezuidenhout
Liz, Murray, Wesley and Dylan Morrison
Vicki, Paul and Alexandra Robins
Heather and Ossie Schoof
Adelé and John Harris
Helen and Tony Walker
Janine and Lyndall de Nyscchen
Reena Batra and Shannon Whateley

CONTENTS

FOREWORD

As a cricket enthusiast, I count it a very great privilege to write a foreword to this book, which forms a very special part of the inspiring tradition of cricket rivalry between South Africa and the sport's mother country. Cricket has been part of our lives since it was introduced to South Africa after the landing of the British Army in Durban in 1842, when the troops pitched not only their tents, but also raised their wickets on the far-flung shores of Natal. The game has had its up and downs and its struggles but has always managed to steadily attract and win people over to be a bridge builder to the world and between communities and individuals who make up South Africa. Always doing more than was asked of it, cricket can now truly claim to be South Africa's national summer sport.

Commenting on cricket's extraordinary "Timeless Test" played between South Africa and England at Durban in 1939 - which lasted for ten days and had to be abandoned as a draw to enable the English team to catch their steamer home Jim Swanton said : "It went on from BBC to AD." However, there have been several interruptions in the evolution of the game in South Africa; periods of division, periods characterised by turmoil, by strife, by war in Europe and Africa, and by politics... The Triangular Tournament between England, South Africa and Australia in 1912 was destined to become South Africa's last cricket tour to England for a decade. The outbreak of World War I effectively ended first-class cricket competition for nearly five years. It was not until 1924 that a South African cricket side led by Herby Taylor arrived in England. When the South African team led by another Herby, Herby Wade, toured England during the summer of 1935 they were not to know that another World War was imminent, and that this was to be the last South African tour to England until Alan Melville's tour in 1947.

We go back a long way and there have been amusing incidents. For example, during the third English tour to our shores in 1895, when Lord Hawke's touring side found themselves caught up in the Jameson Raid. Travelling to

Johannesburg as part of their itinerary, they were "ambushed" by a band of armed and very agitated Transvalers, who had mistaken them for followers of Dr. Leander Starr Jameson. However, on discovering that their prisoners were cricketers, the Boer Commando allowed them to proceed to their destination after Lord Hawke had presented them with a couple of bats. What a difference cricket makes!

Cricket in South Africa is playing a leading role in the building of a new sense of nationhood. Cricketers have come together in a wonderful way.

I know the cricketing world understands that South Africans are playing the game as never before!

I congratulate all concerned with this superb book.

H E KENT DURR
South African Ambassador
London

INTRODUCTION

For the first time since 1965 South Africa will tour the United Kingdom between June and August 1994. This will be the South Africans' fourteenth visit to these shores and will probably be the most significant since their initial Test tour in 1907.

Few cricket enthusiasts below the age of forty will have memories of the last South African tour and few of any age will readily recollect the performances of South African cricketers of the past and the outcome of the several Test Series in England between 1907 and 1965.

Significantly 1994 celebrates the centenary of the first tour to England of a representative South African team of cricketers.

Having been born only a year before the last South African tour it seemed appropriate for me to examine the previous thirteen tours to England from 1894 to 1965 and to record in a single volume for easy reference the detailed outcome of all the previous matches.

This book is a compilation of those tours with particular note of basic details, statistical match scores, records against opponents, grounds played at and historic illustrations.

The author made his first visit to South Africa in 1992 during the Friendship tour between South Africa and India and it is thanks to the support, kindness and interest of many South Africans that this book has evolved.

William A. Powell
Hemel Hempstead
April 1994

ACKNOWLEDGEMENTS

The author would like to thank the following who have assisted in a variety of ways in the preparation of this book including the use of illustrations other than those from the author's own collection:

Ambassador H E Kent Durr, Second Secretary H D Short, Dr. Ali Bacher, Bridget Sprague, Trevor Chesterfield, Murray Morrison, Paul Robins, Denzil Bezuidenhout, Janine de Nyscchen, Shannon Whateley, Tim Lamb, Jill and Vic Lewis, Peter Powell, Ken and John Lodge, Trevor Querk, Trevor Quelch, Ronald Harries, Driaan de la Guerre, Viktor Hergeth, John Keeling, Dr. Peter Johnson, Vivian Ward, Brian Bassano, Garth Lawler, Willie Coetzer, Tony Debenham and David Baggett.

KEY:

* against a player indicates captain.
* against a score indicates not out.
† against a player indicates the wicket-keeper.
‡ against a team name indicates that the match was not first-class

The First South African Team in the United Kingdom, 1894

Following the tours to South Africa by Major R. G. Wharton's and W. W. Read's teams it was decided to send a team to England in 1894.

A. B. Tancred, probably the finest player in the country at the time was prevented by his business commitments from making the trip. Another significant omission was that of J. H. Sinclair who at only eighteen was considered too young to make the trip — subsequently, he was to become one of the country's greatest players.

A relatively young team of 15 was selected with an average age of 25 years, led by wicket-keeper Herbert Castens, the Western Province captain and former South African rugby international.

Twenty-four games were to be played but no representative match, though 1894 was to prove a very wet summer and a substantial financial loss was suffered.

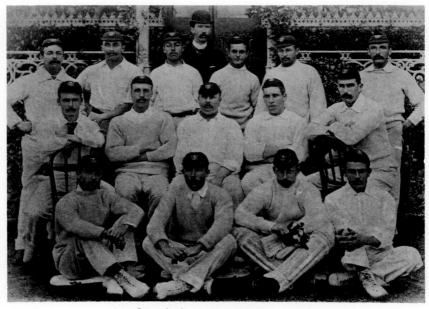

(standing at back) **Mr.W.V.Simkins** (Manager)

(standing) **D.C.Davey T.Routledge C.O.H.Sewell G.A.Rowe G.Glover C.H.Mills**

(sitting) **G.S.Kempis G Cripps H.H.Castens** (Captain) **C.L.Johnson A.W.Seccull**

(on ground) **F.Hearne J.Middleton E.A.Halliwell D.C.Parkin**

Touring party (15):

*† H H Castens (*Western Province/Oxford University*) (Captain)
Age 30. Right-handed opening batsman and wicket-keeper.

F Hearne (*Western Province*)
Age 36. Right-handed opening batsman, right-arm fast round-arm bowler and good cover point fielder.

A W Seccull (*Western Province*)
Age 26. Right-handed batsman, right-arm change bowler and fine short-slip fieldsman.

C H Mills (*Western Province*)
Age 27. Right-handed lower order batsman and right-arm medium pace bowler.

J Middleton (*Western Province*)
Age 29. Left-handed attacking lower order batsman and left-arm slow medium bowler.

G A Rowe (*Western Province*)
Age 20. Left-arm slow bowler and right-handed tail end batsman.

G Cripps (*Western Province*)
Age 29. Dashing right-handed batsman.

D C Parkin (*Eastern Province*)
Age 24. Right-arm round-arm bowler.

C O H Sewell (*Natal/Gloucestershire*)
Age 20. Right-handed hard hitting middle order batsman, right-arm slow bowler and brilliant off side fielder.

D C Davey (*Natal/Essex*)
Age 36. Forceful right-handed opening batsman.

E A Halliwell (*Transvaal*)
Age 30. Right-handed middle order batsman and wicket-keeper.

† T Routledge (*Transvaal*)
Age 26. Right-handed hard hitting batsman and reserve wicket-keeper.

C L Johnson (*Transvaal*)
Age 23. Right-handed batsman and right-arm bowler.

G S Kempis (*Transvaal*)
Age 23. Right-arm medium pace bowler and right-handed late order batsman.

G Glover (*Griqualand West*)
Age 24. Sound right-handed middle order batsman and right-arm slow bowler.

Manager: Mr. W V Simkins

Summary of all matches:
Played 24   Won 12   Lost 5   Drawn 7

First Match vs ‡ Lord Sheffield's XI played at Sheffield Park on 22 and 23 May. Lord Sheffield's XI 233 (Payne 43, B C V Wentworth 41, J Briggs 29, G A Rowe 8 for 52) and 6 for 0 beat South Africans 127 (T Routledge 50, A W Seccull 19, W A Humphreys 5 for 36) and 110 (C O H Sewell 30, E A Halliwell 20, J Briggs 5 for 39) by 10 wickets.

Second Match vs ‡ Hampshire played at County Cricket Ground, Northlands Road, Southampton on 25 and 26 May. Hampshire 408 (A J L Hill 109, C Robson 76, V A Barton 74, R Bencraft 55, C O H Sewell 4 for 46, A W Seccull 2 for 41) drew with South Africans 275 (C H Mills 64, C O H Sewell 46, A W Seccull 42, T Soar 4 for 50, A J L Hill 3 for 55) and 85 for 3 (T Routledge 32, G Cripps 31*).

Third Match vs ‡ Oxford University played at the University Parks, Oxford on 28, 29 and 30 May. South Africans 145 (T Routledge 65, C L Johnson 36, L C V Bathurst 8 for 40) and 73 for 1 (T Routledge 48*) drew with Oxford University 189 (G J Mordaunt 75, H D G Leveson-Gower 31, J Middleton 4 for 51).

Fourth Match vs ‡ Surrey played at Kennington Oval, London on 31 May, 1 and 2 June. Surrey 204 (C Baldwin 68, F C Holland 31*, J Middleton 7 for 45) beat South Africans 52 (G Cripps 18, D L A Jephson 5 for 18) and 146 (H H Castens 58, G Glover 41, A E Street 7 for 40) by an innings and 6 runs.

THE SOUTH AFRICAN CRICKET TEAM 1894

MR H. H. CASTENS
WESTERN PROVINCE

THE SOUTH AFRICAN CRICKET TEAM 1894

MR C. O. H. SEWELL
NATAL

Fifth Match vs ‡ M.C.C. and Ground played at Lord's Cricket Ground, London on 4 and 5 June. South Africans 126 (F Hearne 48, W G Grace 6 for 56) and 60 (E A Halliwell 21, W G Grace 6 for 37, W Mead 4 for 22) beat M.C.C. and Ground 103 (W G Grace 47, J Middleton 6 for 48, G A Rowe 4 for 10) and 72 (H Phillipson 33, C Hesseltine 20, J Middleton 6 for 35, G A Rowe 3 for 37) by 11 runs.

Sixth Match vs ‡ Leicestershire played at County Cricket Ground, Grace Road, Leicester on 11 and 12 June. South Africans 56 (G Cripps 8, A D Pougher 7 for 17, G Walton 3 for 18) and 43 for 3 (C O H Sewell 16, A D Pougher 2 for 19) beat Leicestershire 52 (W Tomlin 12, J Middleton 4 for 26, G A Rowe 4 for 25) and 46 (D Lorrimer 10, G A Rowe 5 for 22, J Middleton 4 for 22) by 7 wickets.

Seventh Match vs ‡ Chatham and District played at Chatham on 18 and 19 June. South Africans 122 (D C Davey 28, P Northcote 6 for 58) and 87 (T Routledge 52, P Northcote 6 for 23) beat Chatham and District 104 (P Northcote 42, J Middleton 7 for 60) and 100 (F M Atkins 27, C H Mills 5 for 28, J Middleton 4 for 44) by 5 runs.

Eighth Match vs ‡ Glamorganshire played at Arms Park, Cardiff on 22 and 23 June. South Africans 238 (A W Seccull 63, G Cripps 51*, A G Eldridge 4 for 61) and 32 for 0 (E A Halliwell 18*) beat Glamorganshire 139 (R B Sweet-Escott 50, J Donovan 33, G A Rowe 5 for 50) and 128 (J J Clark 34, G A Rowe 7 for 56) by 10 wickets.

THE SOUTH AFRICAN CRICKET TEAM 1894

C. MILLS
WESTERN PROVINCE

THE SOUTH AFRICAN CRICKET TEAM 1894

MR G. K. GLOVER
GRIQUALAND WEST

Ninth Match vs ‡ Somerset played at County Cricket Ground, Taunton on 25, 26 and 27 June. Somerset 319 (G Fowler 77, L C H Palairet 69, A E Clapp 66, Nichols 42, G Glover 2 for 37) and 238 for 1 (A E Clapp 84*, L C H Palairet 82, H T Stanley 61*) beat South Africans 176 (E A Halliwell 38*, G Glover 28, C O H Sewell 26, E J Tyler 4 for 57, G B Nichols 4 for 34) and 380 (C O H Sewell 170, G Cripps 54*, G B Nichols 4 for 102) by 9 wickets.

Tenth Match vs ‡ Gloucestershire played at Fry's County Cricket Ground, Bristol on 28, 29 and 30 June. Gloucestershire 301 (W G Grace (Senior) 129, H Wrathall 95, W G Grace (Junior) 33, G A Rowe 4 for 95, D Parkin 4 for 108) and 147 for 5 (R W Rice 35, E Henry 33, G Glover 3 for 24) beat South Africans 185 (F Hearne 56, D C Davey 49, W G Grace (Senior) 9 for 71) and 262 (E A Halliwell 110, F Hearne 104, F G Roberts 4 for 38, J J Ferris 3 for 28) by 5 wickets.

THE SOUTH AFRICAN CRICKET TEAM 1894

MR D. C. PARKIN
EASTERN PROVINCE

THE SOUTH AFRICAN CRICKET TEAM 1894

MR T. W. ROUTLEDGE
TRANSVAAL

Eleventh Match vs ‡ Sussex played at County Cricket Ground, Brighton on 2, 3 and 4 July. Sussex 278 (F W Marlow 75, G Bean 54, G Brann 47, A F Somerset 28, G H Arlington 26, C L Johnson 4 for 62) and 4 for 1 beat South Africans 71 (E A Halliwell 21, W A Humphreys 6 for 34) and 210 (C O H Sewell 52, T Routledge 49, E A Halliwell 48*, W A Humphreys 5 for 86, F Gutteridge 4 for 37) by 9 wickets.

Twelfth Match vs ‡ C W Wright's XI played at United Officer's Services Ground, Portsmouth on 5 and 6 July. C W Wright's XI 241 (N F Druce 54, K S Ranjitsinhji 53, P J T Henery 40, G Glover 3 for 68) and 284 for 7 (K S Ranjitsinhji 146*, C W Wright 36, G J V Weigall 31, C O H Sewell 2 for 43) drew with South Africans 281 (T Routledge 152, E A Halliwell 32, W Morgan 5 for 67).

Thirteenth Match vs ‡ Warwickshire played at Edgbaston Cricket Ground, Birmingham on 9, 10 and 11 July. Warwickshire 252 (A F A Lilley 60, W G Quaife 33, C L Johnson 3 for 40) drew with South Africans 147 (C O H Sewell 47, C H Mills 29, H J Pallett 5 for 25, J E Shilton 4 for 53) and 88 for 4 (F Hearne 35, S Santall 1 for 17).

Fourteenth Match vs ‡ Scotland played at Edinburgh on 13 and 14 July. South Africans 214 (C H Mills 53, F Hearne 36, H H Castens 35, H J Stevenson 4 for 50, A A Palmer 3 for 56, A S Cairns 3 for 77) and 96 for 1 (C H Mills 45*, E A Halliwell 37*) beat Scotland 189 (C T Mannes 65, J Mailer 25, G A Rowe 4 for 46) and 118 (T Johnston 31, G Glover 6 for 39) by 9 wickets.

Fifteenth Match vs ‡ Glasgow and District played at Glasgow on 16, 17 and 18 July. South Africans 169 (C O H Sewell 79, Davies 7 for 34) beat Glasgow and District 74 (T Tripney 31*, G A Rowe 6 for 25, G Glover 4 for 34) and 63 (H Spence 20, G A Rowe 7 for 27) by an innings and 32 runs.

Sixteenth Match vs ‡ Liverpool and District played at Aigburth Cricket Ground, Liverpool on 19, 20 and 21 July. South Africans 287 (C L Johnson 112, D C Davey 50, C O H Sewell 27, G A Rowe 27, A Smith 4 for 53) and 31 for 3 (T Routledge 22*) beat Liverpool and District 110 (D Lorrimer 48, G A Rowe 5 for 52, J Middleton 4 for 22) and 207 (A T Kemble 39, T A Stubbs 32, D Lorrimer 28, T Ainscough 25, G A Rowe 4 for 88, J Middleton 3 for 31) by 7 wickets.

THE SOUTH AFRICAN CRICKET TEAM 1894

F. HEARNE
WESTERN PROVINCE

THE SOUTH AFRICAN CRICKET TEAM 1894

MR C. L. JOHNSON
TRANSVAAL

Seventeenth Match vs ‡ Derbyshire played at the Racecourse Ground, Derby on 26, 27 and 28 July. Derbyshire 325 (W Sugg 121, W Chatterton 53, W Storer 49, J J Hulme 34, G Glover 4 for 58) and 197 (W Chatterton 58*, J P Ward 35, G Glover 4 for 65) drew with South Africans 300 (C O H Sewell 128, C H Mills 36, F Hearne 34, C L Johnson 33, G Glover 32, J J Hulme 4 for 34, G A Davidson 4 for 80) and 48 for 3 (C O H Sewell 24*, J J Hulme 2 for 19).

Eighteenth Match vs ‡ Gentlemen of Ireland played at Dublin on 30 and 31 July. South Africans 250 (C L Johnson 79, C O H Sewell 73, E A Halliwell 39, R H Lambert 5 for 37) and 87 for 1 (C O H Sewell 53*) beat Gentlemen of Ireland 153 (W D Hamilton 68, A D Comyn 32, C L Johnson 3 for 0, G A Rowe 3 for 56) and 181 (A P Gwynne 62, F F Kilkelly 34, G A Rowe 7 for 77) by 9 wickets.

Nineteenth Match vs ‡ Dublin University played at Dublin on 1 and 2 August. South Africans 123 (E A Halliwell 62, J M Meldon 3 for 23, L H Gwynne 3 for 39) and 52 for 1 (C H Mills 21*) beat Dublin University 107 (J M Meldon 38, L H Gwynne 36, G A Rowe 4 for 41) and 69 (L H Gwynne 26, C L Johnson 6 for 33, G A Rowe 4 for 32) by 9 wickets.

THE SOUTH AFRICAN
CRICKET TEAM 1894

MR A. W. SECCULL
WESTERN PROVINCE

THE SOUTH AFRICAN
CRICKET TEAM 1894

MR G. S. KEMPIS
TRANSVAAL

Twentieth Match vs ‡ North of Ireland played at Belfast on 3 and 4 August. North of Ireland 109 (Capt. Hamilton 53, W C Anderson 22, G A Rowe 7 for 32) and 137 (Capt. Hamilton 42, G Combe 27, G A Rowe 6 for 54) drew with South Africans 113 (C L Johnson 22, Baines 8 for 41) and 169 for 8 dec (C L Johnson 50, F Hearne 36, C O H Sewell 31, O Andrews 3 for 29).

Twenty-First Match vs ‡ Leeds and District played at Headingley Cricket Ground, Leeds on 8 and 9 August. South Africans 93 (E A Halliwell 26, W Fletcher 4 for 29, F W Milligan 3 for 6) and 99 for 5 (G Glover 29, W Fletcher 2 for 21) beat Leeds and District 125 (H Hayley 38, J Middleton 5 for 30) and 66 (A Sellars 28, J Middleton 5 for 32, G A Rowe 4 for 28) by 5 wickets.

Twenty-Second Match vs ‡ Scarborough and District played at North Marine Drive, Scarborough on 9, 10 and 11 August. South Africans 124 (G Glover 31, H Hayley 4 for 40, Whatmough 3 for 4) and 96 (G S Kempis 19, H Hayley 8 for 39) beat Scarborough and District 90 (R W Frank 31, G A Rowe 6 for 39) and 123 (H Hayley 36, R W Frank 25, C L Johnson 5 for 17, G A Rowe 4 for 32) by 7 runs.

Twenty-Third Match vs ‡ Lord Cantelupe's XI played at Manor Ground, Bexhill-on-Sea on 13 and 14 August. South Africans 172 (E A Halliwell 65*, Martin 4 for 72) and 43 for 6 (A Hearne 5 for 7) beat Lord Cantelupe's XI 92 (A Payne 25, G Glover 5 for 36, C L Johnson 4 for 27) and 121 (H G Papillon 27, G Glover 4 for 43, C H Mills 3 for 12) by 4 wickets.

Twenty-Fourth Match vs ‡ Warwickshire played at Edgbaston Cricket Ground, Birmingham on 16 and 17 August. Warwickshire 144 (J H G Devey 41, E J Diver 38, C L Johnson 6 for 44) and 185 for 5 dec (E J Diver 68, W Quaife 58, G A Rowe 3 for 58) drew with South Africans 138 (A W Seccull 39, C O H Sewell 29, S J Whitehead 5 for 38, H J Pallett 4 for 52) and 111 for 5 (C O H Sewell 38, D C Parkin 29*, S J Whitehead 2 for 52).

Tour batting averages:

	Inns	NO	Runs	HS	Ave
C O H Sewell	37	3	1,038	170	30.52
E A Halliwell	38	9	759	110	26.17
D C Davey	8	1	146	50*	20.85
T Routledge	43	5	768	152	20.21
A W Seccull	23	0	355	63	15.43
F Hearne	34	1	508	104	15.39
C Mills	33	2	473	64	15.25
C L Johnson	37	3	508	112	14.94
G Cripps	34	7	394	54	14.59
G Glover	31	4	377	41	13.96
G S Kempis	10	0	117	24	11.70
D C Parkin	13	3	98	29	9.80
H H Castens	26	2	235	58	9.79
J Middleton	26	8	127	20	7.05
G A Rowe	30	10	135	27	6.75

Tour bowling averages:

	Overs	Mdns	Runs	Wkts	Ave
G A Rowe	933.3	315	1,754	136	12.89
J Middleton	594.3	173	1,311	83	15.79
G Glover	382.1	95	977	56	17.44
C L Johnson	418	152	892	50	17.84
C Mills	280.4	71	664	28	23.41

Also bowled during the tour:

	Overs	Mdns	Runs	Wkts	Ave
T Routledge	15.1	4	35	3	11.66
C O H Sewell	64	20	172	8	21.50
G Cripps	37.4	5	129	4	32.25

A W Seccull	67.4	18	171	4	42.75
D C Parkin	99	30	250	5	50.00
F Hearne	19	6	56	1	56.00
G S Kempis	60	19	130	2	65.00

Centuries recorded for South Africans during the tour:

C O H Sewell	(2) :	170 vs Somerset (Taunton)
		128 vs Derbyshire (Derby)
E A Halliwell	(1) :	110 vs Gloucestershire (Bristol)
T Routledge	(1) :	152 vs C W Wright's XI (Portsmouth)
C L Johnson	(1) :	112 vs Liverpool & District (Liverpool)

Fielding:

	Catches	Stumpings
E A Halliwell	25	19
F Hearne	24	
J Middleton	20	
C L Johnson	15	
H H Castens	13	1
T Routledge	8	4
C O H Sewell	12	
G A Rowe	11	
A W Seccull	8	
G Glover	7	
D C Parkin	7	
G Cripps	4	
C Mills	3	

THE SOUTH AFRICAN
CRICKET TEAM 1894

Mr W. A. SIMKINS
MANAGER

The Second South African Team in the United Kingdom, 1901

Proposals to make a second tour to England in 1900 were cancelled due to the Boer War but agreement was reached to tour in 1901 despite the fact that the War continued.

Sponsored by a wealthy cricket enthusiast, The Hon. J. D. Logan, who was also a member of the team, the tourists quickly faced on their arrival press comment that they should be fighting in the War rather than playing cricket.

The 14 man squad for this second tour of England in 1901 included eight tourists from the strong Western Province side in Cape Town. It was captained by Murray Bisset and also in the squad was his brother.

Significantly, J. H. Sinclair who had not toured in 1894 was in the team and proved successful — again there was to be no representative match although twenty-five games were played.

(standing) **B.C.Cooley G.A.Rowe C.F.H.Prince J.J.Kotze Mr.G.A.Lohmann** (Manager)
A.Reid A.V.C.Bisset W.A.Shalders

(sitting, middle) **L.J.Tancred J.H.Sinclair E.A.Halliwell M.Bisset** (Captain)
C.M.H.Hathorn

(sitting, front) **J.D.Logan R.Graham C.B.Llewellyn, unknown visitor**

Touring party (14):

* M Bisset (*Western Province*) (Captain)
Age 25. Right-handed middle order batsman, occasional left-arm slow bowler and wicket-keeper.

A Reid (*Western Province*)
Age 24. Right-handed middle order batsman.

A V C Bisset (*Western Province*)
Age 22. Right-handed middle order batsman.

† C F H Prince (*Western Province*)
Age 27. Right-handed middle order batsman and wicket-keeper.

R Graham (*Western Province*)
Age 24. Right-handed lower order batsman and right-arm medium pace bowler.

J D Logan (*Western Province*)
Age 21. Middle order batsman.

J J Kotze (*Western Province*)
Age 22. Right-arm fast bowler, right-handed batsman and poor fieldsman.

G A Rowe (*Western Province*)
Age 27. Left-arm slow bowler and right-handed tail end batsman.

B C Cooley (*Natal*)
Age 27. Right-handed middle order batsman.

C M H Hathorn (*Transvaal*)
Age 23. Right-handed middle order batsman.

L J Tancred (*Transvaal*)
Age 25. Right-handed opening batsman.

† E A Halliwell (*Transvaal/Middlesex/London County*)
Age 37. Right-handed middle order batsman and wicket-keeper.

J H Sinclair (*Transvaal*)
Age 25. Right-handed hard hitting middle order batsman and right-arm medium pace or leg-break bowler.

W A Shalders (*Griqualand West*)
Age 21. Right-handed opening batsman.

Manager: Mr. G A Lohmann

Summary of all matches:

Played 25   Won 13   Lost 9   Drawn 2   Tied 1

Summary of first-class matches:

Played 15   Won 5   Lost 9   Drawn 0   Tied 1

First Match vs Hampshire played at County Cricket Ground, Northlands Road, Southampton on 16, 17 and 18 May. Hampshire 538 (C B Llewellyn 216, A J L Hill 120, Capt. J G Greig 119, J H Sinclair 4 for 170) beat South Africans 346 (C M H Hathorn 103, A V C Bisset 94, E A Halliwell 30, H M Greenhill 3 for 39, H Baldwin 3 for 59) and 141 (M Bisset 35, C B Llewellyn 4 for 6) by an innings and 51 runs.

Second Match vs London County played at Crystal Palace Park, Crystal Palace on 20, 21 and 22 May. South Africans 262 (E A Halliwell 79, C M H Hathorn 74, L J Tancred 37, J H Sinclair 30, L C Braund 5 for 117, W G Grace 3 for 96) and 316 (C B Llewellyn 88, C M H Hathorn 86*, A V C Bisset 30, L Walker 3 for 54) beat London County 316 (L Walker 114, L C Braund 63, W L Murdoch 62, C B Llewellyn 6 for 140) and 201 (W G Grace 37, H S Keigwin 32, L Walker 26, L C Braund 25, C B Llewellyn 7 for 101) by 61 runs.

Third Match vs Kent played at Foxgrove Road, Beckenham on 23 and 24 May. Kent 227 (E Humphreys 60, C J Burnup 50, F D Browne 31, J J Kotze 4 for 46, J H Sinclair 4 for 58) and 139 for 3 (C J Burnup 70, E Humphreys 28, G A Rowe 2 for 50) beat South Africans 225 (A Reid 77*, W A Shalders 31, L J Tancred 28, J R Mason 3 for 45, C Blythe 3 for 48) and 139 (W A Shalders 44, L J Tancred 42, C Blythe 6 for 53, W M Bradley 3 for 43) by 7 wickets.

Fourth Match vs Leicestershire played at Aylestone Road, Leicester on 27 and 28 May. Leicestershire 286 (A E Knight 68, A Woodcock 42, C E de Trafford 40, F Geeson 31, G A Rowe 5 for 121, R Graham 3 for 84) and 38 for 1 (J H King 17*) beat South Africans 132 (J H Sinclair 47, A Reid 25, F Geeson 7 for 33) and 191 (R Graham 63*, W A Shalders 35, M Bisset 35, R T Crawford 4 for 33, J H King 3 for 40) by 9 wickets.

Fifth Match vs Warwickshire played at Edgbaston Cricket Ground, Birmingham on 30 and 31 May. Warwickshire 278 (S P Kinneir 71, A F A Lilley 70, T S Fishlock 31, J J Kotze 5 for 63, G A Rowe 3 for 77) beat South Africans 74 (M Bisset 19, S Santall 5 for 35, S Hargreave 5 for 39) and 135 (L J Tancred 50, A V C Bisset 43*, S Santall 4 for 32, E F Field 4 for 22) by an innings and 69 runs.

Sixth Match vs M.C.C. and Ground played at Lord's Cricket Ground, London on 3 and 4 June. M.C.C. 168 (W Storer 41, H B Chimnery 29, H B Hayman 23, G A Rowe 5 for 68, R Graham 3 for 30) and 170 (A E Trott 42, W Storer 41, H B Hayman 31, G A Rowe 5 for 81, J J Kotze 3 for 49) beat South Africans 150 (W A Shalders 62, H I Young 3 for 23, W Mead 3 for 24) and 135 (M Bisset 55, E A Halliwell 33, W Williams 8 for 53) by 53 runs.

Seventh Match vs Derbyshire played at The Racecourse Ground, Derby on 6, 7 and 8 June. South Africans 392 (M Bisset 184, E A Halliwell 53, A V C Bisset 38, J J Kotze 26*, W Bestwick 3 for 92, J J Hulme 3 for 129) and 84 for 1 (L J Tancred 57*) beat Derbyshire 305 (L G Wright 64, W Storer 64, E Needham 57, C A Ollivierre 44, R Graham 6 for 84) and 170 (C A Ollivierre 54, S W A Cadman 27, J J Hulme 21, R Graham 5 for 47) by 8 wickets.

Eighth Match vs Cambridge University played at Fenner's University Cricket Ground, Cambridge on 10, 11 and 12 June. South Africans 692 (C M H Hathorn 239, B C Cooley 126*, W A Shalders 69, M Bisset 59, E A Halliwell 40, A Reid 40, C F Prince 39, E M Dowson 5 for 191) beat Cambridge University 223 (A E Hind 53, E R Wilson 30, G A Rowe 7 for 65) and 254 (W P Robertson 57, H K Longman 49, S H Day 36, G A Rowe 6 for 90) by an innings and 215 runs.

Ninth Match vs Somerset played at County Cricket Ground, Taunton on 13, 14 and 15 June. Somerset 313 (L C H Palairet 72, A E Lewis 52*, S M J Woods 40, G A Rowe 4 for 80, J J Kotze 3 for 73) and 440 for 9 dec (A E Lewis 100*, G C Gill 85, L C H Palairet 52, L C Braund 50, P R Johnson 46, E Robson 42, B Cranfield 28, J J Kotze 3 for 121) beat South Africans 124 (J H Sinclair 27, L J Tancred 24, W A Shalders 24, G C Gill 5 for 24, B Cranfield 4 for 55) and 288 (W A Shalders 103, E A Halliwell 92, M Bisset 25, R Graham 25, L C Braund 4 for 83, G C Gill 3 for 53) by 341 runs.

Tenth Match vs ‡ Gentlemen of Ireland played at Dublin on 18 and 19 June. South Africans 209 (M Bisset 47, J D Logan 41, L J Tancred 37, T C Ross 5 for 47) and 107 for 5 (L J Tancred 58, C M H Hathorn 28*, T C Ross 2 for 31) beat Gentlemen of Ireland 177 (A D Comyn 58, L H Gwynn 34, G W F Kelly 30, J H Sinclair 6 for 72) and 137 (L H Gwynn 68, G A Rowe 7 for 53) by 5 wickets.

L. J. TANCRED
Transvaal

Eleventh Match vs ‡ Dublin University played at Trinity College, Dublin on 20 and 21 June. South Africans 302 (A Reid 61, J J Kotze 52*, E A Halliwell 51, M Bisset 40, A V C Bisset 30, S H Crawford 3 for 63, J W Crozier 3 for 79, T A Harvey 3 for 92) beat Dublin University 144 (R M Gwynn 30, J T Gwynn 28, H B Mayne 20, J J Kotze 4 for 28, G A Rowe 4 for 53) and 116 (W S Caldwell 56, J T Gwynn 21, R Graham 4 for 41, J H Sinclair 3 for 16) by an innings and 42 runs.

Twelfth Match vs ‡ Liverpool and District played at Aigburth Cricket Ground, Liverpool on 24 and 25 June. South Africans 127 (C B Llewellyn 51, E E Steele 4 for 37, Kitchener 4 for 37) and 204 for 5 (L J Tancred 56, C M H Hathorn 55, E A Halliwell 38*, E E Steele 2 for 49) beat Liverpool and District 141 (T Ainscough 38, J D Johnston 31, C B Llewellyn 6 for 51, G A Rowe 3 for 44) and 189 (T Ainscough 53, J D Johnston 30, W P Barnes 27, C B Llewellyn 6 for 79, J H Sinclair 3 for 27) by 5 wickets.

THE SOUTH AFRICAN
CRICKET TEAM 1894

Mr G. A. ROWE
WESTERN PROVINCE

THE SOUTH AFRICAN
CRICKET TEAM 1894

Mr E. A. HALLIWELL
TRANSVAAL

Thirteenth Match vs ‡ Durham played at Feethams Cricket Ground, Darlington on 27, 28 and 29 June. South Africans 225 (W A Shalders 61, C M H Hathorn 52, J D Logan 39, A V C Bisset 36, G Turnbull 4 for 75) and 502 for 9 dec (A V C Bisset 151, E A Halliwell 97, C M H Hathorn 81, W A Shalders 46, M Bisset 35, R Graham 33, W F Whitwell 4 for 94) beat Durham 188 (E W Elliot 43, J F Whitwell 35, A Burn 31, J H Sinclair 5 for 76, G A Rowe 4 for 52) and 93 (T Prince 36, G Turnbull 21, G A Rowe 6 for 30, J H Sinclair 4 for 50) by 446 runs.

Fourteenth Match vs Lancashire played at Old Trafford, Manchester on 1, 2 and 3 July. Lancashire 125 (J J Broughton 26, E E Steele 23, A Eccles 23, G A Rowe 5 for 48, J H Sinclair 5 for 72) and 172 for 2 (E E Steele 69*, H G Garnett 48, W J Hibbert 36*, R Graham 2 for 38) beat South Africans 155 (E A Halliwell 35, L J Tancred 26, C M H Hathorn 23, S Webb 4 for 33) and 141 (J H Sinclair 22, W A Shalders 20, W J Hibbert 4 for 39, S Webb 4 for 57) by 8 wickets.

Fifteenth Match vs Surrey played at Kennington Oval, London on 8, 9 and 10 July. Surrey 184 (W Brockwell 51, V F S Crawford 35, F C Holland 31, J H Sinclair 6 for 50) and 251 (H S Bush 92, L Walker 64, K E M Barker 45, J H Sinclair 7 for 98) beat South Africans 129 (J H Sinclair 62, T Richardson 6 for 50) and 247 (W A Shalders 63, L J Tancred 56, C M H Hathorn 27, M Bisset 27, J H Sinclair 25, T Richardson 5 for 75) by 59 runs.

Sixteenth Match vs Nottinghamshire played at Trent Bridge, Nottingham on 11, 12 and 13 July. South Africans 165 (A Reid 41, W A Shalders 27, M Bisset 25, A W Hallam 4 for 55, T G Wass 3 for 72) and 278 (W A Shalders 51, M Bisset 49, A Reid 46, E A Halliwell 29, J J Kotze 28, A W Hallam 4 for 86, T G Wass 4 for 94) beat Nottinghamshire 96 (D Harrison 33, T W Oates 25, J J Kotze 7 for 31, J H Sinclair 3 for 51) and 253 (A Shrewsbury 85, T W Oates 44, J Iremonger 31, C E Dench 29, J J Kotze 3 for 51, G A Rowe 3 for 57, J H Sinclair 3 for 110) by 94 runs.

J. H. SINCLAIR
Transvaal

Seventeenth Match vs Worcestershire played at County Cricket Ground, New Road, Worcester on 15, 16 and 17 July. South Africans 293 (C M H Hathorn 90, W A Shalders 51, C F Prince 35, A Reid 34, J J Kotze 29, G Wilson 5 for 123) and 140 (L J Tancred 34, W A Shalders 32, A V C Bisset 23, G Wilson 5 for 39, A F Bannister 3 for 39) tied with Worcestershire 224 (A F Bannister 44, J B Fereday 37, G W Gaukrodger 32, R E Foster 26, J J Kotze 6 for 82) and 209 (G H Simpson-Hayward 52, A W Isaac 42, F L Bowley 36, R Graham 8 for 90).

Eighteenth Match vs Northamptonshire played at County Cricket Ground, Wantage Road, Northampton on 18, 19 and 20 July. South Africans 238 (M Bisset 88*, J H Sinclair 51, G J Thompson 3 for 45, L T Driffield 3 for 74) and 173 (J H Sinclair 77*, M Bisset 35*, W East 3 for 57) beat Northamptonshire 163 (G K Papillon 38, W H Kingston 37, J J Kotze 7 for 48, G A Rowe 3 for 37) and 246 (T Horton 102*, G J Thompson 60, J J Kotze 4 for 107, G A Rowe 3 for 63) by 5 wickets.

Nineteenth Match vs ‡ Staffordshire played at Stoke-on-Trent on 22, 23 and 24 July. South Africans 164 (A Reid 75, Grimshaw 5 for 58, Moss 3 for 64) and 318 (C M H Hathorn 99, C F Prince 95, A Reid 43, Grimshaw 5 for 97, H England 3 for 96) drew with Staffordshire 125 (P Briggs 32, G A Rowe 6 for 30, J H Sinclair 3 for 30) and 43 for 3 (P Briggs 11, J H Sinclair 2 for 27).

Twentieth Match vs ‡ Wiltshire played at County Cricket Ground, Swindon on 26 and 27 July. Wiltshire 123 (J E Stevens 53, G A Rowe 5 for 52, J H Sinclair 4 for 31) drew with South Africans 72 for 6 (W A Shalders 39, Smart 3 for 28, Overton 3 for 30).

Twenty-First Match vs Yorkshire played at St. George's Road, Harrogate on 1, 2 and 3 August. Yorkshire 215 (D Denton 48, J T Brown 47, J Tunnicliffe 45, J H Sinclair 7 for 54, G A Rowe 3 for 60) and 369 (E Wainwright 116, D Denton 83, W Rhodes 35, F Mitchell 30, J Tunnicliffe 25, T L Taylor 25, J H Sinclair 4 for 133, G A Rowe 3 for 97) beat South Africans 193 (J H Sinclair 80, E A Halliwell 35, M Bisset 24, E Smith 6 for 98, W Rhodes 3 for 38) and 240 (L J Tancred 65, A Reid 37, C M H Hathorn 37, E A Halliwell 35, E Smith 4 for 55, W Rhodes 3 for 53) by 151 runs.

Twenty-Second Match vs ‡ The East of Scotland played at Edinburgh on 5, 6 and 7 August. South Africans 337 (L J Tancred 165, C M H Hathorn 47, A Reid 27, Stevenson 7 for 106) beat The East of Scotland 125 (D L A Smith 43, A S Cairns 23, J J Kotze 5 for 27, J H Sinclair 3 for 32) and 170 (G L D Hole 52, D L A Smith 30, J A Campbell 23, R Graham 7 for 40, G A Rowe 3 for 55) by an innings and 42 runs.

Twenty-Third Match vs ‡ The West of Scotland played at Glasgow on 8, 9 and 10 August. South Africans 170 (W A Shalders 33, A Reid 32, M Bisset 30, A Burnett 5 for 16, S Hirst 3 for 32) and 172 (B C Cooley 57, A Reid 29, W A Shalders 21, Henson 4 for 34, A L Graham 2 for 26) beat The West of Scotland 111 (S Hirst 19, J H Orr 18, G A Rowe 5 for 32, J H Sinclair 4 for 47) and 51 (T Mathieson 11, J H Sinclair 7 for 18, G A Rowe 3 for 21) by 180 runs.

Twenty-Fourth Match vs Gloucestershire played at Clifton College, Bristol on 15 and 16 August. South Africans 234 (W A Shalders 90, R Graham 29, A Reid 27, C M H Hathorn 27, A J Paish 6 for 84) beat Gloucestershire 40 (H Wrathall 13, J H Sinclair 7 for 20) and 89 (H Wrathall 28, W S A Brown 27, J H Sinclair 6 for 53, G A Rowe 4 for 34) by an innings and 105 runs.

Twenty-Fifth Match vs ‡ Glamorgan played at Arms Park, Cardiff on 19 and 20 August. South Africans 228 (L J Tancred 91, J H Sinclair 36, M Bisset 26, C M H Hathorn 24, S Lowe 7 for 77) and 202 for 9 dec (M Bisset 67*, J H Sinclair 39, G A Rowe 32, W Russell 7 for 77) beat Glamorgan 168 (Bancroft 50, J H Brain 24, G A Rowe 4 for 54) and 130 (J H Brain 45, W Russell 26, G A Rowe 6 for 42) by 132 runs.

Tour batting averages - all matches:

	Inns	NO	Runs	HS	Ave
C M H Hathorn	39	3	1,261	239	35.02
W A Shalders	39	0	1,085	103	27.82
M Bisset	44	4	1,080	184	27.00
L J Tancred	45	1	1,125	165	25.56
A Reid	31	1	710	77*	23.66
E A Halliwell	40	3	862	97	23.29
A V C Bisset	35	2	704	151	21.33
J H Sinclair	39	1	742	80	19.52
B C Cooley	15	1	242	126*	17.28
C F Prince	13	0	208	95	16.00
J D Logan	12	0	188	41	15.66
R Graham	39	9	391	63*	13.03
J J Kotze	34	9	318	52*	12.72
G A Rowe	40	15	261	32	10.44

Also batted during the tour:

	Inns	NO	Runs	HS	Ave
C B Llewellyn	4	0	153	88	38.25

Tour bowling averages - all matches:

	Overs	Mdns	Runs	Wkts	Ave
C B Llewellyn	121.4	26	371	25	14.84
J H Sinclair	529.4	88	1,786	106	16.84
G A Rowe	948	243	2,522	136	18.54
J J Kotze	518.1	107	1,626	79	20.58
R Graham	426.3	70	1,463	65	22.50
B C Cooley	49.5	6	190	7	27.14
E A Halliwell	51.4	9	153	5	30.60
C M H Hathorn	10	1	40	1	40.00

Also bowled during the tour:

	Overs	Mdns	Runs	Wkts	Ave
W A Shalders	9	2	28	2	14.00
J D Logan	3	0	20	0	-
M Bisset	1	0	14	0	-

Centuries recorded for South Africans during the tour:

C M H Hathorn	(2) :	239	vs Cambridge University (Fenner's)
		103	vs Hampshire (Southampton)
M Bisset	(1) :	184	vs Derbyshire (Derby)
L J Tancred	(1) :	165	vs East of Scotland (Edinburgh)
A V C Bisset	(1) :	151	vs Durham (Darlington)
B C Cooley	(1) :	126*	vs Cambridge University (Fenner's)
W A Shalders	(1) :	103	vs Somerset (Taunton)

Fielding:

	Catches	Stumpings
M Bisset	32	10
E A Halliwell	16	11
R Graham	25	
L J Tancred	20	
J H Sinclair	15	
G A Rowe	13	
W A Shalders	9	
A Reid	8	
A V C Bisset	8	
C F Prince	5	2
B C Cooley	5	
C M H Hathorn	4	
J J Kotze	4	
J D Logan	3	
C B Llewellyn	1	

SOUTH AFRICAN
CRICKET TEAM, 1907.

M. HATHORN.

SOUTH AFRICAN
CRICKET TEAM, 1907.

J. J. KOTZE.

The Third South African Team in the United Kingdom, 1904 (Sir Abe Bailey)

After only a gap of three years the South Africans were to tour again in 1904, this time financed by Sir Abe Bailey.

Of the party of fourteen, six members had previously toured in 1901 and the captain was Frank Mitchell a former captain of Cambridge University (1894-97) and Yorkshire (1894-1903), who had also toured South Africa with Lord Hawke's side in 1898-99. The tourists included Reggie Schwarz of Middlesex (1901-05) and Hampshire also released C. B. Llewellyn to play in several matches.

Reggie Schwarz was to prove a significant member, bowling the googly he had learnt at Lord's from B. J. T. Bosanquet.

(standing) **B.Wallach G.H.Shepstone R.O.Schwarz C.M.H.Hathorn S.E.Horwood S.J.Snooke W.A.Shalders G.C.White**

(sitting) **J.Middleton J.H.Sinclair E.A.Halliwell F.Mitchell (Captain) L.J.Tancred J.J.Kotze**

Touring party (14):

* F Mitchell (*Transvaal/Cambridge University/Yorkshire/London County*)
(Captain)
Age 32. Right-handed attacking middle order batsman and right-arm medium pace bowler.

S E Horwood (*Western Province*)
Age 27. Right-handed middle order batsman.

J Middleton (*Western Province*)
Age 39. Left-handed attacking lower order batsman and left-arm slow medium bowler.

S J Snooke (*Western Province*)
Age 23. Right-handed middle order batsman and right-arm fast medium bowler.

R O Schwarz (*Transvaal/Middlesex*)
Age 29. Right-handed attacking lower order batsman and right-arm medium pace bowler/off-break bowler with leg-break action.

G H Shepstone (*Transvaal*)
Age 28. Right-handed middle order batsman and right-arm fast medium bowler.

G C White (*Transvaal*)
Age 22. Right-handed attractive middle order batsman and leg-break bowler.

† B Wallach (*Transvaal*)
Age 31. Right-handed tail end batsman and wicket-keeper.

J J Kotze (*Western Province*)
Age 25. Right-arm fast bowler, right-handed batsman and poor fieldsman.

C M H Hathorn (*Transvaal*)
Age 26. Right-handed middle order batsman.

L J Tancred (*Transvaal*)
Age 28. Right-handed opening batsman.

† E A Halliwell (*Transvaal/Middlesex/London County*)
Age 40. Right-handed middle order batsman and wicket-keeper.

J H Sinclair (*Transvaal*)
Age 28. Right-handed hard hitting middle order batsman and right-arm medium pace or leg-break bowler.

W A Shalders (*Griqualand West*)
Age 24. Right-handed opening batsman.

Manager: Mr. G Allsop

Summary of all matches:
Played 26   Won 13   Lost 3   Drawn 9   Tied 1

Summary of first-class matches:
Played 22   Won 10   Lost 2   Drawn 9   Tied 1

First Match vs M.C.C. and Ground played at Lord's Cricket Ground, London on 30, 31 May and 1 June. South Africans 194 (C B Llewellyn 68*, W A Shalders 47, J H Sinclair 32, B J T Bosanquet 9 for 107) drew with M.C.C. and Ground 196 for 8 (Capt E G Wynyard 52, G J Thompson 35, W G Grace 27, J J Kotze 3 for 48).

Second Match vs Worcestershire played at County Cricket Ground, New Road, Worcester on 2, 3 and 4 June. Worcestershire 227 (H K Foster 107, G H Simpson-Hayward 58, R D Burrows 22, J Middleton 4 for 73, J J Kotze 3 for 50) and 259 (E G Arnold 85, H K Foster 53, R D Burrows 29, J J Kotze 3 for 41) beat South Africans 161 (F Mitchell 70, W A Shalders 36, E G Arnold 5 for 59) and 188 (L J Tancred 61, F Mitchell 40, W A Shalders 37, R D Burrows 5 for 43, Arnold 3 for 34) by 137 runs.

Third Match vs Cambridge University played at Fenner's University Cricket Ground, Cambridge on 6, 7 and 8 June. South Africans 216 (J H Sinclair 50, G H Shepstone 46, W A Shalders 29, P R May 4 for 61, E P Keigwin 3 for 49) and 246 (F Mitchell 102*, J H Sinclair 46, C M H Hathorn 29, H C McDonell 6 for 84) beat Cambridge University 197 (H C McDonell 58, F B Wilson 40, F J V Hopley 31, J H Sinclair 4 for 45, J Middleton 3 for 46, J J Kotze 3 for 52) and 195 (E S Phillips 47, F B Roberts 34*, H C McDonell 27, J J Kotze 5 for 98, J H Sinclair 4 for 61) by 70 runs.

SOUTH AFRICAN
CRICKET TEAM, 1907.

SOUTH AFRICAN
CRICKET TEAM. 1907.

S. J. SNOOKE.

G. C. WHITE.

Fourth Match vs Oxford University played at The University Parks, Oxford on 9 and 10 June. South Africans 418 (F Mitchell 82, C M H Hathorn 80, G C White 79*, J H Sinclair 65, E G Martin 5 for 115) beat Oxford University 154 (J E Raphael 46, R C W Burn 24, J H Sinclair 8 for 69) and 167 (R W Awdry 69, G M Bennett 26, R O Schwarz 5 for 27, J J Kotze 3 for 51) by an innings and 97 runs.

Fifth Match vs Gloucestershire played at County Cricket Ground, Nevil Road, Bristol on 13, 14 and 15 June. South Africans 339 (L J Tancred 97, R O Schwarz 93, C M H Hathorn 46, W A Shalders 34, H J Huggins 4 for 117, E G Dennett 4 for 144) and 41 for 4 (L J Tancred 26, E G Dennett 2 for 16) drew with Gloucestershire 182 (H Wrathall 88, A W Hill 29*, J H Sinclair 7 for 75) and 225 (H Wrathall 54, F E Thomas 46, C S Barratt 42, G C White 4 for 54, C B Llewellyn 3 for 65).

R. O. SCHWARZ
Transvaal

Sixth Match vs Warwickshire played at Edgbaston Cricket Ground, Birmingham on 16 and 17 June. South Africans 343 (L J Tancred 106, S J Snooke 58, G C White 52, C B Llewellyn 37, S Hargreave 4 for 108) and 42 for 0 (W A Shalders 29*) beat Warwickshire 237 (S P Kinneir 58, T S Fishlock 44, J F Byrne 34, J H Sinclair 5 for 99, C B Llewellyn 4 for 64) and 147 (A C S Glover 73*, S P Kinneir 29, J J Kotze 6 for 58, R O Schwarz 4 for 29) by 10 wickets.

Seventh Match vs Middlesex played at Lord's Cricket Ground, London on 20, 21 and 22 June. Middlesex 272 (B J T Bosanquet 110, C Headlam 44, P F Warner 34, F A Tarrant 31, J J Kotze 5 for 94, C B Llewellyn 3 for 64) and 225 (B J T Bosanquet 44, P F Warner 38, A E Trott 38, R O Schwarz 5 for 48) tied with South Africans 287 (F Mitchell 66, W A Shalders 56, C B Llewellyn 43, C M H Hathorn 32, A E Trott 4 for 80, J T Hearne 3 for 67) and 210 (L J Tancred 75, C B Llewellyn 60, A E Trott 6 for 75).

Eighth Match vs London County played at Crystal Palace Park, Crystal Palace on 23 and 24 June. South Africans 332 (C M H Hathorn 130, J H Sinclair 103, E A Halliwell 37, W Mead 3 for 57, J W H T Douglas 3 for 73) and 6 for 0 beat London County 168 (T B Nicholson 68, L Walker 45, J J Kotze 6 for 67) and 167 (S S Harris 76, L Walker 22, J Middleton 4 for 59, J J Kotze 3 for 46) by 10 wickets.

THE SOUTH AFRICAN CRICKET TEAM 1894

J. MIDDLETON
WESTERN PROVINCE

SOUTH AFRICAN CRICKET TEAM 1907.

W. A. SHALDERS.

Ninth Match vs ‡ Dublin University played at Trinity College, Dublin on 27 and 28 June. South Africans 484 (L J Tancred 148, G C White 117, J H Sinclair 51, W A Shalders 44, F Mitchell 37, S J Snooke 27, E Gibbon 5 for 151, S H Crawford 4 for 146) beat Dublin University 79 (C R Faussett 28, G J Meldon 24, R O Schwarz 5 for 16, G C White 5 for 34) and 115 (C R Faussett 18, R O Schwarz 7 for 36) by an innings and 290 runs.

Tenth Match vs ‡ Gentlemen of Ireland played at Dublin on 30 June, 1 and 2 July. Gentlemen of Ireland 160 (F H Browning 40, A D Comyn 32, R O Schwarz 5 for 66, G C White 3 for 14) and 135 (F H Browning 31, H H Corley 28, S D Lambert 27, G C White 4 for 29, R O Schwarz 3 for 23) beat South Africans 64 (F Mitchell 25, T C Ross 9 for 28) and 138 (G C White 30, S J Snooke 25, H W Harrington 5 for 66, T C Ross 2 for 36) by 93 runs.

Eleventh Match vs Hampshire played at Municipal Ground, Alton on 7 and 8 July. South Africans 380 (L J Tancred 99, R O Schwarz 67, G C White 54, J H Sinclair 31, W A Shalders 30, S J Snooke 27, C B Llewellyn 5 for 160, H Hesketh-Pritchard 3 for 98) beat Hampshire 168 (H A W Bowell 65, J Stone 32*, A S Webb 22, A J L Hill 20, J J Kotze 5 for 66) and 193 (E M Sprot 75, C B Llewellyn 60, J H Sinclair 4 for 104, G C White 3 for 34, J J Kotze 3 for 39) by an innings and 19 runs.

Twelfth Match vs Somerset played at County Cricket Ground, Taunton on 11 and 12 July. South Africans 438 (R O Schwarz 93, W A Shalders 81, L J Tancred 73, E A Halliwell 72*, G H Shepstone 64, A E Lewis 4 for 47, L C Braund 4 for 154) beat Somerset 198 (F M Lee 79*, H Martyn 23, J J Kotze 5 for 82, R O Schwarz 3 for 24) and 154 (F M Lee 39, H Martyn 36, G H Shepstone 4 for 33) by an innings and 86 runs.

Thirteenth Match vs An England XI played at Lord's Cricket Ground, London on 14, 15 and 16 July. South Africans 352 (R O Schwarz 102, F Mitchell 75, C M H Hathorn 59, W A Shalders 46, J T Hearne 3 for 48, J H King 3 for 72) and 207 (C M H Hathorn 69, E A Halliwell 57*, R O Schwarz 26, J T Hearne 5 for 90) beat An England XI 167 (J H King 55, K S Ranjitsinhji 28, R O Schwarz 4 for 30, J H Sinclair 4 for 55) and 203 (J H King 72, G L Jessop 34, K S Ranjitsinhji 29, J H Sinclair 6 for 67, R O Schwarz 4 for 76) by 189 runs.

E. A. HALLIWELL
Transvaal

Fourteenth Match vs ‡ Scotland played at Edinburgh on 18 and 19 July. South Africans 464 for 6 (L J Tancred 250, C M H Hathorn 81, W A Shalders 44, A S Cairns 3 for 28) beat Scotland 128 (W B Sharp 32, M R Dickson 25, J H Sinclair 5 for 68, J J Kotze 4 for 50) and 148 (M R Dickson 69, G C White 5 for 43, R O Schwarz 3 for 19) by an innings and 188 runs.

Fifteenth Match vs ‡ Liverpool and District played at Aigburth Cricket Ground, Liverpool on 21 and 22 July. South Africans 324 (F Mitchell 87, C M H Hathorn 68, S J Snooke 50, E A Halliwell 48, Brown 4 for 81) beat Liverpool and District 111 (A F Spooner 51, C S Hannay 24, R O Schwarz 5 for 40) and 118 (T Ainscough 34, C S Hannay 32, J J Kotze 6 for 53) by an innings and 95 runs.

Sixteenth Match vs Yorkshire played at The Circle Cricket Ground, Hull on 28, 29 and 30 July. South Africans 148 (J H Sinclair 39, G C White 25, C M H Hathorn 23, S Haigh 4 for 58, H Myers 3 for 8) and 158 for 8 (F Mitchell 42, L J Tancred 33, W A Shalders 21, H Myers 4 for 59) drew with Yorkshire 370 (Denton 66, H Wilkinson 60, H Rudston 41, J Tunnicliffe 40, Lord Hawke 34, G H Hirst 31, W Rhodes 31, J H Sinclair 6 for 134).

SOUTH AFRICAN CRICKET TEAM, 1907

J. H. SINCLAIR.

SIR ABE BAILEY
Hon. Vice President
S.A.C.A

Seventeenth Match vs Leicestershire played at Aylestone Road, Leicester on 1, 2 and 3 August. South Africans 464 (C M H Hathorn 128, L J Tancred 109, E A Halliwell 88, G C White 80, J H King 4 for 82, W W Odell 4 for 125) beat Leicestershire 171 (H Whitehead 53, S Coe 27, J H Sinclair 6 for 65, J J Kotze 3 for 54) and 292 (G C Gill 62, C E de Trafford 57, J H King 44, R T Crawford 44, J J Kotze 4 for 98, G C White 3 for 47) by an innings and 1 run.

Eighteenth Match vs Lancashire played at Old Trafford, Manchester on 4, 5 and 6 August. Lancashire 245 (A Ward 42, J S Heap 39, F M Miller 37, J T Tyldesley 36, H L Farr 25, G C White 3 for 63, J Middleton 3 for 85) and 188 (J S Heap 55, W Parker 40, A Ward 37, J J Kotze 4 for 67) drew with South Africans 167 (C M H Hathorn 37, R O Schwarz 30, L J Tancred 23, J S Heap 5 for 66) and 190 for 2 (W A Shalders 79, C M H Hathorn 65*).

Nineteenth Match vs Nottinghamshire played at Trent Bridge, Nottingham on 8, 9 and 10 August. South Africans 611 (G C White 115, L J Tancred 113, S J Snooke 88*, C M H Hathorn 88, W A Shalders 77, E A Halliwell 33, J H Pennington 7 for 223) beat Nottinghamshire 320 (G Gunn 143, R E Hemingway 85, J Hardstaff 37, R O Schwarz 4 for 60, J J Kotze 3 for 55) and 242 (Rev H Staunton 70, J Hardstaff 51, G Gunn 31, R E Hemingway 30, H A Cursham 25*, J J Kotze 5 for 68, J Middleton 4 for 50) by an innings and 49 runs.

Twentieth Match vs M.C.C. and Ground played at Lord's Cricket Ground, London on 11, 12 and 13 August. South Africans 223 (F Mitchell 60, R O Schwarz 28, S E Horwood 23, C M H Hathorn 23, T A Higson 3 for 42) and 90 for 0 (L J Tancred 45*, W A Shalders 30*) beat M.C.C. and Ground 120 (A Page 45, G J V Weigall 27, R O Schwarz 4 for 30, J J Kotze 4 for 32) and 192 (F A Tarrant 61, G J V Weigall 40, J J Kotze 3 for 30, J H Sinclair 3 for 45) by 10 wickets.

Twenty-First Match vs Derbyshire played at the Racecourse Ground, Derby on 15, 16 and 17 August. South Africans 120 (W A Shalders 19, S J Snooke 19, A R Warren 5 for 60) and 90 for 3 (L J Tancred 44*, F Mitchell 34) drew with Derbyshire 283 (E M Ashcroft 93, W Storer 63, L G Wright 32, C A Ollivierre 25, G C White 3 for 47).

Twenty-Second Match vs Sussex played at County Cricket Ground, Brighton on 22, 23 and 24 August. Sussex 357 for 3 dec (K S Ranjitsinhji 178*, C B Fry 74, R B Heygate 44*, R O Schwarz 2 for 72) drew with South Africans 372 for 7 (C M H Hathorn 139, J H Sinclair 79, G C White 47*, G R Cox 3 for 100, K S Ranjitsinhji 3 for 111).

Twenty-Third Match vs Kent played at St. Lawrence Cricket Ground, Canterbury on 25, 26 and 27 August. Kent 285 (Capt R O'Hara Livesay 78, E Humphreys 49, J R Mason 39, A Hearne 37, J H Sinclair 3 for 73) and 196 (S H Day 45, C H B Marsham 35, G C White 5 for 46, R O Schwarz 3 for 46) beat South Africans 188 (R O Schwarz 46, C M H Hathorn 41, F Mitchell 39, E Humphreys 4 for 19, C Blythe 3 for 67) and 189 (C M H Hathorn 39, S E Horwood 34, R O Schwarz 31, G C White 29, C Blythe 6 for 76, A Fielder 3 for 53) by 104 runs.

Twenty-Fourth Match vs Surrey played at Kennington Oval, London on 29, 30 and 31 August. Surrey 236 (E G Goatly 76, J E Raphael 56, E Stedman 44*, L J Tancred 4 for 43, J J Kotze 4 for 86) and 363 for 7 dec (T W Hayward 197, E G Goatly 63, E G Hayes 31, S J Snooke 2 for 39) drew with South Africans 139 (J H Sinclair 41, G C White 27, W A Shalders 25, E H L Nice 5 for 43, H C McDonell 3 for 46) and 17 for 0.

Twenty-Fifth Match vs Yorkshire played at North Marine Drive, Scarborough on 1, 2 and 3 September. South Africans 102 (G C White 49, G H Hirst 5 for 28, W Rhodes 4 for 41) and 232 for 5 (L J Tancred 101, F Mitchell 57*, G H Hirst 2 for 38) drew with Yorkshire 387 (D Denton 119, H Myers 41, Hon. F S Jackson 38, G H Hirst 31, R O Schwarz 5 for 101, G C White 3 for 89).

Twenty-Sixth Match vs South of England at Central Cricket Ground, Hastings on 5, 6 and 7 September. South of England 237 (G L Jessop 159*, R O Schwarz 6 for 68) and 125 for 6 dec (M W Payne 41*, J H Sinclair 3 for 48) drew with South Africans 255 (C B Llewellyn 81, G C White 47, F Mitchell 27, J H Sinclair 27, L C Braund 4 for 74, A E Trott 3 for 55) and 38 for 1 (L J Tancred 15).

Tour batting averages - all matches:

	Inns	NO	Runs	HS	Ave
C B Llewellyn	8	2	338	81	56.33
L J Tancred	38	4	1,640	250	48.23
F Mitchell	34	7	1,009	102*	37.37
C M H Hathorn	38	2	1,339	139	37.19
G C White	35	4	937	117	30.22
W A Shalders	39	3	948	81	26.33
R O Schwarz	31	2	737	102	25.41
E A Halliwell	27	5	514	88*	23.36
J H Sinclair	33	0	713	103	21.60
S J Snooke	28	5	427	88*	18.56
G H Shepstone	10	0	184	64	18.40
B Wallach	6	1	58	30	11.60
S E Horwood	15	1	159	34	11.35
J J Kotze	27	5	190	29	8.63
J Middleton	16	9	34	7	4.85

Tour bowling averages - all matches:

	Overs	Mdns	Runs	Wkts	Ave
R O Schwarz	403.5	48	1,422	96	14.81
J J Kotze	744.5	157	2,263	117	19.34
J H Sinclair	636.3	119	2,285	100	22.85
G C White	359.5	40	1,325	56	23.66
J Middleton	270.2	38	874	35	24.97
C B Llewellyn	111	23	405	16	25.31
S J Snooke	78	12	317	12	26.41
L J Tancred	44	9	160	6	26.66

Also bowled during the tour:

	Overs	Mdns	Runs	Wkts	Ave
G H Shepstone	12.2	3	50	4	12.50
E A Halliwell	4	0	24	0	-

Centuries recorded for South Africans during the tour:

L J Tancred	(6) :	250	vs Scotland (Edinburgh)
		140	vs Dublin University (Dublin)
		113	vs Nottinghamshire (Trent Bridge)
		109	vs Leicestershire (Aylestone Road, Leicester)
		106	vs Warwickshire (Edgbaston)
		101	vs Yorkshire (Scarborough)
C M H Hathorn	(3) :	139	vs Sussex (Brighton)
		130	vs London County (Crystal Palace)
		128	vs Leicestershire (Leicester)
G C White	(2) :	117	vs Dublin University (Dublin)
		115	vs Nottinghamshire (Trent Bridge)
J H Sinclair	(1) :	103	vs Derbyshire (Derby)
F Mitchell	(1) :	102*	vs Cambridge University (Fenner's)
R O Schwarz	(1) :	102	vs An England XI (Lord's)

Fielding:

	Catches	*Stumpings*
E A Halliwell	35	13
F Mitchell	22	
R O Schwarz	18	
B Wallach	10	8
G C White	17	
J H Sinclair	15	
L J Tancred	15	
W A Shalders	14	
S J Snooke	12	
J J Kotze	10	
C M H Hathorn	5	
S E Horwood	4	
C B Llewellyn	3	
J Middleton	3	
G H Shepstone	3	

The Fourth South African Team in the United Kingdom, 1907 (South African Cricket Association)

Finally the South Africans were formally recognised and allocated three three-day Test Matches against England on their 1907 tour to be played at Lord's, Headingley and The Oval.

They were captained by Peter Sherwell who was to be the first to score a Test Century, a second innings 115 at Lord's, which saved the tourists from defeat. However, England were to win at Leeds on a rain affected pitch while a true pitch at The Oval produced a draw.

The consistent improvement of South African cricket was to be noted, and it should be appreciated that so much cricket in South Africa was still played on hard matting wickets so different from the turf pitches to be found in England.

(standing) **R.O.Schwarz H.E.Smith W.A.Shalders J.H.Sinclair A.E.E.Vogler G.C.White A.W.Nourse**

(sitting) **J.J.Kotze L.J.Tancred C.M.H.Hathorn P.W.Sherwell** (Captain) **Mr.G.Allsop** (Manager) **Rev.C.D.Robinson S.J.Snooke**

(on ground) **G.A.Faulkner**

Touring party (15):

*† P W Sherwell (*Transvaal*) (Captain)
Age 26. Right-handed opening/middle order batsman and wicket-keeper.

L J Tancred (*Transvaal*) (Vice-Captain)
Age 30. Right-handed opening batsman.

S D Snooke (*Western Province*)
Age 28. Right-handed middle order batsman and right-arm bowler.

G A Faulkner (*Transvaal*)
Age 25. Right-handed middle order batsman and googly bowler.

A E E Vogler (*Transvaal/Middlesex*)
Age 30. Right-handed middle order batsman and right-arm leg break and googly bowler.

H E Smith (*Transvaal*)
Age 23. Right-handed middle order batsman.

† Rev C D Robinson (*Natal*)
Age 33. Right-handed lower order batsman and wicket-keeper.

A W Nourse (*Natal*)
Age 29. Steady left-handed middle order batsman, left-arm medium pace or slow bowler and good slip fieldsman.

S J Snooke (*Border*)
Age 26. Right-handed middle order batsman and right-arm fast medium bowler.

R O Schwarz (*Transvaal/Middlesex*)
Age 32. Right-handed attacking lower order batsman and right-arm medium pace bowler/off-break bowler with leg-break action.

G C White (*Transvaal*)
Age 25. Right-handed attractive middle order batsman and leg-break bowler.

J J Kotze (*Western Province*)
Age 27. Right-arm fast bowler, right-handed batsman and poor fieldsman.

C M H Hathorn (*Transvaal*)
Age 29. Right-handed middle order batsman.

J H Sinclair (*Transvaal*)
Age 30. Right-handed hard hitting middle order batsman and right-arm medium pace or leg-break bowler.

W A Shalders (*Griqualand West*)
Age 27. Right-handed opening batsman.

Manager: Mr. G Allsop

Summary of all matches:

Played 31   Won 21   Lost 4   Drawn 6

Summary of first-class matches:

Played 27 Won 17 Lost 4 Drawn 6

Summary of Test Matches:

Played 3   Won 0   Lost 1   Drawn 2

First Match vs Leicestershire played at Aylestone Road, Leicester on 20, 21 and 22 May. South Africans 145 (C M H Hathorn 43, A W Nourse 28, T Jayes 4 for 51, W E Astill 3 for 43) and 156 (A W Nourse 41, P W Sherwell 34, G A Faulkner 34, T Jayes 4 for 61, W E Astill 3 for 34) beat Leicestershire 149 (H Whitehead 44, S Coe 26, W W Odell 20, R O Schwarz 6 for 55, A E E Vogler 3 for 25) and 54 (W W Odell 22, A E E Vogler 5 for 37) by 98 runs.

Second Match vs Essex played at County Ground, Leyton on 23, 24 and 25 May. South Africans 355 for 8 dec (G A Faulkner 101*, J H Sinclair 51, A W Nourse 44, A E E Vogler 39, S D Snooke 38, G C White 33, W Mead 3 for 118, J W H T Douglas 3 for 61) beat Essex 89 (C P McGahey 43, J H Sinclair 4 for 23, R O Schwarz 3 for 21) and 167 (S P Metson 46*, S A Trick 26, R O Schwarz 5 for 28, G A Faulkner 3 for 54) by an innings and 99 runs.

Third Match vs M.C.C. and Ground played at Lord's Cricket Ground, London on 27, 28 and 29 May. South Africans 227 (G C White 74, C M H Hathorn 29, F A Tarrant 6 for 73) and 96 for 7 (J H Sinclair 20, F A Tarrant 4 for 36, A E Trott 3 for 43) beat M.C.C. and Ground 142 (L C Collins 33, J H King 31, R O Schwarz 4 for 27) and 177 (F A Tarrant 54, Hubble 43, Thompson 37, A E E Vogler 8 for 67) by 3 wickets.

Fourth Match vs Oxford University at The University Parks, Oxford on 30, 31 May and 1 June. Oxford University 113 (E L Wright 37, R G Barnes 21, R O Schwarz 7 for 41) and 16 for 2 (A E E Vogler 2 for 10) drew with South Africans 182 (G A Faulkner 55, A W Nourse 54, R G Barnes 4 for 44, H A Gilbert 4 for 50).

Fifth Match vs Cambridge University at Fenner's University Cricket Ground, Cambridge on 3, 4 and 5 June. South Africans 201 (G C White 45, J H Sinclair 44, W A Shalders 29, G G Napier 6 for 73) and 11 for 1 drew with Cambridge University 103 (J N Buchanan 24, H J Goodwin 24*, A E E Vogler 5 for 42, J H Sinclair 3 for 46).

Sixth Match vs Northamptonshire at County Cricket Ground, Wantage Road, Northampton on 6, 7 and 8 June. South Africans 115 (R O Schwarz 34, G C White 23, G J Thompson 6 for 41, S G Smith 3 for 22) and 143 (R O Schwarz 38, J H Sinclair 24, S G Smith 7 for 61) beat Northamptonshire 57 (E M Crosse 12, R O Schwarz 6 for 11) and 118 (S G Smith 32, G J Thompson 23, R O Schwarz 4 for 29, G C White 4 for 12) by 83 runs.

Seventh Match vs Middlesex at Lord's Cricket Ground, London on 10, 11 and 12 June. South Africans 212 (A W Nourse 58, L J Tancred 49, F A Tarrant 6 for 97, E Mignon 3 for 41) and 404 for 9 dec (G C White 68, R O Schwarz 51*, J H Sinclair 49, W A Shalders 45, A W Nourse 41, E Mignon 4 for 96) beat Middlesex 112 (F A Tarrant 42, R O Schwarz 6 for 27, J J Kotze 4 for 48) and 226 (G W Beldam 41, J H Hunt 38, C C Page 31, J J Kotze 3 for 48, A E E Vogler 3 for 58) by 278 runs.

Eighth Match vs Hampshire played at County Cricket Ground, Northlands Road, Southampton on 13, 14 and 15 June. South Africans 82 (A E E Vogler 29, H G Smoker 7 for 35, J R Badcock 3 for 26) and 329 for 9 (W A Shalders 105, P W Sherwell 74, C P Mead 3 for 63) drew with Hampshire 111 (C B Llewellyn 61, G A Faulkner 5 for 8).

Ninth Match vs Warwickshire played at Edgbaston Cricket Ground, Birmingham on 17, 18 and 19 June. South Africans 296 (C M H Hathorn 117, S J Snooke 57, R O Schwarz 45, S Santall 7 for 77) and 318 for 6 dec (A W Nourse 127, G A Faulkner 61*, P W Sherwell 46, G C White 37, F Moorhouse 3 for 96) beat Warwickshire 202 (A F A Lilley 63, W G Quaife 52, G C White 4 for 12) and 136 (F Moorhouse 24*, C S Baker 22, A F A Lilley 22, R O Schwarz 5 for 47, A E E Vogler 3 for 41) by 276 runs.

Tenth Match vs Derbyshire played at the Racecourse Ground, Derby on 20, 21 and 22 June. South Africans 376 (A W Nourse 148, S J Snooke 114*, C M H Hathorn 54, F C Bracey 5 for 102) beat Derbyshire 222 (A Morton 72, C A Ollivierre 27, A E E Vogler 4 for 79) and 46 (A E E Vogler 6 for 17, J J Kotze 4 for 23) by an innings and 108 runs.

SOUTH AFRICAN
CRICKET TEAM, 1907.

SOUTH AFRICAN
CRICKET TEAM, 1907.

G. A. FAULKNER.

P. W. SHERWELL

Eleventh Match vs Kent played at St. Lawrence Cricket Ground, Canterbury on 24, 25 and 26 June. South Africans 95 (R O Schwarz 24, C Blythe 5 for 46, W J Fairservice 4 for 17) and 281 (S J Snooke 97, S J Snooke 60, W J Fairservice 5 for 76, C Blythe 5 for 114) beat Kent 273 (W J Fairservice 61, C H B Marsham 46, C Blythe 33, E Humphreys 32, A E E Vogler 4 for 74, R O Schwarz 3 for 49) and 101 (F E Woolley 29, J C Hubble 25, J J Kotze 4 for 19, G C White 4 for 36) by 2 runs.

Twelfth Match vs England (First Test Match) played at Lord's Cricket Ground, London on 1, 2 and 3 July.

England

C B Fry	b Vogler	33
T W Hayward	st Sherwell b Vogler	21
J T Tyldesley	b Vogler	52
* R E Foster	st Sherwell b Vogler	8
L C Braund	c Kotze b Faulkner	104
G H Hirst	b Vogler	7
G L Jessop	c Faulkner b Vogler	93
J N Crawford	c Sherwell b Schwarz	22
E G Arnold	b Schwarz	4
† A F A Lilley	c Nourse b Vogler	48
C Blythe	not out	4
Extras	b 24 lb 6 w 2	32
Total		**428**

Fall 1st inns: 1/54 2/55 3/79 4/140 5/158 6/303 7/335 8/347 9/401 10/428

Bowling		1st inns		
Kotze	12	2	43	0
Schwarz	34	7	90	2
Vogler	47.2	12	128	7
White	15	2	52	0
Nourse	1	0	2	0
Faulkner	12	1	59	1
Sinclair	6	1	22	0

South Africa

*† W A Shalders	c Lilley b Arnold	2	b Hirst	0
P W Sherwell	run out	6	b Blythe	115
C M H Hathorn	c Foster b Hirst	6	c Fry b Blythe	30
A W Nourse	b Blythe	62	not out	11
G A Faulkner	c Jessop b Braund	44	not out	12
S J Snooke	lbw b Blythe	5		
G C White	b Arnold	0		
J H Sinclair	b Arnold	0		
R O Schwarz	not out	0		
A E E Vogler	c Lilley b Arnold	3		
J J Kotze	b Arnold	0		
Extras	b 9 lb 2 w 1	12	b 15 lb 2	17
Total		**140**	**(3 wickets)**	**185**

Fall 1st inns: 1/8 2/8 3/18 4/116 5/134 6/135 7/135 8/137 9/140 10/140
Fall 2nd inns: 1/1 2/140 3/153

Bowling		1st inns				2nd inns		
Hirst	18	7	35	1	16	8	26	1
Arnold	22	7	37	5	13	2	41	0
Jessop	2	0	8	0				
Crawford	8	1	20	0	4	0	19	0
Blythe	8	3	18	2	21	5	56	2
Braund	7	4	10	1	4	0	26	0

Umpires: A Millward and A A White

England drew with South Africa.

Thirteenth Match vs Sussex played at County Cricket Ground, Brighton on 4, 5 and 6 July. South Africans 49 (J H Sinclair 17, E B Dwyer 6 for 25, G R Cox 4 for 21) and 327 (J H Sinclair 92, H E Smith 40*, L J Tancred 38, A E E Vogler 38, Rev C D Robinson 36, G A Faulkner 35, G R Cox 4 for 93, E B Dwyer 3 for 122) beat Sussex 186 (C B Fry 45, R R Relf 20, G A Faulkner 3 for 37) and 151 (G Leach 32, E H Killick 31, J H Sinclair 3 for 34, A E E Vogler 3 for 41, R O Schwarz 3 for 42) by 39 runs.

Fourteenth Match vs Surrey played at Kennington Oval, London on 11, 12 and 13 July. Surrey 239 (J N Crawford 69, T W Hayward 61, A.Marshal 34, A E E Vogler 7 for 92) and 225 (T W Hayward 86, J B Hobbs 41, F C Holland 34, G A Faulkner 4 for 20, A W Nourse 3 for 29) beat South Africans 162 (G C White 27*, C M H Hathorn 25, J H Sinclair 25, N A Knox 6 for 54, J N Crawford 4 for 66) and 217 (J H Sinclair 64, R O Schwarz 30, J N Crawford 4 for 79, N A Knox 3 for 86) by 85 runs.

Fifteenth Match vs Yorkshire played at Park Avenue, Bradford on 15 and 16 July. South Africans 148 (A W Nourse 35, S J Snooke 31, G H Hirst 5 for 34) and 116 for 5 (J H Sinclair 37*, A W Nourse 27, G H Hirst 2 for 26) beat Yorkshire 150 (G H Hirst 35, W Rhodes 24, G C White 4 for 34, G A Faulkner 3 for 28) and 113 (J W Rothery 23, J Tunnicliffe 20, S Haigh 20) by 5 wickets.

Sixteenth Match vs ‡ A Scotland XI played at Glasgow on 18 and 19 July. South Africans 573 (L J Tancred 119, G A Faulkner 107, A W Nourse 105, S J Snooke 36, A E E Vogler 36, A Broadbent 4 for 186) beat A Scotland XI 68 (R G Tait 37, J J Kotze 7 for 43, A W Nourse 3 for 22) and 134 (R G Tait 55*, A Broadbent 22, J J Kotze 5 for 43, S J Snooke 3 for 24) by an innings and 371 runs.

Seventeenth Match vs Scotland played at Edinburgh on 22, 23 and 24 July. South Africans 443 (P W Sherwell 109, A E E Vogler 103, W A Shalders 80, L J Tancred 45, S J Snooke 37, H E Smith 20, B L Peel 4 for 123, A Broadbent 4 for 80) and 28 for 2 (W A Shalders 12*) beat Scotland 209 (B L Peel 74, H D Keigwin 36, A Broadbent 32, R O Schwarz 5 for 58, A E E Vogler 3 for 38) and 258 (B L Peel 65, C T Mannes 62, H D Keigwin 41, R O Schwarz 5 for 18, A E E Vogler 4 for 80) by 8 wickets.

Eighteenth Match vs ‡ Durham played at Ashbrooke Cricket Ground, Sunderland on 25 and 26 July. South Africans 358 (H E Smith 83, W A Shalders 65, S J Snooke 43, Rev C D Robinson 38, G C White 36, A E E Vogler 33, A Stoner 8 for 100) beat Durham 125 (G Turnbull 36, G A Faulkner 4 for 52, G C White 4 for 30) and 204 (E W Elliot 53, G Turnbull 48, J Thackeray 38, G A Faulkner 4 for 41, A E E Vogler 4 for 47) by an innings and 29 runs.

Nineteenth Match vs England (Second Test Match) played at Lord's Cricket Ground, London on 29, 30 and 31 July.

England

C B Fry	b Vogler	2	lbw b White		54
T W Hayward	st Sherwell b Faulkner	24	st Sherwell b Vogler		15
J T Tyldesley	b Faulkner	12	c S J Snooke b Schwarz		30
* R E Foster	b Sinclair	0	lbw b Faulkner		22
L C Braund	lbw b Faulkner	1	c Schwarz b White		0
G H Hirst	c Hathorn b Sinclair	17	b White		2
G L Jessop	c Sherwell b Faulkner	0	c Hathorn b Faulkner		10
E G Arnold	b Faulkner	0	c Schwarz b Faulkner		12
† A F A Lilley	c Schwarz b Faulkner	3	lbw b White		0
C Blythe	not out	5	not out		4
N A Knox	c Faulkner b Sinclair	8	run out		5
Extras	b 1 lb 2 nb 1	4	b 7 lb 1		8
Total		**76**			**162**

Fall 1st inns: 1/9 2/41 3/42 4/42 5/53 6/53 7/57 8/63 9/63 10/76
Fall 2nd inns: 1/37 2/100 3/106 4/107 5/115 6/126 7/151 8/152 9/154 10/162

Bowling	1st inns				2nd inns			
Vogler	8	3	14	1	4	0	18	1
Schwarz	7	0	18	0	5.4	0	18	1
Faulkner	11	4	17	6	20	3	58	3
Sinclair	10.3	2	23	3	4	0	13	0
White					16	3	47	4

South Africa

L J Tancred	st Lilley b Blythe	0	run out		0
*† P W Sherwell	lbw b Blythe	26	c Foster b Blythe		1
C M H Hathorn	c Lilley b Hirst	0	b Arnold		7
A W Nourse	c Arnold b Blythe	18	b Blythe		2
G C White	c Hirst b Blythe	3	c Arnold b Blythe		7
G A Faulkner	c Braund b Blythe	6	c Foster b Blythe		11
J H Sinclair	st Lilley b Blythe	2	c Braund b Blythe		15
S J Snooke	c Lilley b Knox	13	c Hirst b Blythe		14
W A Shalders	c Fry b Blythe	21	lbw b Hirst		5
A E E Vogler	c Hayward b Blythe	11	c Tyldesley b Blythe		9
R O Schwarz	not out	5	not out		0
Extras	b 3 lb 1 nb 1	5	b 3 nb 1		4
Total		**110**			**75**

Fall 1st inns: 1/6 2/9 3/34 4/47 5/49 6/56 7/59 8/73 9/102 10/110
Fall 2nd inns: 1/0 2/3 3/10 4/16 5/18 6/38 7/56 8/66 9/75 10/75

Bowling	1st inns				2nd inns			
Hirst	9	3	22	1	9	2	21	1
Blythe	15.5	1	59	8	12.4	9	40	7
Arnold	4	1	11	0	13	7	10	1
Knox	3	0	13	1				

Umpires: J Moss and J Carlin

England beat South Africa by 53 runs.

Twentieth Match vs Lancashire played at Old Trafford, Manchester on 1 and 2 August. South Africans 429 (G A Faulkner 106*, A W Nourse 71, P W Sherwell 69, A E E Vogler 69, H E Smith 31, A Kermode 5 for 94) beat Lancashire 169 (R H Spooner 57, J Sharp 52, R O Schwarz 6 for 45, A E E Vogler 3 for 56) and 95 (H D Stanning 35, A W Nourse 5 for 44, S J Snooke 3 for 46) by an innings and 165 runs.

Twenty-First Match vs Gentlemen of Ireland played at Dublin on 5, 6 and 7 August. South Africans 218 (C M H Hathorn 73*, G A Faulkner 26, W A Shalders 25, T C Ross 5 for 99, W Harrington 4 for 79) and 162 (W A Shalders 48, G A Faulkner 28, A E E Vogler 27*, W Harrington 5 for 48) beat Gentlemen of Ireland 153 (R H Lambert 51, F H Browning 41, A E E Vogler 6 for 73) and 76 (T C Ross 23*, G A Faulkner 6 for 39, R O Schwarz 4 for 20) by 151 runs.

Twenty-Second Match vs ‡ S H Cochrane's XI played at Bray, Ireland on 8 and 9 August. South Africans 251 (L J Tancred 56, W A Shalders 53, H E Smith 24*, W Brearley 5 for 113, J T Newstead 4 for 54) beat S H Cochrane's XI 88 (J T Newstead 18, R O Schwarz 6 for 31, A W Nourse 5 for 44) and 97 (G J Meldon 32, A E E Vogler 6 for 50, S J Snooke 4 for 38) by an innings and 66 runs.

Twenty-Third Match vs Nottinghamshire played at Trent Bridge, Nottingham on 14 and 15 August. Nottinghamshire 296 (J Hardstaff 124, C C James 43, G Gunn 41, A E E Vogler 5 for 55, R O Schwarz 4 for 82) and 164 for 5 (J Iremonger 92*, J Hardstaff 48, R O Schwarz 2 for 24) beat South Africans 258 (A W Nourse 66, G A Faulkner 51, W A Shalders 34, A E E Vogler 32, J R Gunn 4 for 92, T G Wass 3 for 102) and 199 (A E E Vogler 48, R O Schwarz 39*, G C White 32, R O Schwarz 2 for 24) by 5 wickets.

Twenty-Fourth Match vs Essex played at County Ground, Leyton on 16 and 17 August. South Africans 293 (G C White 76, A E E Vogler 57, S J Snooke 55, J H Sinclair 27, W Reeves 5 for 104) and 155 (A W Nourse 38, R O Schwarz 29, J W H T Douglas 3 for 23) beat Essex 186 (F L Fane 34, J W H T Douglas 26, S P Metson 24, A E E Vogler 5 for 66) and 158 (W Reeves 46, F L Fane 28, J W H T Douglas 24, G C White 4 for 44, A E E Vogler 3 for 43) by 104 runs.

SOUTH AFRICAN
CRICKET TEAM, 1907.

SOUTH AFRICAN
CRICKET TEAM, 1907.

A. D. NOURSE.

H. SMITH.

Twenty-Fifth Match vs England (Third Test Match) played at Kennington Oval, London on 19, 20 and 21 August.

England

T W Hayward	lbw b Vogler	0	c Sherwell b Nourse		3
C B Fry	c & b Faulkner	129	b Vogler		3
J T Tyldesley	b Faulkner	8	c White b Nourse		11
* R E Foster	lbw b Vogler	51	c & b S J Snooke		35
L C Braund	b Schwarz	18	c Schwarz b Vogler		34
G H Hirst	c S J Snooke b Schwarz	4	hit wicket b Schwarz		16
G L Jessop	c S D Snooke b Sinclair	2	st Sherwell b Schwarz		11
J N Crawford	c S D Snooke b Schwarz	2	c Nourse b Vogler		2
† A F A Lilley	b Nourse	42	not out		9
C Blythe	b Nourse	10	b Schwarz		0
N A Knox	not out	8	b Vogler		3
Extras	b 6 lb 12 w 1 nb 2	21	b 3 lb 6 nb 2		11
Total		**295**			**138**

Fall 1st inns: 1/0 2/19 3/105 4/154 5/170 6/177 7/181 8/271 9/274 10/295
Fall 2nd inns: 1/6 2/6 3/20 4/89 5/100 6/108 7/118 8/131 9/131 10/138

Bowling		1st inns				2nd inns		
Vogler	31	7	86	2	14.3	2	49	4
Faulkner	27	2	78	2	3	1	6	0
Schwarz	27	8	45	3	14	7	21	3
White	9	2	28	0				
Sinclair	14	4	27	1				
Nourse	4	1	10	2	18	6	43	2
S J Snooke					5	3	8	1

South Africa

*† P W Sherwell	b Blythe	6	(1) b Hirst		42
G A Faulkner	c & b Hirst	2	(2) c Foster b Blythe		36
S J Snooke	c Jessop b Hirst	63	(6) not out		0
A W Nourse	c Lilley b Knox	34	(3) b Hirst		28
J H Sinclair	c Crawford b Knox	22	(7) not out		24
W A Shalders	c Jessop b Blythe	31	(4) b Blythe		19
A E E Vogler	b Blythe	5			
R O Schwarz	b Hirst	2			
G C White	st Lilley b Blythe	4	(5) b Hirst		1
C M H Hathorn	not out	3			
S D Snooke	c Foster b Blythe	0			
Extras	b 3 lb 1 nb 2	6	b 5 lb 3 nb 1		9
Total		**178**	**(5 wickets)**		**159**

Fall 1st inns: 1/8 2/8 3/69 4/105 5/149 6/160 7/163 8/174 9/175 10/178
Fall 2nd inns: 1/61 2/72 3/76 4/110 5/159

Bowling		1st inns				2nd inns		
Blythe	20.3	5	61	5	12.3	3	36	2
Hirst	22	7	39	3	13	1	42	3
Crawford	11	2	33	0	6	3	14	0
Knox	10	2	39	2	8	0	53	0
Braund					1	0	5	0

Umpires: W Richards and W A J West

England drew with South Africa.

SOUTH AFRICAN
CRICKET TEAM, 1907.

S. D. SNOOKE.

SOUTH AFRICAN
CRICKET TEAM, 1907.

A. E. VOGLER.

Twenty-Sixth Match vs Gloucestershire played at Wagon Works Ground, Gloucester on 23 August. South Africans 372 (G C White 162, R O Schwarz 71, G A Faulkner 46, L J Tancred 28, E G Dennett 4 for 98) beat Gloucestershire 183 (J H Board 69, T Langdon 54, G L Jessop 26, R O Schwarz 5 for 46) and 151 (T Langdon 78, G L Jessop 20, G A Faulkner 4 for 23, A E E Vogler 3 for 36) by an innings and 38 runs.

Twenty-Seventh Match vs ‡ South Wales played at Arms Park, Cardiff on 27 and 28 August. South Africans 289 (S J Snooke 87, W A Shalders 62, P W Sherwell 47, Nash 6 for 75, Creber 3 for 140) and 131 (A J Silverlock 33, A Gibson 29*, Diver 23, G C White 4 for 29, A W Nourse 3 for 14) by an innings and 66 runs.

Twenty-Eighth Match vs Somerset played at the Recreation Ground, Bath on 30 and 31 August. South Africans 233 (G A Faulkner 73, G C White 37, P W Sherwell 35, A E Lewis 3 for 34, O C Mordaunt 3 for 78, E Robson 3 for 39) and 348 (S J Snooke 157, L J Tancred 67, R O Schwarz 38, G C White 33, H F Montgomery 3 for 22, A E Lewis 3 for 97) beat Somerset 118 (V H B Majendie 28, R O Schwarz 6 for 46, J J Kotze 3 for 35) and 105 (S M J Woods 37, G C White 5 for 19) by 358 runs.

Twenty-Ninth Match vs M.C.C. and Ground played at Lord's Cricket Ground, London on 5, 6 and 7 September. M.C.C. and Ground 318 (A E Lawton 89, B S Foster 86, P F Warner 44, G C White 6 for 91) beat South Africans 135 (L J Tancred 61*, A E E Vogler 22, F A Tarrant 5 for 65) and 174 (L J Tancred 42, G A Faulkner 36, S J Snooke 35, F A Tarrant 5 for 57) by an innings and 9 runs.

Thirtieth Match vs J C Bamford's XI played at Uttoxeter on 7 September. South Africans 257 (A W Nourse 68, G A Faulkner 52, L J Tancred 37, E G Dennett 4 for 69) beat J C Bamford's XI 92 (A F A Lilley 26, A C MacLaren 21, G C White 7 for 33, R O Schwarz 3 for 40) and 151 (A E Lawton 47, J N Crawford 38, G C White 4 for 36, G A Faulkner 4 for 44) by an innings and 14 runs.

Thirty-First Match vs C I Thornton's (England) XI played at North Marine Drive, Scarborough on 10 September. C I Thornton's (England) XI 397 (W Rhodes 81, J B Hobbs 78, R H Spooner 73, J T Tyldesley 40, G H Hirst 38, A E E Vogler 3 for 74, R O Schwarz 3 for 96) and 232 for 2 dec (T W Hayward 105*, J T Tyldesley 99) drew with South Africans 319 (W A Shalders 76, A W Nourse 70, J J Kotze 60, W Rhodes 3 for 74, N A Knox 3 for 105) and 192 for 5 (L J Tancred 84, R O Schwarz 49).

SOUTH AFRICAN
CRICKET TEAM, 1907.

SOUTH AFRICAN
CRICKET TEAM, 1907.

R. O. SCHWARZ.

GEO. ALSOP.
MANAGER.

Test Match batting averages:

	Inns	NO	Runs	HS	Ave
A W Nourse	6	2	127	62	31.75
P W Sherwell	5	0	154	115	30.80
S J Snooke	5	0	131	63	26.20
G A Faulkner	6	1	117	44	23.40
W A Shalders	6	1	83	31	16.60
J H Sinclair	5	0	67	28	13.40
C M H Hathorn	5	1	46	30	11.50
A E E Vogler	5	0	47	19	9.40
R O Schwarz	4	3	7	5*	7.00
G C White	5	0	15	7	3.00

The following did not bat: J J Kotze, S D Snooke and L J Tancred

Test Match bowling averages:

	Overs	Mdns	Runs	Wkts	Ave
A W Nourse	23	7	55	4	13.75
G A Faulkner	73	11	218	12	18.16
A E E Vogler	104.5	24	295	15	19.66
J H Sinclair	34.3	7	85	4	21.25
R O Schwarz	87.4	22	192	9	21.33
G C White	40	7	127	4	31.75
J J Kotze	12	2	43	-	-

Also bowled during Tests:

	Overs	Mdns	Runs	Wkts	Ave
S J Snooke	5	3	8	1	8.00

Tour batting averages - all matches:

	Inns	NO	Runs	HS	Ave
S J Snooke	41	5	1,127	157	31.30
G A Faulkner	48	6	1,288	107	30.66
A W Nourse	47	2	1,329	148	29.53
W A Shalders	42	4	974	105	25.63
P W Sherwell	41	4	871	115	23.54
L J Tancred	35	1	784	119	23.05
A E E Vogler	42	4	831	103	21.86
G C White	46	3	939	162*	21.83
H E Smith	19	3	337	83	21.06
R O Schwarz	40	8	656	71	21.50
J H Sinclair	40	1	779	92	19.97
Rev C D Robinson	13	6	117	38*	16.70
C M H Hathorn	40	4	584	117	16.22
J J Kotze	16	5	131	60	11.90
S D Snooke	21	5	175	38*	10.93

Tour bowling averages - all matches:

	Overs	Mdns	Runs	Wkts	Ave
R O Schwarz	718.3	157	1,647	143	11.51
G C White	322.3	59	971	72	13.48
A E E Vogler	647.5	133	2,029	133	15.25
G A Faulkner	409.3	88	1,133	73	15.52
A W Nourse	164.3	40	427	27	15.81
J J Kotze	212.5	36	770	37	20.81
J H Sinclair	308.3	67	930	39	23.84
S J Snooke	158	27	445	16	27.81

Also bowled during the tour:

	Overs	Mdns	Runs	Wkts	Ave
S D Snooke	8	4	11	1	11.00
W A Shalders	12	1	32	0	-

Centuries recorded for South Africans during the tour:

A W Nourse   (3) :   148   vs Derbyshire (Derby)
                                 127   vs Warwickshire (Edgbaston)
                                 105   vs A Scottish XI (Glasgow)
G A Faulkner   (3) :   107   vs A Scottish XI (Glasgow)
                              106* vs Lancashire (Old Trafford)
                              101* vs Essex (Leyton) (1st Match)
S J Snooke   (2) :   157   vs Somerset (Bath)
                              114* vs Derbyshire (Derby)
P W Sherwell   (2) :   115   vs England (Lord's) (First Test Match)
                               109   vs Scotland (Edinburgh)
G C White   (1) :   162* vs Gloucestershire (Bristol)
L J Tancred   (1) :   119   vs A Scottish XI (Glasgow)
C M H Hathorn (1) :   117   vs Warwickshire (Edgbaston)
W A Shalders   (1) :   105   vs Hampshire (Southampton)
A E E Vogler   (1) :   103   vs Scotland (Edinburgh)

Fielding:

	Catches	*Stumpings*
P W Sherwell	24	17
A E E Vogler	24	
A W Nourse	20	
R O Schwarz	19	
G A Faulkner	18	
Rev C D Robinson	8	10
S J Snooke	18	
G C White	11	
S D Snooke	9	
C M H Hathorn	8	
J J Kotze	8	
W A Shalders	8	
H E Smith	7	
J H Sinclair	5	
L J Tancred	3	

The Fifth South African Team in the United Kingdom, 1912 Triangular Tournament (South African Cricket Association)

It was the initiative of Sir Abe Bailey that brought about the Triangular Tournament of 1912 between England, Australia and South Africa. Each of these three main cricketing nations was to play three Tests against each other.

The poor weather contributed to what proved to be a tournament of disappointing cricket, and in addition Australia were missing a number of their top players while the South Africans were below the strength of the 1907 tourists.

In this tournament South Africa were to lose five of their six Tests, three against England, who were to win the tournament, and two against Australia, gaining a draw at Trent Bridge in a rain spoilt game.

Once again it appears to have been the English turf wickets which were to prove significant in the downfall of the South African tourists.

Following this tour two players were lost to South Africa as S. J. Pegler remained in England to play Minor County cricket and G. A. Faulkner remained to start a business. Both were to be recalled into the 1924 touring party although in the case of Faulkner for a single Test appearance at Lord's.

(standing) **L.A.Stricker R.O.Schwarz R.Beaumont T.Campbell G.P.D.Hartigan J.L.Cox**

(sitting) **S.J.Pegler L.J.Tancred F.Mitchell** (Captain) **G.A.Faulkner S.J.Snooke A.W.Nourse**

(on ground) **H.W.Taylor T.A.Ward C.P.Carter**

Touring party (17):

* F Mitchell (*Transvaal/Cambridge University/Yorkshire/London County*)
(Captain)
Age 39. Right-handed attacking middle order batsman and right-arm medium
pace bowler.

L J Tancred (*Transvaal*) (Vice-Captain)
Age 35. Right-handed opening batsman.

L A Stricker (*Transvaal*)
Age 28. Right-handed opening batsman.

R Beaumont (*Transvaal*)
Age 28. Right-handed hard hitting middle order batsman and fine fieldsman.

S J Pegler (*Transvaal*)
Age 24. Right-handed lower order batsman, right-arm medium pace and leg break
bowler.

† T A Ward (*Transvaal*)
Age 24. Steady right-handed middle/late order batsman and wicket-keeper.

† T Campbell (*Transvaal*)
Age 30. Right-handed middle/lower order batsman and wicket-keeper.

H W Taylor (*Natal*)
Age 23. Attractive right-handed opening batsman and fine fielder.

C P Carter (*Natal*)
Age 31. Right-handed lower order batsman and left-arm bowler.

C B Llewellyn (*Natal*)
Age 35. Left-handed attacking middle order batsman, left-arm slow medium
bowler and fine mid off fieldsman.

J L Cox (*Natal*)
Age 25. Right-handed lower order batsman, right-arm medium-fast bowler and
good slip fielder.

G P D Hartigan (*Border*)
Age 27. Right-handed middle order batsman, leg-break bowler and good
fieldsman.

G A Faulkner (*Transvaal*)
Age 31. Right-handed middle order batsman and googly bowler.

A W Nourse (*Natal*)
Age 34. Steady left-handed middle order batsman, left-arm medium pace or slow
bowler and good slip fieldsman.

S J Snooke (*Transvaal/Border*)
Age 31. Right-handed middle order batsman and right-arm fast medium bowler.

R O Schwarz (*Transvaal/Middlesex*)
Age 37. Right-handed attacking lower order batsman and right-arm medium pace
bowler/off-break bowler with leg-break action.

G C White (*Transvaal*)
Age 30. Right-handed attractive middle order batsman and leg-break bowler.

Manager: Mr. G Allsop

Summary of all / first-class matches:

Played 37   Won 13   Lost 8   Drawn 16

Summary of Test Matches:

Played 3   Won 0   Lost 3   Drawn 0   (against England)
Played 3   Won 0   Lost 2   Drawn 1   (against Australia)

First Match vs Derbyshire played at the Racecourse Ground, Derby on 4, 6 and 7 May. South Africans 136 (L J Tancred 39, S J Snooke 31, A Morton 6 for 52, A G Slater 3 for 25) and 138 for 3 (G A Faulkner 46, A W Nourse 31*, S J Snooke 28*) beat Derbyshire 143 (S W A Cadman 53, C J Corbett 24, C P Carter 3 for 29) and 129 (A R Warren 44, J Humphries 29, G A Faulkner 5 for 46, C P Carter 4 for 36) by 7 wickets.

Second Match vs Surrey played at Kennington Oval, London on 9, 10 and 11 May. South Africans 252 (R O Schwarz 70, F Mitchell 37, S J Snooke 32, C P Carter 29, J W Hitch 4 for 76, T Rushby 3 for 56, E G Hayes 3 for 62) and 175 (A W Nourse 49, R O Schwarz 38, J W Hitch 6 for 57) beat Surrey 163 (E G Hayes 44, T W Hayward 23, A Ducat 22, A W Nourse 4 for 44, R O Schwarz 4 for 64) and 212 (T W Hayward 67, H S Harrison 38, M C Bird 24, C P Carter 3 for 11, R O Schwarz 3 for 77) by 52 runs.

Third Match vs M.C.C. played at Lord's Cricket Ground, London on 13, 14 and 15 May. M.C.C. 293 (F A Tarrant 104, A P Day 50, R H Spooner 36, C B Fry 30, R R Relf 25, S J Pegler 5 for 75 G P D Hartigan 3 for 69) and 221 (R H Spooner 72, F A Tarrant 52, C B Fry 38, S J Pegler 6 for 44) beat South Africans 176 (A W Nourse 35, R O Schwarz 35, F Mitchell 30, F A Tarrant 6 for 55) and 230 (S J Snooke 86, A W Nourse 32, J W Hearne 4 for 122) by 108 runs.

Fourth Match vs Yorkshire played at Fartown, Huddersfield on 16, 17 and 18 May. South Africans 170 (G P D Hartigan 57, G C White 49, S Haigh 5 for 33, G H Hirst 3 for 50) and 288 (F Mitchell 91*, H W Taylor 40, S J Pegler 35, W Rhodes 6 for 102) drew with Yorkshire 317 (D Denton 82, G H Hirst 65, S Haigh 62*, O Drake 46, S J Pegler 5 for 77) and 10 for 1.

Fifth Match vs Oxford University played at the University Parks, Oxford on 20, 21 and 22 May. Oxford University 278 (H H Gaekwad 62, A J Evans 56, K Lister-Kaye 35, J L S Vidler 33, S J Pegler 4 for 50, G A Faulkner 3 for 52) and 244 for 5 dec (A J Evans 107, F H Knott 70, G R R Colman 40*, J L Cox 3 for 74) drew with South Africans 179 (A W Nourse 94, A J Evans 5 for 73) and 138 for 3 (H W Taylor 55, A W Nourse 40*, J L S Vidler 2 for 31).

Sixth Match vs Worcestershire played at County Cricket Ground, New Road, Worcester on 23, 24 and 25 May. South Africans 298 (G P D Hartigan 103, H W Taylor 83, S J Snooke 45, G C White 25, G H Simpson-Hayward 5 for 19) beat Worcestershire 50 (J A Cuffe 29, S J Pegler 7 for 31, G A Faulkner 3 for 19) and 206 (R D Burrows 45, E W Bale 43, F L Bowley 31, R O Schwarz 4 for 59) by an innings and 42 runs.

Seventh Match vs Australia (First Test Match) (Triangular Tournament - 1st Match) played at Old Trafford, Manchester on 27 and 28 May.

Australia

C B Jennings	c Schwarz b Pegler	32
C Kelleway	c Ward b Pegler	114
C G Macartney	b Pegler	21
W Bardsley	c & b White	121
* S E Gregory	st Ward b Pegler	37
R B Minnett	c & b Schwarz	12
T J Matthews	not out	49
S H Emery	b Schwarz	1
G R Hazlitt	lbw b Schwarz	0
† W Carkeek	b Pegler	4
W J Whitty	st Ward b Pegler	33
Extras	b 14 lb 9 w 1	24
Total		**448**

Fall 1st inns: 1/62 2/92 3/294 4/314 5/328 6/375 7/376 8/376 9/385 10/448

Bowling		1st inns		
Faulkner	16	2	55	0
Nourse	14	1	62	0
Pegler	45.3	9	105	6
Schwarz	32	0	142	3
Hartigan	9	0	31	0
White	6	1	29	1

South Africa

G P D Hartigan	c Carkeek b Emery	25	b Kelleway	4
H W Taylor	c Carkeek b Whitty	0	(5) b Matthews	21
A W Nourse	b Whitty	17	c Bardsley b Whitty	18
S J Snooke	b Whitty	7	b Whitty	9
G A Faulkner	not out	122	(2) b Kelleway	0
G C White	lbw b Whitty	22	c Carkeek b Kelleway	9
* F Mitchell	b Whitty	11	b Kelleway	0
R O Schwarz	b Hazlitt	19	c & b Matthews	0
R Beaumont	b Matthews	31	(10) b Kelleway	17
S J Pegler	lbw b Matthews	0	(11) not out	8
† T A Ward	lbw b Matthews	0	(9) c & b Matthews	0
Extras	b 2 lb 5 w 1 nb 3	11	b 5 lb 1 nb 3	9
Total		**265**		**95**

Fall 1st inns: 1/4 2/30 3/42 4/54 5/143 6/167 7/200 8/265 9/265 10/265
Fall 2nd inns: 1/1 2/22 3/22 4/43 5/70 6/70 7/70 8/70 9/78 10/95

Bowling		1st inns				2nd inns		
Hazlitt	16	4	46	1				
Whitty	34	12	55	5	6	3	15	2
Emery	37	10	94	1				
Kelleway	11	3	27	0	14.2	4	33	5
Matthews	12	3	16	3	8	1	38	3
Minnett	6	2	16	0				

Umpires: G Webb and A A White

Australia beat South Africa by an innings and 88 runs.

Eighth Match vs Northamptonshire played at County Ground, Wantage Road, Northampton on 30, 31 May and 1 June. South Africans 428 (A W Nourse 137, R Beaumont 75, S J Pegler 52*, S J Snooke 47, H W Taylor 35, W Wells 4 for 121, G J Thompson 3 for 108) drew with Northamptonshire 156 (W Wells 39*, S G Smith 29, W H Denton 28, G P D Hartigan 3 for 27) and 286 (W H Denton 54, R A Haywood 52, S G Smith 39, G A T Vials 30, G A Faulkner 4 for 95).

G. P. D. HARTIGAN
Border

L. A. STRICKER
Transvaal

Ninth Match vs Cambridge University played at Fenner's University Cricket Ground, Cambridge on 3, 4 and 5 June. South Africans 260 (L J Tancred 94, L A Stricker 42, G P D Hartigan 38, H W Taylor 36, Hon G J Mulholland 3 for 33, F S G Calthorpe 3 for 58) and 3 for 0 beat Cambridge University 130 (R Knight 66, G A Faulkner 5 for 53, C P Carter 5 for 17) and 132 (W N Riley 40, E L Kidd 31, G A Faulkner 5 for 48) by 10 wickets.

Tenth Match vs Surrey played at Kennington Oval, London on 6, 7 and 8 June. Surrey 169 (E G Hayes 44, J B Hobbs 43, A W Nourse 4 for 54, S J Pegler 4 for 74) drew with South Africans.

Eleventh Match vs England (First Test Match) (Triangular Tournament - 2nd Match) played at Lord's Cricket Ground, London on 10, 11 and 12 June.

England

J B Hobbs	b Nourse	4
W Rhodes	b Nourse	36
R H Spooner	c Llewellyn b Nourse	119
* C B Fry	b Pegler	29
P F Warner	st Campbell b Pegler	39
F E Woolley	b Pegler	73
G L Jessop	b Pegler	3
F R Foster	lbw b Pegler	11
† E J Smith	b Pegler	2
S F Barnes	not out	0
W Brearley	b Pegler	0
Extras	b 11 lb 9 w 1	21
Total		**337**

Fall 1st inns: 1/4 2/128 3/183 4/207 5/320 6/323 7/324 8/330 9/337 10/337

Bowling		1st inns		
Nourse	16	5	46	3
Pegler	31	8	65	7
Faulkner	29	6	72	0
Carter	4	0	15	0
Llewellyn	9	0	60	0
Schwarz	20	3	44	0
Hartigan	10	2	14	0

South Africa

G P D Hartigan	c Foster b Barnes	0	b Foster	1
H W Taylor	lbw b Barnes	1	b Barnes	5
A W Nourse	b Foster	13	run out	17
C B Llewellyn	b Foster	9	c Smith b Foster	75
G A Faulkner	b Foster	7	b Barnes	15
S J Snooke	b Barnes	2	b Foster	16
* F Mitchell	c & b Barnes	1	b Barnes	1
R O Schwarz	c Foster b Barnes	4	b Barnes	28
S J Pegler	b Foster	4	b Barnes	10
C P Carter	b Foster	0	not out	27
† T Campbell	not out	0	c Jessop b Barnes	3
Extras	b 12 lb 3 nb 2	17	b 17 lb 1 nb 1	19
Total		**58**		**217**

Fall 1st inns: 1/2 2/3 3/28 4/35 5/36 6/42 7/45 8/54 9/55 10/58
Fall 2nd inns: 1/5 2/17 3/36 4/104 5/132 6/135 7/147 8/176 9/197 10/217

Bowling		1st inns				2nd inns		
Foster	13.1	7	16	5	27	10	54	3
Barnes	13	3	25	5	34	9	85	6
Brearley					6	2	4	0
Woolley					4	0	19	0
Hobbs					11	2	36	0

Umpires: W Richards and W A J West

England beat South Africa by an innings and 62 runs.

Twelfth Match vs Nottinghamshire played at Trent Bridge, Nottingham on 13, 14 and 15 June. Nottinghamshire 261 (J Gunn 95, G Gunn 73, J Hardstaff 29, S J Pegler 5 for 67) and 269 for 7 dec (A O Jones 79, J R Gunn 76, G Gunn 40, A W Nourse 2 for 44) drew with South Africans 276 (L A Stricker 79, S J Pegler 35, G P D Hartigan 28, C P Carter 26, A W Nourse 26, J Iremonger 5 for 99) and 203 for 2 (L J Tancred 100*, H W Taylor 77, J Iremonger 2 for 44).

Thirteenth Match vs Somerset played at the Recreation Ground, Bath on 17, 18 and 19 June. South Africans 96 (L J Tancred 28, S J Snooke 21, W T Gresswell 5 for 44, E Robson 5 for 33) and 300 for 3 dec (A W Nourse 113, S J Snooke 77*, H W Taylor 71) drew with Somerset 127 (E Robson 28, L C Braund 27, S J Pegler 6 for 42, C P Carter 4 for 47) and 128 for 7 (J Daniell 62*, M P Bajana 29, J L Cox 3 for 36, C P Carter 3 for 25).

T. CAMPBELL
Transvaal

F. MITCHELL
Wanderers C.C.

Fourteenth Match vs South Wales played at St. Helen's Cricket Ground, Swansea on 20, 21 and 22 June. South Africans 352 (S J Pegler 79, L A Stricker 69, H W Taylor 32, S J Snooke 30, F Mitchell 30, T A Ward 30*, H A Gilbert 3 for 90, H Creber 3 for 121) and 204 (F Mitchell 44, S J Snooke 43, L A Stricker 21, W S Hacker 5 for 65, J Maxwell 3 for 74) beat South Wales 192 (T A L Whittington 57, N C Phillips 49, H G Symonds 41, A W Nourse 5 for 50, S J Pegler 5 for 53) and 134 (J Maxwell 34, N V H Riches 30) by 230 runs.

Fifteenth Match vs Scotland played at Glasgow on 24, 25 and 26 June. South Africans 326 for 9 dec (G A Faulkner 145, T A Ward 43, R Beaumont 34, F Mitchell 27, T A Bowie 3 for 34) beat Scotland 136 (R G Tait 34, T A Bowie 22, S J Pegler 5 for 53, G A Faulkner 5 for 37) and 93 (C E Benham 32, S J Pegler 4 for 34, J L Cox 4 for 39) by an innings and 97 runs.

S. J. SNOOKE
Border

L. J. TANCRED
Transvaal

Sixteenth Match vs Scotland played Edinburgh on 27, 28 and 29 June. South Africans 263 (A W Nourse 73, G A Faulkner 39, C P Carter 32, R W Sievwright 6 for 121) beat Scotland 94 (R G Tait 29, G A Faulkner 6 for 35, C P Carter 3 for 35) and 72 (J A Ferguson 19, G A Faulkner 5 for 32, C P Carter 5 for 37) by an innings and 97 runs.

Seventeenth Match vs Middlesex played at Lord's Cricket Ground, London on 1, 2 and 3 July. South Africans 263 (A D Nourse 44, L J Tancred 40, C B Llewellyn 32, G C White 29, J W Hearne 3 for 46, F A Tarrant 3 for 58) drew with Middlesex 110 for 7 (F T Mann 38*, H R Murrell 34, S J Pegler 5 for 37).

Eighteenth Match vs Warwickshire played at Edgbaston Cricket Ground, Birmingham on 4 and 5 July. South Africans 189 (A W Nourse 50, G A Faulkner 45, G C White 34, C Charlesworth 6 for 56) and 86 for 4 (G A Faulkner 28, E F Field 2 for 22) beat Warwickshire 92 (S P Kinneir 38, S J Pegler 4 for 20, C P Carter 3 for 39, L A Stricker 3 for 13) and 179 (W Quaife 63, C S Baker 50, C P Carter 5 for 43, S J Pegler 4 for 76) by 6 wickets.

Nineteenth Match vs England (Second Test Match) (Triangular Tournament - 4th Match) played at Headingley Cricket Ground, Leeds on 8, 9 and 10 July.

England

J B Hobbs	c Ward b Nourse	27	c Nourse b Faulkner	55
W Rhodes	c & b Pegler	7	b Pegler	10
R H Spooner	c Stricker b Nourse	21	b Faulkner	82
* C B Fry	lbw b Pegler	10	c Nourse b Pegler	7
J W Hearne	b Pegler	45	b Nourse	35
F E Woolley	b Nourse	57	c Nourse b Pegler	4
G L Jessop	b Faulkner	16	b Nourse	1
F R Foster	c Pegler b Nourse	30	b Nourse	0
† E J Smith	run out	13	c Ward b Faulkner	11
S F Barnes	b Faulkner	0	not out	15
H Dean	not out	2	b Faulkner	8
Extras	b 12 lb 2	14	b 5 lb 5	10
Total		**242**		**238**

Fall 1st inns: 1/20 2/44 3/67 4/68 5/179 6/181 7/198 8/226 9/227 10/242
Fall 2nd inns: 1/46 2/78 3/95 4/165 5/180 6/181 7/181 8/207 9/224 10/238

Bowling		1st inns				2nd inns		
Nourse	26.1	8	52	4	30	11	52	3
Pegler	35	6	112	3	31	0	110	3
Faulkner	13	2	50	2	24.2	2	50	4
Carter	4	0	14	0	5	1	16	0

South Africa

* L J Tancred	c Spooner b Barnes	15	st Smith b Barnes	39
H W Taylor	c Hobbs b Dean	31	c Smith b Foster	2
A W Nourse	b Barnes	5	(6) c Foster b Dean	15
C B Llewellyn	c Smith b Barnes	0	b Barnes	4
G A Faulkner	c & b Barnes	5	b Barnes	0
L A Stricker	b Dean	10	(7) run out	0
G C White	c Barnes b Woolley	6	(3) c & b Foster	17
S J Snooke	b Barnes	23	b Dean	8
S J Pegler	not out	35	b Hearne	32
C P Carter	c Dean b Barnes	5	b Barnes	31
† T A Ward	b Dean	0	not out	0
Extras	b 4 lb 3 nb 5	12	b 5 lb 3 nb 3	11
Total		**147**		**159**

Fall 1st inns: 1/18 2/25 3/25 4/43 5/69 6/76 7/80 8/130 9/146 10/147
Fall 2nd inns: 1/18 2/38 3/44 4/49 5/67 6/69 7/85 8/110 9/159 10/159

Bowling		1st inns				2nd inns		
Foster	16	7	29	0	23	4	51	2
Barnes	22	7	52	6	21.2	5	63	4
Dean	12.3	1	41	3	8	3	15	2
Woolley	6	2	13	1				
Rhodes					4	1	14	0
Hearne					2	0	5	1

Umpires: W Richards and A A White

England beat South Africa by 174 runs.

Twentieth Match vs Australia (Second Test Match) (Triangular Tournament - 5th Match) played at Lord's Cricket Ground, London on 15, 16 and 17 July.

South Africa

G A Faulkner	lbw b Whitty	5	(6) c & b Matthews	6
L J Tancred	lbw b Matthews	31	c Bardsley b Hazlitt	19
G C White	c Carkeek b Minnett	0	b Matthews	18
C B Llewellyn	c Jennings b Minnett	8	b Macartney	59
A W Nourse	b Hazlitt	11	lbw b Kelleway	10
H W Taylor	c Kelleway b Hazlitt	93	(7) not out	10
L A Stricker	lbw b Kelleway	48	(1) b Hazlitt	13
* F Mitchell	b Whitty	12	b Matthews	3
R O Schwarz	b Whitty	0	c Macartney b Matthews	1
S J Pegler	c Bardsley b Whitty	25	c Kelleway b Macartney	14
† T A Ward	not out	1	b Macartney	7
Extras	b 12 lb 14 w 1 nb 2	29	b 9 lb 4	13
Total		**263**		**173**

Fall 1st inns: 1/24 2/25 3/35 4/56 5/74 6/171 7/203 8/213 9/250 10/263
Fall 2nd inns: 1/28 2/54 3/62 4/102 5/134 6/136 7/142 8/146 9/163 10/173

Bowling		1st inns				2nd inns		
Minnett	15	6	49	2				
Whitty	31	9	68	4	9	0	41	0
Hazlitt	19	9	47	2	13	1	39	2
Matthews	13	5	32	1	13	2	29	4
Kelleway	11	3	38	1	8	1	22	1
Macartney					14.1	5	29	3

Australia

C B Jennings	b Nourse	0	not out	22
C Kelleway	lbw b Faulkner	102		
C G Macartney	b Nourse	9		
W Bardsley	lbw b Llewellyn	164		
* S E Gregory	b Llewellyn	5		
E R Mayne	st Ward b Pegler	23	(2) not out	25
R B Minnett	b Pegler	39		
T J Matthews	c Faulkner b Pegler	9		
G R Hazlitt	b Nourse	0		
† W Carkeek	not out	6		
W J Whitty	lbw b Pegler	3		
Extras	b 24 lb 3 w 2 nb 1	30	b 1	1
Total		**390**	**(no wicket)**	**48**

Fall 1st inns: 1/0 2/14 3/256 4/277 5/316 6/353 7/375 8/379 9/381 10/390

Bowling		1st inns				2nd inns		
Nourse	36	12	60	3	6.1	2	22	0
Pegler	29.5	7	79	4	4	1	15	0
Schwarz	11	1	44	0				
Faulkner	28	3	86	1	2	0	10	0
Llewellyn	19	2	71	2				
Taylor	2	0	12	0				
Stricker	3	1	8	0				

Umpires: J Moss and A E Street

Australia beat South Africa by 10 wickets.

Twenty-First Match vs Kent played at Mote Park, Maidstone on 18, 19 and 20 July. South Africans 360 (H W Taylor 96, L A Stricker 54, S J Snooke 52, R Beaumont 47, G C White 30, W J Fairservice 3 for 55, C Blythe 3 for 92) and 152 for 8 dec (H W Taylor 46, C P Carter 23*, F E Woolley 3 for 45, W J Fairservice 3 for 51) drew with Kent 245 (E Humphreys 62, F E Woolley 43, J C Hubble 31, G A Faulkner 6 for 48) and 185 for 4 (F E Woolley 59*, H T W Hardinge 54, J Seymour 53, G A Faulkner 2 for 32).

G. C. WHITE
Transvaal

R. BEAUMONT
Transvaal

Twenty-Second Match vs Woodbrook Club and Ground at Bray, Ireland on 22, 23 and 24 July. South Africans 326 (L J Tancred 131, G A Faulkner 56, J L Cox 34, G C White 31, R H Lambert 3 for 64) and 212 for 7 dec (H W Taylor 71, G C White 39*, R Beaumont 33, A E E Vogler 3 for 56) drew with Woodbrook Club and Ground 290 (A Baker 90, P F Quinlan 80, S J Pegler 3 for 79, H W Taylor 3 for 9).

Twenty-Third Match vs Ireland played at Bray, Ireland on 25, 26 and 27 July. South Africans 395 (A W Nourse 113, S J Snooke 81, L J Tancred 61, G A Faulkner 43, R H Lambert 5 for 51) beat Ireland 108 (P C Ross 26, R A Lloyd 22, H W Taylor 4 for 36, G A Faulkner 3 for 20) and 118 (R A Lloyd 27, C P Carter 5 for 44, G A Faulkner 4 for 18) by an innings and 169 runs.

Twenty-Fourth Match vs Minor Counties XI played at Longton, Stoke-on-Trent on 29, 30 and 31 July. Minor Counties 127 (N V H Riches 51, G A Faulkner 5 for 59, S J Pegler 3 for 27) drew with South Africans 22 for 3 (A Morris 3 for 5).

Twenty-Fifth Match vs Lancashire played at Aigburth Cricket Ground, Liverpool on 1, 2 and 3 August. Lancashire 242 (J Sharp 121, F R R Brooke 30, G A Faulkner 5 for 98) and 151 (R H Spooner 33, F R R Brooke 27, G A Faulkner 5 for 55, S J Pegler 3 for 33) beat South Africans 124 (G A Faulkner 44, R Beaumont 26, W Huddleston 7 for 42) and 44 (G C White 12*, H Dean 7 for 22, W Huddleston 3 for 20) by 225 runs.

Twenty-Sixth Match vs Australia (Third Test Match) (Triangular Tournament - 7th Match) played at Trent Bridge, Nottingham on 5, 6 and 7 August.

South Africa

* L J Tancred	c Kelleway b Matthews	30
H W Taylor	b Whitty	2
A W Nourse	b Whitty	64
G A Faulkner	c Kelleway b Emery	15
C B Llewellyn	b Emery	12
L A Stricker	lbw b Macartney	37
S J Snooke	b Kelleway	20
G C White	not out	59
R Beaumont	b Hazlitt	2
S J Pegler	b Hazlitt	26
† T A Ward	c Emery b Matthews	24
Extras	b 30 lb 7 nb 1	38
Total		**329**

Fall 1st inns: 1/2 2/79 3/116 4/140 5/154 6/196 7/225 8/232 9/282 10/329

Bowling		1st inns		
Whitty	30	10	64	2
Minnett	8	3	12	0
Hazlitt	28	10	48	2
Matthews	20.5	7	27	2
Emery	21	1	87	2
Kelleway	8	2	18	1
Macartney	13	2	35	1

Australia

C B Jennings	run out	9
C Kelleway	c Faulkner b Pegler	37
C G Macartney	c Faulkner b Llewellyn	34
W Bardsley	run out	56
* S E Gregory	b Pegler	18
R B Minnett	c Nourse b Faulkner	31
T J Matthews	b Pegler	21
S H Emery	b Faulkner	5
G R Hazlitt	not out	2
W J Whitty	b Pegler	0
† W Carkeek	st Ward b Faulkner	1
Extras	b 2 lb 3	5
Total		**219**

Fall 1st inns: 1/19 2/61 3/101 4/127 5/171 6/199 7/212 8/216 9/216 10/219

Bowling		1st inns		
Pegler	36	6	80	4
Faulkner	20.1	2	43	3
Taylor	12	5	19	0
Llewellyn	22	3	60	1
Nourse	4	1	12	0

Umpires: G Webb and W A J West

Australia drew with South Africa.

Twenty-Seventh Match vs Leicestershire played at Aylestone Road, Leicester on 8 and 9 August. South Africans 125 (G A Faulkner 33, G C White 20, J H King 5 for 52, H M Bannister 4 for 23) and 73 (G C White 18, J H King 7 for 45, H M Bannister 3 for 24) beat Leicestershire 46 (A E Knight 23, G A Faulkner 6 for 21, S J Pegler 4 for 20) and 92 (C J B Wood 28, G A Faulkner 5 for 38, S J Pegler 3 for 37) by 60 runs.

Twenty-Eighth Match vs England (Third Test Match) (Triangular Tournament - 8th Match) played at Kennington Oval, London on 12 and 13 August.

South Africa

* L J Tancred	c Foster b Woolley	23	(2) st Smith b Woolley	0
H W Taylor	b Barnes	0	(1) lbw b Barnes	6
A W Nourse	lbw b Woolley	8	c & b Foster	42
G A Faulkner	c Hayes b Barnes	9	(5) b Barnes	10
L A Stricker	b Barnes	5	(4) c Spooner b Barnes	0
C B Llewellyn	c Rhodes b Woolley	0	c Hitch b Barnes	0
G C White	b Barnes	4	c Smith b Barnes	1
S J Snooke	c Foster b Woolley	23	c Hearne b Barnes	7
R Beaumont	c Hearne b Barnes	3	b Barnes	6
S J Pegler	c Hitch b Woolley	3	b Barnes	0
† T A Ward	not out	6	not out	0
Extras	b 8 lb 3	11	b 18 lb 3	21
Total		**95**		**93**

Fall 1st inns: 1/2 2/31 3/38 4/47 5/50 6/53 7/76 8/86 9/86 10/95
Fall 2nd inns: 1/0 2/10 3/10 4/54 5/54 6/58 7/70 8/89 9/93 10/93

Bowling		1st inns				2nd inns		
Foster	6	2	15	0	7	2	19	1
Barnes	21	10	28	5	16.4	4	29	8
Woolley	15.3	1	41	5	9	2	24	1

England

J B Hobbs	c & b Faulkner	68	not out	9
W Rhodes	b Faulkner	0		
R H Spooner	c Nourse b Llewellyn	26		
* C B Fry	c Snooke b Faulkner	9		
E G Hayes	b Faulkner	4		
F E Woolley	b Pegler	13		
J W Hearne	lbw b Faulkner	20	(2) not out	5
F R Foster	st Ward b Faulkner	8		
† E J Smith	b Faulkner	9		
S F Barnes	c Taylor b Pegler	8		
J W Hitch	not out	0		
Extras	b 10 lb 1	11		
Total		**176**	**(no wicket)**	**14**

Fall 1st inns: 1/4 2/65 3/85 4/89 5/111 6/127 7/135 8/163 9/176 10/176

Bowling		1st inns				2nd inns		
Pegler	19	3	53	2				
Faulkner	27.1	4	84	7	2	0	4	0
Llewellyn	10	1	28	1				
Nourse					2.3	0	10	0

Umpires: W Richards and A A White

England beat South Africa by 10 wickets.

Twenty-Ninth Match vs Sussex played at County Cricket Ground, Brighton on 15, 16 and 17 August. South Africans 118 (G A Faulkner 47*, A E Relf 6 for 49) and 179 for 6 (G A Faulkner 53*, L J Tancred 28, H L Simms 3 for 86) beat Sussex 76 (V W C Jupp 27*, A E Relf 21, A W Nourse 6 for 33, S J Pegler 3 for 42) and 220 (A E Relf 104, J Vine 60, S J Pegler 7 for 55, G A Faulkner 3 for 71) by 4 wickets.

C. B. LLEWELLYN
Accrington C.C.

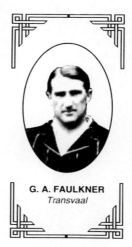

G. A. FAULKNER
Transvaal

Thirtieth Match vs Yorkshire played at Bramall Lane, Sheffield on 19, 20 and 21 August. South Africans 180 (L J Tancred 51, L A Stricker 29, G H Hirst 4 for 44, R Kilner 3 for 37) and 40 for 1 (R Beaumont 20) drew with Yorkshire 149 (R Kilner 54, S J Pegler 6 for 29, G C White 3 for 31).

Thirty-First Match vs Lancashire played at Old Trafford, Manchester on 22, 23 and 24. Lancashire 170 (J Sharp 34, A H Hornby 28, G A Faulkner 6 for 78) drew with South Africans 69 for 1 (H W Taylor 27*, A W Nourse 27*).

Thirty-Second Match vs Essex played at County Ground, Leyton on 26, 27 and 28 August. Essex 127 (F L Fane 47, W Reeves 28, S J Pegler 4 for 46, G A Faulkner 3 for 39) and 168 (W Reeves 68, S J Pegler 5 for 42, G A Faulkner 5 for 65) drew with South Africans 166 (A W Nourse 49, W Mead 4 for 46) and 102 for 5 (A W Nourse 29, H W Taylor 22, C P Buckenham 2 for 24).

Thirty-Third Match vs Gloucestershire played at County Cricket Ground, Nevil Road, Bristol on 29, 30 and 31 August. South Africans 79 (L J Tancred 27*, G H Dennett 5 for 40, C W L Parker 5 for 35) and 114 for 8 (A W Nourse 35, G H Dennett 4 for 51, G L Jessop 4 for 33) beat Gloucestershire 126 (T Langdon 36, A W Roberts 33, G C White 5 for 21, S J Pegler 3 for 41) and 64 (G L Jessop 16, S J Pegler 5 for 33, G A Faulkner 4 for 26) by 2 wickets.

Thirty-Fourth Match vs Hampshire played at Dean Park, Bournemouth on 2, 3 and 4 September. South Africans 162 (L A Stricker 99, K H C Woodruffe 5 for 33, J A Newman 3 for 59) and 432 (A W Nourse 213*, H W Taylor 63, G C White 36, C P Carter 30, H C McDonell 4 for 56, A S Kennedy 3 for 125) drew with Hampshire 137 (C P Mead 64*, S J Pegler 4 for 53, G A Faulkner 3 for 57) and 187 for 6 (C P Mead 77*, Capt. E I M Barratt 28, E M Sprot 28, G A Faulkner 3 for 49).

Thirty-Fifth Match vs Lionel Robinson's XI played at Old Buckenham Hall, Attleborough on 5, 6 and 7 September. Lionel Robinson's XI 153 (A J Evans 48, M Falcon 29, S J Pegler 6 for 45, A W Nourse 3 for 48) and 255 (E H Hendren 80, F A Tarrant 49, J Sharp 39, S J Pegler 5 for 75) beat South Africans 151 (F Mitchell 33*, C P Carter 27, S J Pegler 26, M Falcon 6 for 47) and 66 (H W Taylor 21, H L Simms 5 for 24, F A Tarrant 5 for 8) by 191 runs.

C. P. CARTER
Transvaal

R. O. SCHWARZ
Transvaal

Thirty-Sixth Match vs Lord Londesborough's XI played at North Marine Drive, Scarborough on 9, 10 and 11 September. South Africans 100 (L J Tancred 22, G C White 20, S F Barnes 6 for 32, G H Hirst 4 for 56) drew with Lord Londesborough's XI 63 for 4 (R H Spooner 23, C P Mead 23*, G A Faulkner 3 for 13).

Thirty-Seventh Match vs Gentlemen of England played at Central Cricket Ground, Hastings on 12, 13 and 14 September. South Africans 178 (A W Nourse 58, G C White 34, S G Smith 6 for 46) and 273 for 4 (H W Taylor 67, G A Faulkner 61, G C White 43*, A W Nourse 40, L A Stricker 40*, H L Simms 3 for 89) beat Gentlemen of England 286 (J W H T Douglas 94, G L Jessop 59, S G Smith 48, E L Kidd 28, G A Faulkner 3 for 49) and 164 (B J T Bosanquet 62, R H Spooner 42, S G Smith 31, S J Pegler 4 for 48, G A Faulkner 4 for 43) by 6 wickets.

Test Match batting averages:

	Inns	NO	Runs	HS	Ave
C P Carter	4	1	63	31	21.00
A W Nourse	11	0	220	64	20.00
H W Taylor	11	1	194	93	19.40
G A Faulkner	11	1	194	122*	19.40
L J Tancred	7	0	134	39	19.14
C B Llewellyn	9	0	167	75	18.55
S J Pegler	11	2	157	35*	17.44
G C White	9	1	136	59*	17.00
L A Stricker	7	0	113	48	16.14
S J Snooke	9	0	115	23	12.77
R Beaumont	5	0	59	31	11.80
R O Schwarz	6	0	52	28	8.66
T A Ward	9	4	38	24	7.60
G P D Hartigan	4	0	30	25	7.50
F Mitchell	6	0	28	12	4.66
T Campbell	2	1	3	3	3.00

Test Match bowling averages:

	Overs	Mdns	Runs	Wkts	Ave
S J Pegler	231.2	40	619	29	21.34
A W Nourse	134.5	40	316	13	24.30
G A Faulkner	161.4	21	454	17	26.70
G C White	6	1	29	1	29.00
C B Llewellyn	60	6	219	4	54.75
R O Schwarz	63	4	230	3	76.66
G P D Hartigan	19	2	45	0	-
H W Taylor	14	5	31	0	-
C P Carter	13	1	45	0	-
L A Stricker	3	1	8	0	-

Tour batting averages - all matches:

	Inns	NO	Runs	HS	Ave
A W Nourse	55	5	1,762	213*	35.24
H W Taylor	57	5	1,340	96	25.76
G P D Hartigan	18	3	372	103	24.80
G A Faulkner	51	6	1,075	145*	23.88
S J Snooke	38	2	790	86	21.94
G C White	41	7	717	59*	21.08
L J Tancred	50	2	974	131	20.29
C B Llewellyn	10	0	199	75	19.90
L A Stricker	46	2	875	99	19.88
R Beaumont	31	3	510	75	18.21
R O Schwarz	14	0	249	70	17.78
F Mitchell	33	4	504	91*	17.37
S J Pegler	48	6	643	79	15.30
T A Ward	34	14	223	43	11.05
C P Carter	41	5	398	32	11.05

J L Cox	16	6	92	34	9.20
T Campbell	17	4	115	27*	8.84

Tour bowling averages - all matches:

	Overs	Mdns	Runs	Wkts	Ave
S J Pegler	1,287.5	347	2,883	189	15.25
G A Faulkner	1,054.5	207	2,514	163	15.42
C P Carter	460.1	128	1,116	67	16.65
L A Stricker	27	4	67	4	16.75
H W Taylor	120.1	35	292	14	20.85
A W Nourse	575.3	190	1,232	50	24.64
G C White	120	15	456	18	25.33
S J Snooke	34	3	112	4	28.00
J L Cox	170.1	46	403	14	28.78
G P D Hartigan	156	20	470	14	33.57
R O Schwarz	185.1	17	672	18	37.33
C B Llewellyn	60	6	219	4	54.75

Centuries recorded for South Africans during the tour:

A W Nourse	(4) :	213* vs Hampshire (Bournemouth)
		137 vs Northamptonshire (Northampton)
		113 vs Somerset (Bath)
		113 vs Ireland (Bray)
G A Faulkner	(2) :	145* vs Scotland (Glasgow)
		122* vs Australia (Old Trafford)
L J Tancred	(2) :	131 vs Woodbrook Club (Bray)
		100* vs Nottinghamshire (Trent Bridge)
G P D Hartigan	(1) :	103 vs Worcestershire (Worcester)

Fielding:

	Catches	Stumpings
T A Ward	24	18
G A Faulkner	28	
C P Carter	25	
L A Stricker	19	2
A W Nourse	19	
S J Pegler	15	
F Mitchell	11	
L J Tancred	11	
T Campbell	7	2
S J Snooke	8	
G P D Hartigan	6	
G C White	6	
R Beaumont	5	
R O Schwarz	4	
H W Taylor	4	
J L Cox	1	

The Sixth South African Team in the United Kingdom, 1924

This was to prove a rather unsatisfactory tour. Once again an exceptionally wet summer was coupled with the continued lack of experience on turf wickets and a strangely selected party with an average age of 33, of which only six members were subsequently selected to represent their country again.

There was allegedly a lack of team spirit and two former members of the 1912 tourists, Pegler and Faulkner, who had settled in England were called to join the tourists, as was another expatriate South African cricketer, G. M. Parker, who was playing in the Bradford League.

This was also the first tour with five Test Matches of which England were to win three while the other two at Old Trafford and The Oval were affected by rain and ended in draws.

The team in fact won only eight matches, drew twenty-one times and lost on nine occasions. Such a disastrous tour was finally to emphasize the need for South Africa to develop turf pitches.

(standing) **H.G.Deane P.A.M.Hands C.D.Dixon M.J.Susskind G.F.Bissett E.P.Nupen A.W.Nourse Mr.G.Allsop** (Manager)

(sitting) **J.M.Blanckenberg J.M.M.Commaille H.W.Taylor** (Captain) **S.J.Pegler T.A.Ward**

(on ground) **R.H.Catterall C.P.Carter G.A.L.Hearne D.J.Meintjes**

69

Touring party (16):

* H W Taylor (*Natal*) (Captain)
Age 35. Attractive right-handed opening batsman and fine fielder.

J M M Commaille (*Western Province*) (Vice-Captain)
Age 41. Right-handed opening batsman.

A W Nourse (*Natal*)
Age 46. Steady left-handed middle order batsman, left-arm medium pace or slow bowler and good slip fieldsman.

J M Blanckenberg (*Natal*)
Age 30. Right-handed middle order batsman and right-arm medium pace bowler.

C P Carter (Natal)
Age 43. Right-handed lower order batsman and left-arm bowler.

H G Deane (*Transvaal*)
Age 28. Right-handed middle order batsman and specialist close fieldsman.

† M J Susskind (*Transvaal/Cambridge University/Middlesex*)
Age 33. Steady right-handed middle order batsman and occasional wicket-keeper.

E P Nupen (*Transvaal*)
Age 22. Right-handed lower order batsman and right-arm fast medium bowler.

D J Meintjes (*Transvaal*)
Age 34. Right-handed lower order batsman and right-arm fast medium bowler.

C D Dixon (*Transvaal*)
Age 33. Right-handed lower order batsman and right-arm medium pace bowler.

† T A Ward (*Transvaal*)
Age 36. Steady right-handed middle/late order batsman and wicket-keeper.

S J Pegler (*Transvaal*)
Age 36. Right-handed lower order batsman, right-arm medium pace and leg break bowler.

P A M Hands (*Western Province*)
Age 34. Right-handed middle order batsman.

R H Catterall (*Rhodesia*)
Age 23. Right-handed opening/middle order batsman, right-arm medium pace bowler and fine deep fieldsman.

G F Bissett (*Griqualand West*)
Age 18. Right-arm fast bowler and right-handed tail end batsman.

G A L Hearne (*Western Province*)
Age 36. Right-handed opening/middle order batsman.

Manager: Mr. G Allsop

Summary of all matches:

Played 38   Won 8   Lost 9   Drawn 21

Summary of first-class matches:

Played 35   Won 8   Lost 9   Drawn 18

Summary of Test Matches:

Played 5   Won 0   Lost 3   Drawn 2

First Match vs Leicestershire played at Aylestone Road, Leicester on 3, 5 and 6 May. South Africans 153 (H W Taylor 60*, R H Catterall 44, W E Astill 5 for 70) and 167 (P A M Hands 60, A W Nourse 32, A Skelding 4 for 43, W E Astill 4 for 39) drew with Leicestershire 90 (A T Sharp 21, T E Sidwell 20, J M Blanckenberg 5 for 23) and 118 for 9 (W E Astill 24, E P Nupen 4 for 30, C P Carter 3 for 28).

Second Match vs Derbyshire played at County Cricket Ground, Derby on 7, 8 and 9 May. South Africans 161 for 7 dec (J M M Commaille 43, H W Taylor 33, R H Catterall 29, W Bestwick 3 for 37) drew with Derbyshire 78 for 5 (H Storer 28, J M Blanckenberg 2 for 13, E P Nupen 2 for 16).

Third Match vs Surrey played at Kennington Oval, London on 10, 12 and 13 May. Surrey 223 (P G H Fender 102, T Shepherd 30, S J Pegler 6 for 63) and 136 for 2 dec (J B Hobbs 79*, W T Cook 38) drew with South Africans 223 (A W Nourse 62, H W Taylor 44, J M M Commaille 34, H A Peach 4 for 44) and 85 for 2 (H W Taylor 35*).

Fourth Match vs Nottinghamshire played at Trent Bridge, Nottingham on 14, 15 and 16 May. Nottinghamshire 185 (W Whysall 45, T Oates 33, H Turland 29, S J Pegler 5 for 47) and 238 for 7 (J R Gunn 89*, G Gunn 58, S J Pegler 4 for 47) beat South Africans 186 (A W Nourse 52, R H Catterall 24, F Barratt 5 for 59, L Richmond 3 for 49) and 236 (A W Nourse 147*, E P Nupen 33, S J Staples 5 for 78) by 3 wickets.

Fifth Match vs Lancashire played at Old Trafford, Manchester on 17, 19 and 20 May. Lancashire 293 (F Watson 117, J Sharp 55, E Tyldesley 47, S J Pegler 6 for 68) beat South Africans 60 (A W Nourse 22, R K Tyldesley 7 for 28) and 155 (G A L Hearne 33, J M M Commaille 28, C H Parkin 5 for 61, R K Tyldesley 5 for 50) by an innings and 78 runs.

Sixth Match vs Gloucestershire played at County Cricket Ground, Nevil Road, Bristol on 21, 22 and 23 May. South Africans 162 (A W Nourse 58, J M Blanckenberg 41, C W L Parker 4 for 41) and 126 for 8 dec (M J Susskind 69*, P T Mills 4 for 54, E G Dennett 3 for 34) drew with Gloucestershire 92 (F G Rogers 47, J M Blanckenberg 4 for 29, C P Carter 3 for 17) and 19 for 1 (A G Dipper 12*).

Seventh Match vs M.C.C. played at Lord's Cricket Ground, London on 24, 26 and 27 May. M.C.C. 145 (J W Hearne 59, S J Pegler 8 for 54) and 191 for 4 dec (A C Russell 45, J W Hearne 45, E H Hendren 44*, S J Pegler 2 for 75) drew with South Africans 192 (H W Taylor 42, J M M Commaille 39*, R H Catterall 37, J W H T Douglas 6 for 65) and 90 for 1 (H W Taylor 50*).

Eighth Match vs Scotland played at Edinburgh on 29 and 30 May. Scotland 177 (J A Ferguson 33, R S Clark 29, W N Walker 23, C P Carter 5 for 51) and 163 for 4 dec (J Kerr 80*, C S Patterson 47*, C P Carter 3 for 58) drew with South Africans 186 (J M Blanckenberg 47, H G Deane 30, H W Taylor 27, W N Walker 3 for 31, C S Scobie 3 for 67) and 59 for 2 (M J Susskind 29*, G A L Hearne 25*).

Ninth Match vs Scotland played at Glasgow on 31 May, 2 and 3 June. South Africans 389 for 5 dec (H G Deane 80*, R H Catterall 72, G A L Hearne 63*, M Commaille 52, M J Susskind 40, A W Nourse 39, J M Blanckenberg 36, W N Walker 3 for 96) beat Scotland 36 (R S Clark 10, D J Meintjes 4 for 19, C D Dixon 4 for 14) and 67 (W N Walker 25, C D Dixon 6 for 39) by an innings and 286 runs.

Tenth Match vs Yorkshire played at Bramall Lane, Sheffield on 4, 5 and 6 June. Yorkshire 236 (E Oldroyd 67, W Rhodes 52, J M Blanckenberg 4 for 58, S J Pegler 3 for 61) and 142 for 3 dec (H Sutcliffe 67*, M Leyland 20) drew with South Africans 111 (J M M Commaille 25, R Kilner 4 for 30, G G Macaulay 4 for 47) and 141 for 6 (M J Susskind 60*, R Kilner 3 for 31).

H.G.Deane   J.M.Blanckenberg

Eleventh Match vs Cambridge University played at Fenner's Cricket Ground, Cambridge on 7, 9 and 10 June. South Africans 334 (A W Nourse 144, P A M Hands 34, J M M Commaille 30, G F Bissett 25, R J O Meyer 4 for 134) and 179 (M J Susskind 41, J M M Commaille 29, R H Catterall 26, R J O Meyer 5 for 70) beat Cambridge University 191 (T C Lowry 67, R J O Meyer 25, G F Bissett 3 for 36, E P Nupen 3 for 57) and 197 (A H White 53*, E W Dawson 37, T C Lowry 25, C P Carter 5 for 64) by 125 runs.

Twelfth Match vs Oxford University played at University Parks, Oxford on 11, 12 and 13 June. Oxford University 117 for 9 (K G Blaikie 26, J L Guise 25, G M Parker 4 for 34) drew with South Africans.

Thirteenth Match vs England (First Test Match) played at Edgbaston Cricket Ground, Birmingham on 14, 16 and 17 June.

England

J B Hobbs	lbw b Blanckenberg	76
H Sutcliffe	b Parker	64
* F E Woolley	c Ward b Parker	64
E H Hendren	c Nourse b Parker	74
A P F Chapman	b Parker	8
P G H Fender	c Taylor b Blanckenberg	36
R Kilner	c & b Pegler	59
M W Tate	c Taylor b Parker	19
A E R Gilligan	b Pegler	13
† G E C Wood	b Parker	1
C H Parkin	not out	8
Extras	b 4 lb 11 nb 1	16
Total		**438**

Fall 1st inns: 1/136 2/164 3/247 4/255 5/315 6/356 7/386 8/407 9/410 10/438

Bowling		1st inns		
Parker	37	2	152	6
Pegler	36	8	106	2
Blanckenberg	32	5	95	2
Nupen	18	2	66	0
Nourse	1	0	3	0

South Africa

* H W Taylor	b Tate	7	c & b Tate	34
R H Catterall	b Gilligan	0	c Hobbs b Tate	120
M J Susskind	c Kilner b Tate	3	b Gilligan	51
A W Nourse	lbw b Gilligan	1	c Wood b Gilligan	34
J M M Commaille	not out	1	c Hendren b Tate	29
J M Blanckenberg	b Tate	4	c Chapman b Gilligan	56
H G Deane	b Gilligan	2	run out	5
E P Nupen	b Gilligan	0	lbw b Tate	5
S J Pegler	b Tate	0	c Hobbs b Gilligan	6
† T A Ward	b Gilligan	1	b Gilligan	19
G M Parker	lbw b Gilligan	0	not out	2
Extras	b 1 lb 7 nb 3	11	b 4 lb 18 w 1 nb 6	29
Total		**30**		**390**

Fall 1st inns: 1/1 2/4 3/6 4/14 5/20 6/23 7/23 8/24 9/30 10/30
Fall 2nd inns: 1/54 2/101 3/152 4/161 5/275 6/284 7/295 8/350 9/372 10/390

Bowling		1st inns				2nd inns		
Gilligan	6.3	4	7	6	28	6	83	5
Tate	6	1	12	4	54.4	19	103	4
Parkin					16	5	38	0
Kilner					22	10	40	0
Fender					17	5	56	0
Woolley					10	2	41	0

Umpires: H Butt and W Reeves

England beat South Africa by an innings and 18 runs.

Fourteenth Match vs Essex played at Castle Park, Colchester on 18, 19 and 20 June. South Africans 263 (H W Taylor 126, A W Nourse 48, G A L Hearne 43, G M Louden 6 for 71) and 239 for 9 (P A M Hands 64, A W Nourse 36, G F Bissett 28*, S J Pegler 23*, G M Louden 4 for 82) beat Essex 155 (A C Russell 34, S J Pegler 4 for 34) and 345 (A C Russell 108, J O'Conner 51, Capt. F W H Nicholas 50, J W H T Douglas 40*, C P Carter 5 for 70) by 1 wicket.

M.J.Susskind

D.J.Meintjes

Fifteenth Match vs Hampshire played at County Cricket Ground, Northlands Road, Southampton on 21, 23 and 24 June. South Africans 336 (A W Nourse 121, J M Blanckenberg 69, J M M Commaille 62, S J Pegler 27*, J A Newman 4 for 118) and 275 for 5 (H W Taylor 93, M J Susskind 44, J M Blanckenberg 34*, P A M Hands 33*, A W Nourse 30, J M M Commaille 25, G S Boyes 3 for 80) beat Hampshire 279 (H L V Day 100, J Newman 58, J M Blanckenberg 6 for 121) and 330 (J Newman 60, G Brown 55, Capt. R St. L Fowler 50, Hon. L H Tennyson 34, G F Bissett 5 for 102) by 5 wickets.

Sixteenth Match vs H D G Leveson-Gower's XI played at Reigate on 25, 26 and 27 June. H D G Leveson-Gower's XI 230 (A G Doggart 47, M Howell 43, G E V Crutchley 30, A P F Chapman 25, J M Blanckenberg 5 for 53) and 196 for 7 (M Leyland 53, E Robinson 29*, J L Bryan 27, A G Doggart 27, G E V Crutchley 25, G F Bissett 2 for 46) beat South Africans 253 (H W Taylor 81, J M M Commaille 42, E P Nupen 37, J M Blanckenberg 36, W Rhodes 6 for 56) and 171 (R H Catterall 45, M J Susskind 44, H W Taylor 33, A G Doggart 5 for 58, W Rhodes 4 for 39) by 3 wickets.

Seventeenth Match vs England (Second Test Match) played at Lord's Cricket Ground, London on 28 and 30 June and 1 July.

South Africa

	1st innings			2nd innings	
* H W Taylor	c Wood b Gilligan	4	b Gilligan	8
J M M Commaille	b Gilligan	0	lbw b Tyldesley	37
M J Susskind	c Tate b Hearne	64	lbw b Tyldesley	53
A W Nourse	c Woolley b Tate	4	lbw b Gilligan	11
R H Catterall	b Gilligan	120	c Gilligan b Tyldesley	45
J M Blanckenberg	b Tate	12	c Hobbs b Fender	15
H G Deane	b Tyldesley	33	c Sutcliffe b Hearne	24
G A Faulkner	b Fender	25	run out	12
† T A Ward	b Tyldesley	1	not out	3
S J Pegler	c Fender b Tyldesley	0	b Tate	8
G M Parker	not out	1	b Tate	0
Extras	b 3 lb 2 nb 4	9	b 13 lb 8 nb 3	24
Total		**273**		**240**

Fall 1st inns: 1/4 2/5 3/17 4/129 5/182 6/212 7/265 8/271 9/272 10/273
Fall 2nd inns: 1/50 2/78 3/103 4/117 5/171 6/204 7/224 8/231 9/240 10/240

Bowling		1st inns			2nd inns	
Gilligan	31	7	70	3	24	6	54	2
Tate	34	12	62	2	26.4	8	43	2
Tyldesley	24	10	52	3	36	18	50	3
Hearne	18	3	35	1	19	4	35	1
Fender	9	1	45	1	14	5	25	1
Woolley					4	1	9	0

England

J B Hobbs	c Taylor b Parker	211
H Sutcliffe	b Parker	122
* F E Woolley	not out	134
E H Hendren	not out	50
Extras	b 11 lb 1 nb 2	14
Total	**(2 wickets, declared)**	**531**

J W Hearne, A P F Chapman, P G H Fender, M W Tate, R K Tyldesley, A E R Gilligan and † G E C Wood did not bat.
Fall 1st inns: 1/268 2/410

Bowling		1st inns		
Parker	24	0	121	2
Blanckenberg	28	3	113	0
Pegler	31	4	120	0
Nourse	15	1	57	0
Faulkner	17	0	87	0
Catterall	3	0	19	0

Umpires: F Chester and H Young

England beat South Africa by an innings and 18 runs.

Eighteenth Match vs Yorkshire played at Park Avenue, Bradford on 2, 3 and 4 July. Yorkshire 285 (E Robinson 95*, W Rhodes 54, E P Nupen 3 for 53) and 147 for 4 (H Sutcliffe 36, E Oldroyd 35*, P Holmes 30, C D Dixon 3 for 32) drew with South Africans 279 (H W Taylor 79, A W Nourse 68, E P Nupen 29, G G Macaulay 6 for 66) and 64 for 3 (M J Susskind 25*).

E.P.Nupen

G.F.Bissett

Nineteenth Match vs Northamptonshire played at County Cricket Ground, Wantage Road, Northampton on 5 and 7 July. South Africans 380 (H W Taylor 113, A W Nourse 62, E P Nupen 57, S J Pegler 50*, M J Susskind 25, A E Thomas 8 for 96) beat Northamptonshire 157 (V W C Jupp 84, F Walden 23, J M Blanckenberg 7 for 57) and 87 (C N Woolley 30, W H Denton 27, S J Pegler 6 for 22, J M Blanckenberg 3 for 17) by an innings and 136 runs.

Twentieth Match vs Warwickshire played at Edgbaston Cricket Ground, Birmingham on 9, 10 and 11 July. South Africans 317 (H W Taylor 94, A W Nourse 49, M J Susskind 45, J M M Commaille 44, G A Jennings 5 for 92) and 384 (H W Taylor 116, J M M Commaille 69, J M Blanckenberg 33, R E S Wyatt 2 for 77) drew with Warwickshire 440 (F R Santall 102, Hon. F S G Calthorpe 76, L A Bates 76, N Kilner 48, J H Parsons 43, H Howell 26*, S J Pegler 3 for 75, J M Blanckenberg 3 for 104).

Twenty-First Match vs England (Third Test Match) played at Headingley Cricket Ground, Leeds on 12, 14 and 15 July.

England

J B Hobbs	c Pegler b Nourse	31	b Blanckenberg	7
H Sutcliffe	c Nupen b Blanckenberg	83	not out	29
J W Hearne	lbw b Pegler	20	not out	23
* F E Woolley	b Pegler	0		
E H Hendren	c Deane b Nupen	132		
E Tyldesley	run out	15		
M W Tate	c Taylor b Carter	29		
A E R Gilligan	c Catterall b Pegler	28		
R K Tyldesley	c Carter b Pegler	29		
† G E C Wood	run out	6		
G G Macaulay	not out	0		
Extras	b 13 lb 8 w 1 nb 1	23	lb 1	1
Total		**396**	**(one wicket)**	**60**

Fall 1st inns: 1/72 2/130 3/130 4/201 5/248 6/305 7/350 8/365 9/386 10/396
Fall 2nd inns: 1/17

Bowling			1st inns				2nd inns	
Nupen	30	8	85	1	1	0	6	0
Pegler	34	6	116	4	11.2	3	30	0
Nourse	24	7	67	1				
Blanckenberg	12	0	58	1	10	2	23	1
Carter	15	2	47	1				

South Africa

H G Deane	c & b Tate	2	not out	47
J M M Commaille	run out	4	st Wood b R K Tyldesley	31
† T A Ward	b Tate	17	lbw b Hearne	25
M J Susskind	b Gilligan	4	lbw b R K Tyldesley	23
A W Nourse	run out	3	c Wood b R K Tyldesley	30
* H W Taylor	not out	59	run out	56
R H Catterall	c Wood b Tate	29	b Tate	56
E P Nupen	c Wood b Tate	0	b Macaulay	11
S J Pegler	lbw b Tate	0	run out	14
J M Blanckenberg	b Tate	0	b Tate	6
C P Carter	c Hendren b Macaulay	11	b Tate	0
Extras	lb 1 nb 2	3	b 14 lb 7 nb 3	24
Total		**132**		**323**

Fall 1st inns: 1/6 2/10 3/16 4/30 5/34 6/88 7/88 8/90 9/90 10/132
Fall 2nd inns: 1/35 2/81 3/82 4/135 5/234 6/238 7/244 8/276 9/318 10/323

Bowling			1st inns				2nd inns	
Gilligan	10	3	27	1	18	7	37	0
Tate	17	4	42	6	30	6	64	3
Macaulay	11.3	2	23	1	27	8	60	1
R K Tyldesley	13	4	37	0	24	8	63	3
Hearne					19	3	54	1
Woolley					9	2	21	0

Umpires: W Reeves and A E Street

England beat South Africa by 9 wickets.

Twenty-Second Match vs Lancashire played at Aigburth Cricket Ground, Liverpool on 16, 17 and 18 July. Lancashire 445 for 6 dec (C Hallows 124, J L Hopwood 105*, Major L Green 79, F Watson 63, J Sharp 26, J M Blanckenberg 4 for 94) drew with South Africans 259 for 3 (A W Nourse 103*, J M M Commaille 85, H W Taylor 37*, E A McDonald 2 for 79).

C.D.Dixon

J.M.M.Commaille

Twenty-Third Match vs Middlesex played at Lord's Cricket Ground, London on 19, 21 and 22 July. Middlesex 328 (J W Hearne 85, G T S Stevens 81, H L Hales 51, H W Lee 47, J M Blanckenberg 5 for 79, S J Pegler 3 for 110) drew with South Africans 139 for 2 (M J Susskind 48*, T A Ward 44).

Twenty-Fourth Match vs ‡ Durham played at Ashbrooke Cricket Ground, Sunderland on 23 and 24 July. Durham 195 (L H Weight 43, H C Ferens 33, J Carr 28, T Kinch 26, C P Carter 5 for 76, H G Deane 3 for 38) and 12 for 0 drew with South Africans 173 (H G Deane 38, J M M Commaille 31, T K Dobson 4 for 49, A G Doggart 3 for 21).

Twenty-Fifth Match vs England (Fourth Test Match) played at Old Trafford, Manchester on 26, 28 and 29 July.

South Africa

J M M Commaille	lbw b Tate	8
† T A Ward	b Tate	50
M J Susskind	lbw b Tyldesley	5
A W Nourse	b Tate	18
* H W Taylor	not out	18
R H Catterall	not out	6
Extras	b 8 lb 3	11
Total	**(4 wickets)**	**116**

H G Deane, P A M Hands, S J Pegler, J M Blanckenberg and C P Carter did not bat.
Fall 1st inns: 1/8 2/40 3/71 4/98

Bowling		1st inns		
Tate	24	8	34	3
Douglas	8	2	20	0
Geary	11	5	21	0
Tyldesley	11.5	4	11	1
Kilner	12	6	19	0

England
J W H T Douglas, J C W MacBryan, A Sandham, H Sutcliffe, * F E Woolley, E H Hendren, M W Tate, G Geary, R Kilner, † G Duckworth and R K Tyldesley did not bat.

Umpires: H Butt and A E Street

England drew with South Africa.

Twenty-Sixth Match vs Sussex played at County Cricket Ground, Brighton on 30 and 31 July and 1 August. South Africans 337 (A W Nourse 73, P A M Hands 58*, T A Ward 47, J M Blanckenberg 47, J M M Commaille 42, S J Pegler 25, R R Relf 3 for 80, J H Parks 3 for 91) and 217 for 4 dec (M J Susskind 88, A W Nourse 44*, T A Ward 43, R R Relf 3 for 43) drew with Sussex 334 (E H Bowley 106, R A Young 53, M W Tate 39, R R Relf 32, H L Wilson 27, J M Blanckenberg 5 for 102, S J Pegler 3 for 112) and 96 for 6 (R A Young 35*, P A M Hands 3 for 9).

Twenty-Seventh Match vs Glamorgan played at Arms Park, Cardiff on 2, 4 and 5 August. Glamorgan 178 (J T Bell 38, D Davies 34, T Arnott 31, J M Blanckenberg 8 for 97) drew with South Africans 15 for 1.

Twenty-Eighth Match vs Surrey played at Kennington Oval, London on 6, 7 and 8 August. Surrey 300 (T Shepherd 127, P G H Fender 56, A Sandham 51, A D Nourse 3 for 27, J M Blanckenberg 3 for 37) and 203 for 3 (D J Knight 68, D R Jardine 38*, T Shepherd 34, A Sandham 29, J M Blanckenberg 2 for 84) drew with South Africans 418 (M J Susskind 137, R H Catterall 63, H G Deane 42, H W Taylor 39, J M M Commaille 27, S Fenley 6 for 148).

Twenty-Ninth Match vs Combined Services played at United Services Officers Sports Ground, Portsmouth on 9, 11 and 12 August. South Africans 182 (G A L Hearne 68, H W Taylor 62, R H Catterall 36, Capt. T O Jameson 4 for 92, Lieut. A C Gore 3 for 47) and 420 (R H Catterall 137, H W Taylor 118, H G Deane 41*, G A L Hearne 34, M J Susskind 29, Capt. T O Jameson 7 for 152, Capt. M B Burrows 3 for 111) drew with Combined Services 418 (Lieut. G J Bryan 229, Squadron Leader C H B Blount 61, Lieut. A C Wilkinson 31, J M Blanckenberg 4 for 92, S J Pegler 3 for 109) and 88 for 2 (Major R A D Brooks 35*).

Thirtieth Match vs ‡ Harlequins played at The Saffrons, Eastbourne on 13 and 14 August. South Africans 162 (H W Taylor 67, J M M Commaille 45, R H Bettington 7 for 52) and 125 for 4 (J M M Commaille 68, V R Price 3 for 44) beat Harlequins 73 (R H Bettington 15, J M Blanckenberg 5 for 34, S J Pegler 5 for 34) and 213 (A J Evans 42, D R Jardine 40, R H Twining 32, C H Knott 28, C P Carter 6 for 40) by 6 wickets.

G.A.L.Hearne

P.A.M.Hands

Thirty-First Match vs England (Fifth Test Match) played at Kennington Oval, London on 16, 18 and 19 August.

South Africa

J M M Commaille	b Tate	3
G A L Hearne	run out	4
M J Susskind	c Woolley b Hearne	65
A W Nourse	c Sutcliffe b Woolley	37
* H W Taylor	c & b Tyldesley	11
R H Catterall	c sub b Tate	95
H G Deane	c Strudwick b Hearne	30
J M Blanckenberg	not out	46
† T A Ward	lbw b Tate	5
S J Pegler	b Tyldesley	25
C P Carter	c Sandham b Hearne	4
Extras	b 4 lb 9 w 1 nb 3	17
Total		**342**

Fall 1st inns: 1/ 7 2/7 3/86 4/108 5/181 6/259 7/259 8/268 9/337 10/342

Bowling		1st inns		
Gilligan	16	5	44	0
Tate	29	10	64	3
Howell	20	5	69	0
Tyldesley	22	6	36	2
Hearne	22	3	90	3
Woolley	14	4	22	1

England

J B Hobbs	c Ward b Pegler	30
H Sutcliffe	c Ward b Nourse	5
J W Hearne	c Susskind b Pegler	35
* F E Woolley	b Carter	51
A Sandham	c Ward b Nourse	46
E H Hendren	c Nourse b Carter	142
M W Tate	b Carter	50
A E R Gilligan	c Nourse b Pegler	36
R K Tyldesley	not out	1
† H Strudwick	not out	2
Extras	b 8 lb 13 nb 2	23
Total	**(8 wickets)**	**421**

H Howell did not bat.

Fall 1st inns: 1/5 2/72 3/79 4/137 5/238 6/328 7/402 8/418

Bowling		1st inns		
Nourse	24	3	63	2
Blanckenberg	36	2	122	0
Carter	23	2	85	3
Pegler	48	14	128	3

Umpires: H Butt and F Chester

England drew with South Africa.

Thirty-Second Match vs Minor Counties played at Lakenham Cricket Ground, Norwich on 20, 21 and 22 August. Minor Counties 196 (J M Coldham 40, A G Doggart 28, R J O Meyer 26, S J Pegler 5 for 46, D J Meintjes 4 for 104) and 272 (C H Titchmarsh 80, A P F Chapman 68, R J O Meyer 30, J M Blanckenberg 4 for 56, C P Carter 3 for 42) beat South Africans 149 (D J Meintjes 26*, M J Susskind 25, R J O Meyer 6 for 60) and 294 (A W Nourse 91, H W Taylor 47, G A L Hearne 45, D J Meintjes 26, M J Susskind 25, M Falcon 5 for 103, W A Beadsmoore 4 for 53) by 25 runs.

Thirty-Third Match vs Kent played at St. Lawrence Cricket Ground, Canterbury on 23 and 25 August. Kent 418 for 6 dec (F E Woolley 176, H T W Hardinge 118, C H Knott 63, G C Collins 25*, J M Blanckenberg 3 for 82) beat South Africans 135 (H G Deane 43, H W Taylor 29, C Wright 5 for 39) and 194 (J M Blanckenberg 51*, H G Deane 42, E P Nupen 32, S J Pegler 27, A P Freeman 6 for 68) by an innings and 89 runs.

Thirty-Fourth Match vs Somerset played at County Cricket Ground, Taunton on 27 and 28 August. South Africans 268 (R H Catterall 90, H W Taylor 45, H G Deane 38, S J Pegler 25, J J Bridges 6 for 61, R C Robertson-Glasgow 3 for 70) and 79 for 1 (M J Susskind 43*) beat Somerset 208 (J C W MacBryan 59, J C White 37, G Hunt 28, J M Blanckenberg 6 for 76, S J Pegler 3 for 63) and 138 (J C W MacBryan 35, A Young 28, C P Carter 6 for 50, A W Nourse 3 for 41) by 9 wickets.

Thirty-Fifth Match vs Worcestershire played at County Cricket Ground, New Road, Worcester on 30 August and 1 September. South Africans 276 (A W Nourse 90, H W Taylor 38, R H Catterall 29, S J Pegler 29, J M M Commaille 27, C F Root 5 for 83, F Pearson 3 for 90) beat Worcestershire 87 (C F Root 24, J M Blanckenberg 6 for 40, S J Pegler 4 for 41) and 161 (J F Maclean 27, F Pearson 26, S J Pegler 3 for 21, D J Meintjes 3 for 38, C P Carter 3 for 44) by an innings and 28 runs.

Thirty-Sixth Match vs South of England played at Central Cricket Ground, Hastings on 3, 4 and 5 September. South of England 312 for 9 dec (Hon. F S G Calthorpe 69, J B Hobbs 56, A Sandham 44, E H Bowley 44, D J Knight 30, M W Tate 25*, A W Nourse 3 for 55, S J Pegler 3 for 69) and 218 for 8 dec (Hon. F S G Calthorpe 52, A E R Gilligan 35*, J B Hobbs 34, A Sandham 33, F E Woolley 26, R H Catterall 3 for 48, D J Meintjes 3 for 83) drew with South Africans 269 (A W Nourse 69, T A Ward 68, R H Catterall 39, M J Susskind 29, F E Woolley 4 for 69, R R Relf 4 for 24) and 219 for 7 (M J Susskind 101, H W Taylor 30, H G Deane 30*, J M Blanckenberg 29, P G H Fender 3 for 58).

Thirty-Seventh Match vs ‡ North Wales played at The Oval, Llandudno on 8 and 9 September. North Wales 49 (Pell 13, J M Blanckenberg 6 for 12, S J Pegler 3 for 22) drew with South Africans 111 for 7 (J M Blanckenberg 27, S F Barnes 5 for 32).

Thirty-Eighth Match vs C I Thornton's XI played at North Marine Drive, Scarborough on 10, 11 and 12 September. C I Thornton's XI 461 for 6 dec (P Holmes 202*, E H Hendren 101, W Rhodes 56, A P F Chapman 37, A W Nourse 2 for 51, S J Pegler 2 for 51) beat South Africans 143 (J M Blanckenberg 37*, A D Nourse 25, G O B Allen 7 for 61) and 273 (A W Nourse 84, M J Susskind 39, J M M Commaille 38, G A L Hearne 31, G O B Allen 3 for 57) by an innings and 45 runs.

Test Match batting averages:

	Inns	NO	Runs	HS	Ave
R H Catterall	8	1	471	120	67.28
M J Susskind	8	0	268	65	33.50
H W Taylor	8	2	197	59*	32.83
H G Deane	7	1	143	47*	23.83
J M Blanckenberg	7	1	139	56	23.16
T A Ward	8	1	121	50	17.28
A W Nourse	8	0	138	37	17.25
J M M Commaille	8	1	113	37	16.14
S J Pegler	7	0	53	25	7.57
C P Carter	3	0	15	11	5.00
E P Nupen	4	0	16	11	4.00

Also batted during Tests:

G A Faulkner 25 and 12; G A L Hearne 4; G M Parker 2*, 1*, 0 and 0; P A M Hands did not bat.

Test Match bowling averages:

	Overs	Mdns	Runs	Wkts	Ave
C P Carter	38	4	132	4	33.00
G M Parker	61	2	273	8	34.12
S J Pegler	160.2	35	500	9	55.55
A W Nourse	64	11	190	3	63.33
J M Blanckenberg	118	12	411	4	102.75
E P Nupen	49	10	157	1	157.00

Also bowled during Tests:

	Overs	Mdns	Runs	Wkts	Ave
R H Catterall	3	0	19	0	-
G A Faulkner	17	0	87	0	-

Tour batting averages - all matches:

	Inns	NO	Runs	HS	Ave
H W Taylor	54	8	1,925	126	41.84
A W Nourse	55	5	1,943	147*	38.56
M J Susskind	52	7	1,469	137	32.64
R H Catterall	53	2	1,389	137	27.23
J M M Commaille	52	4	1,202	85	25.04
H G Deane	35	5	689	80*	22.96
J M Blanckenberg	48	9	848	69	21.74
G A L Hearne	24	2	463	68	21.04
P A M Hands	29	5	470	64	19.58
E P Nupen	27	4	384	57	16.69
S J Pegler	38	7	454	50*	14.64

T A Ward	38	3	490	68	14.00
G F Bissett	13	3	122	28*	12.20
D J Meintjes	23	3	186	26*	9.30
C D Dixon	16	4	71	9	5.91
C P Carter	28	8	99	19	4.95

Also batted during the tour:

G A Faulkner 25 and 12; G M Parker 2*, 1* and 0.

Tour bowling averages - all matches:

	Overs	*Mdns*	*Runs*	*Wkts*	*Ave*
C P Carter	466.3	85	1,291	65	19.86
J M Blanckenberg	1,040	247	2,718	127	21.40
S J Pegler	1,063	299	2,574	111	23.18
G M Parker	77	7	307	12	25.58
C D Dixon	415.3	113	961	37	25.97
H G Deane	19	0	88	3	29.33
E P Nupen	345.4	81	896	30	29.86
G F Bissett	204.4	23	618	20	30.90
H W Taylor	25	2	96	3	32.00
A W Nourse	405.3	121	963	27	35.66
D J Meintjes	377.2	64	1,150	30	38.33
R H Catterall	86.5	12	276	6	46.00
M J Susskind	6	0	51	1	51.00

Also bowled during the tour:

G A Faulkner	17	0	87	0	-
P A M Hands	1.5	0	9	3	3.00
G A L Hearne	18	2	46	0	-
T A Ward	2	0	11	0	-

Centuries recorded for South Africans during the tour:

A W Nourse	(4) :	147*	vs Nottinghamshire (Trent Bridge)
		144	vs Cambridge University (Fenner's)
		121	vs Hampshire (Southampton)
		103*	vs Lancashire (Old Trafford)
H W Taylor	(4) :	126	vs Essex (Colchester)
		118	vs Combined Services (Portsmouth)
		116	vs Warwickshire (Edgbaston)
		113	vs Northamptonshire (Northampton)
R H Catterall	(3) :	137	vs Combined Services (Portsmouth)
		120	vs England (Edgbaston) (First Test Match)
		120	vs England (Lord's) (Second Test Match)
M J Susskind	(2) :	137	vs Surrey (The Oval)
		101	vs South of England (Hastings)

Fielding:

	Catches	Stumpings
T A Ward	35	12
M J Susskind	25	3
J M Blanckenberg	21	
A W Nourse	21	
S J Pegler	15	
C P Carter	13	
H W Taylor	12	
R H Catterall	12	
H G Deane	11	
E P Nupen	10	
P A M Hands	9	
C D Dixon	8	
G F Bissett	6	
J M M Commaille	6	
G A L Hearne	6	
D J Meintjes	6	

R.H.Catterall

The Seventh South African Team in the United Kingdom, 1929

The errors of the past appear to have been heeded when the selectors came to decide the touring party. In contrast to 1924 they selected a young squad with an average age of 26 years with only two players over thirty, and they were the only two survivors of the 1924 team, Herby Taylor and H G 'Nummy' Deane who was captain. Deane proved an able and popular captain whose superb fielding set an example for all the team.

The tourists included a number of players of very considerable talent - Taylor, Owen-Smith, Morkel, Siedle, Mitchell, Cameron, Catterall, McMillan, Bell, Vincent, Quinn and Ochse. A total of twenty-one centuries were scored while seven of the tourists hit more than a thousand runs. All this combined to suggest that a great future was in store for South African cricket.

Regrettably a long list of injuries prevented the team from reaching their full potential. Of the 34 first-class matches, nine were won, seven lost and eighteen drawn, while in the Tests three were lost and two drawn.

(standing) **I.J.Siedle B.Mitchell A.L.Ochse A.J.Bell D.P.B.Morkel J.A.J.Christy N.A.Quinn Q.McMillan E.L.Dalton Mr.A.S.Frames** (Secretary)

(sitting) **H.B.Cameron H.W.Taylor Mr.H.O.Frielinghaus** (Manager) **H.G.Deane** (Captain) **R.H.Catterall C.L.Vincent**

(on ground) **H.G.O.Owen-Smith E.A.van der Merwe**

Touring party (16):

* H G Deane (*Transvaal*) (Captain)
Age 33. Right-handed middle order batsman and specialist close fieldsman.

H W Taylor (*Transvaal*) (Vice-Captain)
Age 40. Attractive right-handed opening batsman and fine fielder.

† H B Cameron (*Transvaal*)
Age 23. Right-handed middle order batsman and wicket-keeper.

R H Catterall (*Orange Free State*)
Age 28. Right-handed opening/middle order batsman, right-arm medium pace bowler and fine deep fieldsman.

J A J Christy (*Transvaal*)
Age 24. Stylish right-handed opening/middle order batsman and right-arm medium pace bowler.

E L Dalton (*Natal*)
Age 22. Right-handed middle order batsman and leg break bowler.

A J Bell (*Western Province*)
Age 23. Right-arm fast-medium bowler and right-handed tail end batsman.

B Mitchell (*Transvaal*)
Age 20. Stylish right-handed opening batsman, leg-break bowler and good slip fieldsman.

D P B Morkel (*Western Province*)
Age 23. Right-handed attacking middle order batsman, right-arm fast-medium bowler and good slip fieldsman.

Q McMillan (*Transvaal*)
Age 24. Right-handed hard hitting batsman and leg-break and googly bowler.

A L Ochse (*Eastern Province*)
Age 29. Right-handed lower order batsman and right-arm fast bowler.

H G O Owen-Smith (*Western Province*)
Age 20. Right-handed middle order batsman, slow leg-break bowler and excellent outfielder.

N A Quinn (*Griqualand West*)
Age 21. Right-handed lower order batsman and left-arm medium fast bowler.

I J Siedle (*Natal*)
Age 26. Right-handed opening batsman.

† E A van der Merwe (*Transvaal*)
Age 24. Right-handed lower order batsman and wicket-keeper.

C L Vincent (*Transvaal*)
Age 27. Right-handed lower order batsman and left-arm slow bowler.

Hon. General Manager: Mr. H O Frielinghaus

Secretary: Mr. A S Frames

Scorer and Baggage-Master: Mr. W H Ferguson

Summary of all matches:

Played 37   Won 11   Lost 7   Drawn 19

Summary of first-class matches:

Played 34   Won 9   Lost 7   Drawn 18

Summary of Test Matches:

Played 5   Won 0   Lost 2   Drawn 3

First Match vs ‡ Reginald Earle's XI played at Godalming on 25 April. Mr. R. Earle's XI 138 (T Shepherd 30, A L Ochse 4 for 35, N A Quinn 4 for 12) drew with South Africans 129 for 7 (I J Siedle 33, T J Durston 3 for 35, H A Peach 3 for 33).

Second Match vs ‡ P F Warner's XI played at Bearsted on 29 April. South Africans 199 for 6 dec (E L Dalton 41, H B Cameron 39, J A J Christy 36, I A R Peebles 3 for 75) drew with P F Warner's XI 117 for 7 (B H Lyon 26, A L Ochse 5 for 44).

Third Match vs Worcestershire played at County Cricket Ground, New Road, Worcester on 1, 2 and 3 May. South Africans 444 for 8 dec (H W Taylor 103, H B Cameron 102, B Mitchell 83*, H G Deane 42, R H Catterall 35, I J Siedle 26, Capt. D V Hill 3 for 72) drew with Worcestershire 284 (W V Fox 88, M F S Jewell 68, L Wright 32, Capt. D V Hill 25, N A Quinn 6 for 75) and 262 for 7 (W V Fox 58, L Wright 50, C V Tarbox 50*, M Nichol 32, M F S Jewell 30*, B Mitchell 3 for 64).

Fourth Match vs Leicestershire played at Aylestone Road, Leicester on 4, 6 and 7 May. South Africans 354 for 8 dec (I J Siedle 169*, H G Deane 68, T E Shipman 2 for 24) drew with Leicestershire 208 (E W Dawson 58, A Shipman 58, B Mitchell 3 for 49) and 191 for 7 (E W Dawson 48, L G Berry 45*, A Shipman 30, C L Vincent 3 for 47).

Fifth Match vs Surrey played at Kennington Oval, London on 8, 9 and 10 May. Surrey 229 (P G H Fender 79, T H Barling 34, A Sandham 33, H A Peach 27, C L Vincent 6 for 62) and 292 for 9 dec (P G H Fender 98, A Sandham 61, R J Gregory 36, D P B Morkel 4 for 121) beat South Africans 111 (R H Catterall 41, M J C Allom 2 for 18, H A Peach 2 for 18, T Shepherd 2 for 21) and 285 (D P B Morkel 86, H G Deane 43, I J Siedle 31, R H Catterall 31, Q McMillan 29*, P G H Fender 4 for 56, S Fenley 4 for 68) by 125 runs.

Sixth Match vs Middlesex played at Lord's Cricket Ground, London on 11, 13 and 14 May. South Africans 291 (H G Deane 62, B Mitchell 51, I J Siedle 46, R H Catterall 38, D P B Morkel 34, N E Haig 2 for 36, I A R Peebles 2 for 49, T J Durston 2 for 43) and 85 for 2 (J A J Christy 41*, B Mitchell 28) beat Middlesex 132 (N E Haig 28, E T Killick 24, D P B Morkel 7 for 61) and 240 (E T Killick 111, N E Haig 57, N A Quinn 4 for 54, H G Owen-Smith 4 for 80) by 8 wickets.

Seventh Match vs Oxford University played at University Parks, Oxford on 15, 16 and 17 May. South Africans 298 (R H Catterall 67, D P B Morkel 62, H G Deane 48, J A J Christy 38, I J Siedle 32, E M Wellings 4 for 81, H M Garland-Wells 3 for 39) and 181 for 6 (I J Siedle 90, D P B Morkel 30*, H W Taylor 24, C K Hill-Wood 3 for 27) beat Oxford University 152 (A M Crawley 79, C L Vincent 4 for 57, N A Quinn 3 for 25) and 325 (A M Crawley 81, H M Garland-Wells 58, A T Barber 51, N M Ford 30, N A Quinn 6 for 94) by 4 wickets.

Eighth Match vs Glamorgan played at Ynysangharad Park, Pontypridd on 18, 20 and 21 May. South Africans 212 (H G Deane 58, B Mitchell 28, D P B Morkel 26, J Mercer 8 for 60) and 186 (H W Taylor 57, H G Deane 33, J Mercer 6 for 59, W Jones 4 for 44) beat Glamorgan 113 (A H Howard 33, J C Clay 25, C L Vincent 7 for 36) and 115 (T Arnott 30, Q McMillan 5 for 36, C L Vincent 4 for 53) by 170 runs.

Ninth Match vs Gloucestershire played at County Cricket Ground, Nevil Road, Bristol on 22, 23 and 24 May. Gloucestershire (R A Sinfield 112, A E Dipper 94, C J Barnett 33, C C Dacre 32, A J Bell 6 for 68) and 129 for 4 (W R Hammond 63*, C C Dacre 36, A J Bell 2 for 45) beat South Africans 225 (H B Cameron 60, E L Dalton 38, I J Siedle 34, J A J Christy 32, T W J Goddard 6 for 68) and 232 (J A J Christy 76, D P B Morkel 43, R H Catterall 38, I J Siedle 26, C W L Parker 5 for 56) by 6 wickets.

Tenth Match vs Yorkshire played at Bramall Lane, Sheffield on 25, 27 and 28 May. South Africans 441 for 5 dec (I J Siedle 168, B Mitchell 101, D P B Morkel 59*, H B Cameron 55*, H W Taylor 30, C Turner 2 for 81) and 277 (H B Cameron 85*, D P B Morkel 68, I J Siedle 41, H G Deane 31, C Turner 3 for 81) drew with Yorkshire 338 (A Mitchell 126, H Sutcliffe 113, N A Quinn 3 for 73, C L Vincent 3 for 96).

Eleventh Match vs Cambridge University at Fenner's University Cricket Ground, Cambridge on 29 and 30 May. South Africans 360 (H B Cameron 120, I J Siedle 51, D P B Morkel 46, H G Deane 33, Q McMillan 25, P K Webster 4 for 86) beat Cambridge University 98 (M J L Turnbull 33, E T Killick 25, D P B Morkel 4 for 13, A L Ochse 4 for 37) and 143 (E T Killick 77, G C Grant 28, Q McMillan 5 for 45, A L Ochse 4 for 34) by an innings and 119 runs.

Twelfth Match vs M.C.C. played at Lord's Cricket Ground, London on 1, 3 and 4 June. South Africans 311 (D P B Morkel 70, R H Catterall 44, H B Cameron 44, B Mitchell 34, E L Dalton 30, J C White 5 for 87) and 269 for 6 dec (B Mitchell 61, I J Siedle 54, D P B Morkel 42, H B Cameron 29, M Falcon 2 for 42, G T S Stevens 2 for 54) drew with M.C.C. 336 (K S Duleepsinhji 74, G O B Allen 52, J C White 39, Capt. R T Stanyforth 39, E H Hendren 31, Q McMillan 4 for 76) and 72 for 1 (G O B Allen 41*).

Thirteenth Match vs Derbyshire played at County Cricket Ground, Derby on 5, 6 and 7 June. South Africans 166 (H G Deane 47, H W Taylor 37, I J Siedle 20, T B Mitchell 4 for 46, L F Townsend 4 for 62) drew with Derbyshire 208 for 6 (D Smith 46, G M Lee 37, H Storer 35, G R Jackson 27, C L Vincent 2 for 61).

Fourteenth Match vs Lancashire played at Old Trafford, Manchester on 8, 10 and 11 June. Lancashire 191 (F Watson 50, R K Tyldesley 31, T M Halliday 27, A L Ochse 4 for 46) and 145 for 4 (T M Halliday 60*, J Iddon 48, A L Ochse 2 for 39) beat South Africans 185 (R H Catterall 46, H G Deane 35, H G O Owen-Smith 30, F M Sibbles 4 for 31) and 150 (I J Siedle 75, R K Tyldesley 3 for 19, G Hodgson 3 for 35) by 6 wickets.

Fifteenth Match vs Minor Counties played at Stoke-on-Trent on 12, 13 and 14 June. Minor Counties 201 (Hon. P F Remnant 62, W T Cook 45, H W Hodgson 25, H G O Owen-Smith 6 for 38) and 183 for 6 dec (W T Cook 92, T W Dobson 35, A J Bell 4 for 47) drew with South Africans 139 (H W Taylor 28, H G O Owen-Smith 26, S F Barnes 8 for 41) and 40 for 1.

H.G.O.Owen-Smith

A.J.Bell

Sixteenth Match vs England (First Test Match) played at Edgbaston Cricket Ground, Birmingham on 15, 17 and 18 June.

England

Batsman	1st innings	Runs	2nd innings	Runs
H Sutcliffe	c Cameron b Ochse	26	b Morkel	114
E T Killick	c Morkel b Ochse	31	b Quinn	23
* W R Hammond	b Quinn	18	not out	138
K S Duleepsinhji	c Vincent b Morkel	12	lbw b Ochse	1
E H Hendren	b Morkel	70	(6) not out	8
M Leyland	c Taylor b Ochse	3		
P G H Fender	c Cameron b Quinn	6	(5) c Vincent b Ochse	12
M W Tate	c Mitchell b Morkel	40		
H Larwood	lbw b Ochse	6		
J C White	run out	5		
† G Duckworth	not out	11		
Extras	b 9 lb 3 w 4 nb 1	17	b 10 w 2	12
Total		**245**	**(4 wickets, declared)**	**308**

Fall 1st inns: 1/59 2/66 3/92 4/96 5/111 6/128 7/215 8/215 9/222 10/245
Fall 2nd inns: 1/34 2/255 3/278 4/280

Bowling	1st inns				2nd inns			
Morkel	20	4	40	3	22	6	54	1
Quinn	27	8	62	2	20	2	55	1
Ochse	25.1	2	79	4	28	2	88	2
Vincent	7	0	37	0	19	3	55	0
Mitchell	2	0	10	0				
Owen-Smith					6	0	29	0
Christy					5	1	15	0

South Africa

Batsman	1st innings	Runs	2nd innings	Runs
R H Catterall	lbw b Fender	67	c White b Fender	98
B Mitchell	b Tate	88	not out	61
J A J Christy	b Larwood	1		
H W Taylor	b Larwood	2		
D P B Morkel	b Tate	5		
* H G Deane	c & b Fender	29		
† H B Cameron	b Larwood	5		
H G O Owen-Smith	b Tate	25		
C L Vincent	not out	14		
N A Quinn	b Larwood	1		
A L Ochse	b Larwood	2		
Extras	b 6 lb 2 w 1 nb 2	11	b 9 nb 3	12
Total		**250**	**(1 wicket)**	**171**

Fall 1st inns: 1/119 2/120 3/122 4/130 5/174 6/182 7/224 8/239 9/248 10/250
Fall 2nd inns: 1/171

Bowling	1st inns				2nd inns			
Larwood	42.4	17	57	5	11	6	12	0
Tate	44	14	65	3	16	4	43	0
Fender	32	10	64	2	15.4	3	55	1
Hammond	22	12	25	0	3	0	19	0
White	32	19	28	0	13	5	23	0
Duleepsinhji					1	0	7	0

Umpires: T Oates and J Hardstaff

England drew with South Africa.

Seventeenth Match vs Yorkshire played at The Circle Cricket Ground, Hull on 19, 20 and 21 June. South Africans 265 (H G Deane 60*, H G O Owen-Smith 52, H W Taylor 37, D P B Morkel 36, S Douglas 3 for 55, F Dennis 3 for 65) and 260 for 4 dec (D P B Morkel 109, H W Taylor 83*, S Douglas 2 for 63) drew with Yorkshire 335 (W Barber 108, E Robinson 48, C Turner 44, Capt. W A Worsley 37, J A J Christy 3 for 46) and 86 for 2 (Capt. W A Worsley 29*).

Eighteenth Match vs Surrey played at Kennington Oval, London on 22, 24 and 25 June. South Africans 426 for 8 dec (R H Catterall 124, I J Siedle 66, H W Taylor 59, H G Deane 54, C L Vincent 35*, R J Gregory 2 for 61, A R Gover 2 for 65) and 202 for 2 dec (R H Catterall 98, H W Taylor 49*, D P B Morkel 30*) drew with Surrey 305 (T Shepherd 113, R J Gregory 48, A Ducat 42, P G H Fender 30, A L Ochse 4 for 103) and 111 for 3 (A Ducat 62*, D P B Morkel 3 for 8).

D.P.B.Morkel   **J.A.J.Christy**

Nineteenth Match vs ‡ Norfolk played at Lakenham Cricket Ground, Norwich on 26 and 27 June. South Africans 420 (H W Taylor 170, C L Vincent 62, Q McMillan 46, J A J Christy 35, H B Cameron 26, M Falcon 3 for 65, R C Rought-Rought 3 for 101) beat Norfolk 126 (B W Rought-Rought 30, A J Bell 5 for 37) and 250 (F R Bell 69, R H Gladden 50, B W Rought-Rought 39, H G O Owen-Smith 3 for 56) by an innings and 44 runs.

Twentieth Match vs England (Second Test Match) at Lord's Cricket Ground, London on 29 June, 1 and 2 July.

England

E T Killick	b Morkel	3	c Morkel b Christy	24
H Sutcliffe	c Mitchell b Bell	100	c Catterall b Morkel	10
* W R Hammond	c Christy b Morkel	8	b Morkel	5
J O'Connor	b Morkel	0	c Cameron b Ochse	11
E H Hendren	b Morkel	43	b Morkel	11
M Leyland	b Bell	73	c Cameron b Ochse	102
M W Tate	c Cameron b Bell	15	not out	100
R W V Robins	c Mitchell b Bell	4	c Mitchell b Ochse	0
H Larwood	b Bell	35	b Ochse	9
J C White	b Bell	8	not out	18
† G Duckworth	not out	8		
Extras	lb 4 w 1	5	b 11 lb 6 w 2 nb 3	22
Total		**302**	**(8 wickets, declared)**	**312**

Fall 1st inns: 1/8 2/18 3/18 4/111 5/199 6/243 7/249 8/252 9/287 10/302
Fall 2nd inns: 1/28 2/46 3/83 4/93 5/117 6/246 7/250 8/260

Bowling	1st inns				2nd inns			
Ochse	24	5	51	0	20	0	99	4
Morkel	31	6	93	4	24	6	63	3
Bell	30.4	7	99	6	18.2	2	60	0
Christy	6	2	20	0	3	0	15	1
McMillan	7	0	31	0	13	0	34	0
Owen-Smith	1	0	3	0				
Mitchell					4	0	19	0

South Africa

R H Catterall	b Larwood	0	b Tate	3
B Mitchell	st Duckworth b Hammond	29	c Hendren b Robins	22
J A J Christy	run out	70	c Hendren b Robins	41
D P B Morkel	lbw b Tate	88	not out	17
* H G Deane	b Tate	1	st Duckworth b Robins	2
† H B Cameron	c Leyland b Robins	32	retired hurt	0
H G O Owen-Smith	not out	52	(8) not out	1
E L Dalton	b Tate	6	(7) c Killick b Larwood	1
Q McMillan	c Killick b White	17		
A L Ochse	c Duckworth b White	1		
A J Bell	b Robins	13		
Extras	b 9 lb 4	13	b 2 lb 1	3
Total		**322**	**(5 wickets)**	**90**

Fall 1st inns: 1/0 2/82 3/125 4/126 5/189 6/237 7/253 8/272 9/279 10/322
Fall 2nd inns: 1/9 2/60 3/77 4/82 5/85

Bowling	1st inns				2nd inns			
Larwood	20	4	65	1	12	3	17	1
Tate	39	9	108	3	11	3	27	1
Hammond	8	3	19	1				
White	35	12	61	2	9	3	11	0
Robins	24	5	47	2	19	4	32	3
Leyland	5	2	9	0				

Umpires: F Chester and W Bestwick

England drew with South Africa.

Twenty-First Match vs Northamptonshire played at County Cricket Ground, Wantage Road, Northampton on 3, 4 and 5 July. South Africans 219 (B Mitchell 73, J A J Christy 34, Q McMillan 33, E C Clark 6 for 41, V W C Jupp 3 for 90) and 11 for 0 drew with Northamptonshire 268 (A H Bakewell 80, V W C Jupp 61, E F Towell 27, A J Bell 3 for 50).

N.A.Quinn

A.L.Ochse

Twenty-Second Match vs Nottinghamshire played at Trent Bridge, Nottingham on 6, 8 and 9 July. Nottinghamshire 476 (A W Carr 194, W Payton 134*, W Walker 53, D P B Morkel 5 for 72) and 177 for 4 dec (W Whysall 58, A W Carr 43, D P B Morkel 2 for 47) drew with South Africans 304 (J A J Christy 148, H G O Owen-Smith 42, A L Ochse 30, H G Deane 26, A Staples 4 for 64, H Larwood 3 for 91) and 191 for 6 (D P B Morkel 64*, J A J Christy 50, B Mitchell 38, H Larwood 2 for 41, R D F Bland 2 for 47).

Twenty-Third Match vs Wales played at Rhos Road, Colwyn Bay on 10, 11 and 12 July. South Africans 192 (R H Catterall 117, I J Siedle 33, S F Barnes 6 for 28, E Davies 4 for 27) and 239 (H G Deane 64, I J Siedle 45, B Mitchell 44, R H Catterall 35, S F Barnes 4 for 62, J Mercer 4 for 67) beat Wales 159 (D E Davies 53, A L Ochse 4 for 28, Q McMillan 4 for 82) and 262 (W Bates 102, J T Bell 68, J Jones 34, C L Vincent 5 for 70) by 10 runs.

Twenty-Fourth Match vs England (Third Test Match) played at Headingley Cricket Ground, Leeds on 13, 15 and 16 July.

South Africa

R H Catterall	b Freeman	74	b Tate		10
I J Siedle	b Larwood	0	c White b Freeman		14
B Mitchell	b Tate	22	lbw b White		24
D P B Morkel	st Duckworth b Freeman	17	lbw b Freeman		14
J P Duminy	b Freeman	2	b Woolley		12
* H G Deane	c Duckworth b Tate	20	b White		4
H G O Owen-Smith	c Hammond b Freeman	6	c Sutcliffe b Woolley		129
C L Vincent	b Freeman	60	b Woolley		0
N A Quinn	c Leyland b Freeman	5	st Duckworth b White		28
† E A van der Merwe	c Hammond b Freeman	19	c Duckworth b Freeman		1
A J Bell	not out	2	not out		26
Extras	b 9	9	b 6 lb 6 nb 1		13
Total		**236**			**275**

Fall 1st inns: 1/1 2/75 3/120 4/124 5/125 6/143 7/151 8/170 9/219 10/236
Fall 2nd inns: 1/15 2/25 3/66 4/66 5/73 6/116 7/116 8/167 9/172 10/275

Bowling	1st inns				2nd inns			
Larwood	17	4	35	1				
Tate	26	8	40	2	26	5	50	1
Freeman	32.3	6	115	7	35	7	92	3
Hammond	8	2	13	0	7	0	19	0
White	17	6	24	0	23	7	40	3
Bowley					4	1	7	0
Woolley					13.1	3	35	3
Leyland					3	0	19	0

England

H Sutcliffe	c Mitchell b Quinn	37	c Owen-Smith b Morkel		4
E H Bowley	c Bell b Quinn	31	c Mitchell b Vincent		46
* W R Hammond	c van der Merwe b Quinn	65	c & b Morkel		0
† G Duckworth	b Bell	21			
F E Woolley	b Vincent	83	(4) not out		95
E H Hendren	c van der Merwe b Quinn	0	(5) c Owen-Smith b Vincent		5
M Leyland	c Duminy b Quinn	45	(6) b Vincent		0
M W Tate	c Owen-Smith b Vincent	3	(7) not out		24
J C White	not out	20			
H Larwood	c Deane b Mitchell	0			
A P Freeman	b Quinn	15			
Extras	b 2 lb 4 nb 2	8	b 8 lb 4		12
Total		**328**	**(5 wickets)**		**186**

Fall 1st inns: 1/42 2/94 3/149 4/170 5/170 6/276 7/285 8/295 9/300 10/328
Fall 2nd inns: 1/13 2/13 3/98 4/110 5/110

Bowling	1st inns				2nd inns			
Morkel	19	5	41	0	14	1	43	2
Bell	14	0	58	1	2	0	12	0
Quinn	29.5	5	92	6	17	2	46	0
Vincent	13	5	76	2	19	0	67	3
Owen-Smith	2	0	8	0				
Mitchell	13	1	45	1	0.4	0	6	0

Umpires: L C Braund and W R Parry

England beat South Africa by 5 wickets.

Twenty-Fifth Match vs Lancashire played at Aigburth Cricket Ground, Liverpool on 17, 18 and 19 July. Lancashire 384 (P T Eckersley 78, J L Hopwood 65, W Farrimond 55, C Hallows 42, J Iddon 39, R K Tyldesley 39, C L Vincent 4 for 125, Q McMillan 3 for 83) and 36 for 0 beat South Africans 218 (I J Siedle 64, H W Taylor 31, J P Duminy 26*, J Iddon 5 for 34, G Hodgson 3 for 47) and 200 (R H Catterall 58, J P Duminy 31, H W Taylor 29, R K Tyldesley 7 for 52) by 10 wickets.

E.A.van der Merwe   I.J.Siedle

Twenty-Sixth Match vs Scotland played at North Inch, Perth on 20 and 22 July. South Africans 297 (H W Taylor 125, I J Siedle 52, E A van der Merwe 35, A P Baxter 4 for 91) beat Scotland 148 (A D Innes 48, J Kerr 42, N A Quinn 6 for 43) and 144 (W O'B Lindsay 23, N A Quinn 5 for 33) by an innings and 5 runs.

Twenty-Seventh Match vs ‡ Durham played at Ashbrooke Cricket Ground, Sunderland on 24 and 25 July. South Africans 243 (H G O Owen-Smith 102, H B Cameron 63, H Howell 5 for 74) beat Durham 112 (C L Adamson 39, T D Olver 31, Q McMillan 5 for 43, C L Vincent 4 for 22) and 71 (H Howell 30, A L Ochse 4 for 18, H G O Owen-Smith 4 for 24) by an innings and 60 runs.

Twenty-Eighth Match vs England (Fourth Test Match) played at Old Trafford, Manchester on 27, 29 and 30 July.

England

H Sutcliffe	b Morkel	9
E H Bowley	b Bell	13
R E S Wyatt	c Cameron b Vincent	113
* F E Woolley	c & b Vincent	154
E H Hendren	b Quinn	12
M Leyland	c Cameron b Mitchell	55
A W Carr	c Bell b Quinn	10
G Geary	not out	31
F Barratt	not out	2
Extras	b 16 lb 10 nb 2	28
Total	**(7 wickets, declared)**	**427**

A P Freeman and † G Duckworth did not bat.
Fall 1st inns: 1/30 2/36 3/281 4/304 5/342 6/365 7/424

Bowling	1st inns			
Morkel	18	5	61	1
Quinn	31	3	95	2
Bell	32	3	113	1
Vincent	36	4	93	2
Owen-Smith	5	0	16	0
Mitchell	8	3	21	1

South Africa

I J Siedle	lbw b Freeman	6	b Barratt	1
R H Catterall	c Sutcliffe b Barratt	3	b Geary	1
B Mitchell	c Geary b Freeman	1	b Geary	2
H W Taylor	b Freeman	28	c Leyland b Freeman	70
* H G Deane	st Duckworth b Freeman	0	c Duckworth b Wyatt	29
† H B Cameron	c Bowley b Freeman	13	c Woolley b Freeman	83
D P B Morkel	lbw b Geary	63	st Duckworth b Woolley	36
H G O Owen-Smith	c Barratt b Freeman	6	st Duckworth b Freeman	7
C L Vincent	c Geary b Freeman	6	c Duckworth b Freeman	4
N A Quinn	not out	1	b Freeman	11
A J Bell	c Duckworth b Geary	0	not out	0
Extras	lb 2 nb 1	3	b 13 lb 3 nb 5	21
Total		**130**		**265**

Fall 1st inns: 1/4 2/7 3/34 4/34 5/39 6/65 7/84 8/98 9/130 10/130
Fall 2nd inns: 1/1 2/3 3/13 4/66 5/113 6/145 7/180 8/245 9/256 10/265

Bowling	1st inns				2nd inns			
Barratt	10	4	8	1	20	7	30	1
Geary	22.3	13	18	2	37	18	50	2
Freeman	32	12	71	7	39.4	13	100	5
Woolley	9	3	22	0	18	5	51	1
Wyatt	2	1	8	0	4	0	13	1

Umpires: W R Parry and J Hardstaff

England beat South Africa by an innings and 32 runs.

Twenty-Ninth Match vs Somerset played at County Cricket Ground, Taunton on 31 July, 1 and 2 August. South Africans 302 for 4 dec (B Mitchell 127, I J Siedle 59, E L Dalton 35, D P B Morkel 29, J W Lee 1 for 43) beat Somerset 122 (G Hunt 27, C C Case 26*, Q McMillan 8 for 50) and 146 (A W Wellard 46, J C W MacBryan 33, A J Bell 3 for 23, N A Quinn 3 for 30) by an innings and 34 runs.

Thirtieth Match vs Glamorgan played at St. Helen's Cricket Ground, Swansea on 3, 5 and 6 August. Glamorgan 237 (J T Morgan 103, J Mercer 42, J Hills 33, D P B Morkel 3 for 29) drew with South Africans 98 for 5 (H W Taylor 36*, J Mercer 5 for 41).

Thirty-First Match vs Warwickshire played at Edgbaston Cricket Ground, Birmingham on 7, 8 and 9 August. South Africans 263 (Q McMillan 58*, H G O Owen-Smith 34, R H Catterall 31, B Mitchell 29, A J Bell 29, R E S Wyatt 3 for 55, G A E Paine 3 for 55) and 336 for 7 (H G Owen-Smith 126, B Mitchell 69, Q McMillan 44, I J Siedle 37, H W Taylor 30, J H Mayer 3 for 77) drew with Warwickshire 399 (A J Croom 109, L A Bates 94*, N Kilner 64, Rev J H Parsons 47, F R Santall 39, C L Vincent 3 for 85).

Thirty-Second Match vs Essex played at County Ground, Leyton on 10, 12 and 13 August. South Africans 389 for 7 dec (H W Taylor 95, H G O Owen-Smith 64, R H Catterall 61, H G Deane 58*, I J Siedle 51, M S Nichols 2 for 75, A B Hipkin 2 for 88) and 281 for 8 dec (H G O Owen-Smith 90, H W Taylor 67, Q McMillan 29*, M S Nichols 4 for 112) beat Essex 237 (A C Russell 90, M S Nichols 33, C J Bray 31, Q McMillan 5 for 81) and 106 (L G Crawley 47, Q McMillan 4 for 56) by 327 runs.

E.L.Dalton

B.Mitchell

Thirty-Third Match vs Hampshire played at County Cricket Ground, Northlands Road, Southampton on 14, 15 and 16 August. South Africans 259 (Q McMillan 53, H G O Owen-Smith 51, H W Taylor 42, E L Dalton 31, O W Herman 5 for 76) and 408 for 8 dec (H G Deane 133*, E L Dalton 67, H B Cameron 45, H W Taylor 34, C L Vincent 33, G S Boyes 3 for 137) drew with Hampshire 279 (G Brown 75, C P Mead 57, Lord Tennyson 32, A Kennedy 26, A J Bell 4 for 77) and 158 for 3 (L Harfield 59*, C P Mead 50*).

Thirty-Fourth Match vs England (Fifth Test Match) played at Kennington Oval on 17, 19 and 20 August.

England

J B Hobbs	c Quinn b McMillan	10	c Mitchell b Vincent		52
H Sutcliffe	c Owen-Smith b Vincent	104	not out		109
* W R Hammond	st Cameron b Vincent	17	not out		101
F E Woolley	hit wicket b Vincent	46			
R E S Wyatt	c Deane b Vincent	6			
M Leyland	b Vincent	16			
A W Carr	c Morkel b McMillan	15			
† L E G Ames	c Mitchell b McMillan	0			
G Geary	not out	12			
A P Freeman	c Cameron b Quinn	15			
E W Clark	b Quinn	7			
Extras	b 9 nb 1	10	b 1 lb 1		2
Total		**258**	**(1 wicket)**		**264**

Fall 1st inns: 1/38 2/69 3/140 4/166 5/194 6/217 7/221 8/222 9/239 10/258
Fall 2nd inns: 1/77

Bowling	1st inns				2nd inns			
Morkel	9	2	20	0	16	6	43	0
Quinn	15.3	4	30	2	24	3	61	0
Vincent	45	10	105	5	15	3	42	1
McMillan	28	7	78	3	10	1	39	0
Owen-Smith	4	0	15	0	8	0	42	0
Mitchell					4	0	17	0
Catterall					3	0	18	0

South Africa

R H Catterall	c Carr b Clark	0
I J Siedle	b Geary	14
B Mitchell	b Geary	2
H W Taylor	c Ames b Clark	121
* H G Deane	c Woolley b Wyatt	93
† H B Cameron	c Freeman b Geary	62
D P B Morkel	c Ames b Clark	81
H G O Owen-Smith	b Woolley	26
Q McMillan	not out	50
C L Vincent	not out	24
Extras	b 4 lb 12 w 2 nb 1	19
Total	**(8 wickets, declared)**	**492**

N A Quinn did not bat.
Fall 1st inns: 1/0 2/9 3/20 4/234 5/246 6/326 7/397 8/439

Bowling	1st inns			
Clark	36	8	79	3
Geary	49	15	121	3
Freeman	49	9	169	0
Woolley	13	4	25	1
Leyland	9	4	25	0
Wyatt	16	4	54	1

Umpires: T Oates and W Bestwick

England drew with South Africa.

Thirty-Fifth Match vs Kent played at St. Lawrence Cricket Ground, Canterbury on 24, 26 and 27 August. South Africans 491 for 7 dec (E L Dalton 157, H G O Owen-Smith 87, Q McMillan 86, I J Siedle 73, A C Wright 2 for 65) and 237 (E L Dalton 116*, A L Ochse 27, W Ashdown 5 for 79) drew with Kent 436 (L E G Ames 145, W Ashdown 87, F E Woolley 50, H T W Hardinge 45, A J Bell 4 for 104, Q McMillan 3 for 114) and 123 for 1 (H T W Hardinge 49*, F E Woolley 49*).

Thirty-Sixth Match vs Sussex played at County Cricket Ground, Brighton on 28, 29 and 30 August. South Africans 330 (E L Dalton 102, H W Taylor 57, H G O Owen-Smith 56, C L Vincent 39*, Q McMillan 34, E H Bowley 5 for 61, M W Tate 4 for 41) and 290 (B Mitchell 140, E L Dalton 44*, D P B Morkel 34, J H Parks 4 for 46, A F Wensley 3 for 73) beat Sussex 239 (James Langridge 62, M W Tate 55, A F Wensley 35, T E R Cook 32, A J Bell 4 for 78, Q McMillan 4 for 54) and 164 (T E R Cook 41*, E H Bowley 37, Q McMillan 5 for 54) by 217 runs.

Thirty-Seventh Match vs ‡ Sir Julien Cahn's XI played at West Bridgford, Nottingham on 31 August and 2 September. South Africans 275 (D P B Morkel 65, E L Dalton 59, H B Cameron 37, R H Catterall 32, L Richmond 6 for 114) drew with Sir Julien Cahn's XI 252 (Capt. F W H Nicholas 55, D H Baulkhead 46, C Flood 40, G F H Heane 34, D P B Morkel 7 for 61).

Thirty-Eighth Match vs C I Thornton's XI played at North Marine Drive, Scarborough on 4, 5 and 6 September. C I Thornton's XI 388 (J B Hobbs 151, E H Hendren 114, R E S Wyatt 31, Q McMillan 6 for 106, C L Vincent 3 for 129) and 130 for 3 dec (J B Hobbs 70*, E H Hendren 45) drew with South Africans 211 (B Mitchell 56, I J Siedle 37, H G O Owen-Smith 34, Q McMillan 28, W E Astill 4 for 84, N E Haig 3 for 32, M W Tate 3 for 55) and 273 for 8 (J A J Christy 61, E L Dalton 53, H G O Owen-Smith 40, Q McMillan 40*, M W Tate 3 for 71, N E Haig 3 for 73).

Thirty-Ninth Match vs An England XI played at Cheriton Road, Folkestone on 7 and 9 September. An England XI 450 (J W Hearne 143, F E Woolley 111, F J Seabrook 40, R W V Robins 32, Lord Tennyson 30, A P Freeman 25, A J Bell 4 for 105) beat South Africans 153 (H G O Owen-Smith 51, B Mitchell 31, P G H Fender 3 for 49, A P Freeman 3 for 56) and 281 (D P B Morkel 59, R H Catterall 51, B Mitchell 35, A J Bell 32*, H B Cameron 29, A P Freeman 6 for 135, F J Durston 3 for 59) by an innings and 16 runs.

Test Match batting averages:

	Inns	NO	Runs	HS	Ave
H W Taylor	4	0	221	121	55.25
D P B Morkel	8	1	321	88	45.85
H G O Owen-Smith	8	2	252	129	42.00
H B Cameron	6	1	195	83	39.00
J A J Christy	3	0	112	70	37.33
B Mitchell	9	1	251	88	31.37
R H Catterall	9	0	256	98	28.44
C L Vincent	6	2	108	60	27.00
H G Deane	8	0	178	93	22.25
N A Quinn	5	1	46	28	11.50
I J Siedle	5	0	35	14	7.00

Also batted during Tests:

A J Bell 13, 2*, 26* and 0*; E L Dalton 6 and 1; J P Duminy 2 and 12; Q McMillan 17 and 50*; E A van der Merwe 19 and 1; A L Ochse 2 and 1.

Test Match bowling averages:

	Overs	Mdns	Runs	Wkts	Ave
A L Ochse	97.1	9	317	10	31.70
D P B Morkel	173	41	458	14	32.71
N A Quinn	164.2	27	441	13	33.92
C L Vincent	154	25	475	13	36.53
A J Bell	97	12	342	8	42.75
J A J Christy	14	3	50	1	50.00
B Mitchell	31.4	4	118	2	59.00
Q McMillan	58	8	182	3	60.66
H G O Owen-Smith	26	0	113	0	-

Also bowled during Tests:

R H Catterall	3	0	18	0	-

Tour batting averages - all matches:

	Inns	NO	Runs	HS	Ave
H W Taylor	48	5	1,755	170	40.81
H G O Owen-Smith	39	3	1,282	129	35.61
D P B Morkel	9	6	1,508	109	35.06
I J Siedle	48	2	1,600	169*	34.78
H G Deane	42	5	1,254	133*	33.89
B Mitchell	53	3	1,637	140	32.74
H B Cameron	38	5	1,077	120	32.63
E L Dalton	32	3	908	157	31.31
R H Catterall	52	1	1,455	124	28.33
Q McMillan	40	10	801	86	26.70

J A J Christy	32	1	781	148	25.19
J P Duminy	5	1	81	31	20.25
C L Vincent	35	8	422	62	15.62
N A Quinn	23	6	208	28	12.23
E A van der Merwe	20	7	154	35*	11.84
A J Bell	29	14	162	32*	10.80
A L Ochse	2	7	147	30	9.80

Tour bowling averages - all matches:

	Overs	Mdns	Runs	Wkts	Ave
H G O Owen-Smith	288.3	47	905	39	23.20
N A Quinn	683.2	161	1,587	65	24.41
D P B Morkel	701.2	174	1,856	76	24.42
Q McMillan	803.4	114	2,455	98	25.05
A J Bell	684.1	116	1,810	70	25.85
C L Vincent	749	153	2,022	73	27.69
A L Ochse	635	92	1,938	62	31.25
R H Catterall	20	3	64	2	32.00
J A J Christy	107	18	311	9	34.55
B Mitchell	277.4	39	934	24	38.91
E L Dalton	18	2	55	0	-

Also bowled during the tour:

H B Cameron	13	2	37	1	37.00
J P Duminy	6.3	0	27	0	-
I J Siedle	2	0	21	0	-

Centuries recorded for South Africans during the tour:

E L Dalton	(3) :	157	vs Kent (Canterbury)
		116*	vs Kent (Canterbury)
		102	vs Sussex (Brighton)
B Mitchell	(3) :	140	vs Sussex (Brighton)
		127	vs Somerset (Taunton)
		101	vs Yorkshire (Sheffield)
H W Taylor	(4) :	125	vs Scotland (Perth)
		121	vs England (The Oval) (Fifth Test Match)
		103	vs Worcestershire (Worcester)
		170	vs Norfolk (Norwich)
H B Cameron	(2) :	120	vs Cambridge University (Fenner's)
		102	vs Worcestershire (Worcester)
R H Catterall	(2) :	124	vs Surrey (The Oval)
		117	vs Wales (Colwyn Bay)
H G O Owen-Smith	(3) :	129	vs England (Headingley) (Third Test Match)
		126	vs Warwickshire (Edgbaston)
		102	vs Durham (Sunderland)
I J Siedle	(2) :	169*	vs Leicestershire (Aylestone Road, Leicester)
		168	vs Yorkshire (Sheffield)
J A J Christy	(1) :	148	vs Nottinghamshire (Trent Bridge)
H G Deane	(1) :	133*	vs Hampshire (Southampton)

Fielding:

	Catches	Stumpings
H B Cameron	48	12
B Mitchell	36	
E A van der Merwe	19	15
D P B Morkel	30	
H G O Owen-Smith	17	
Q McMillan	16	
C L Vincent	16	
I J Siedle	15	
J A J Christy	11	
H G Deane	11	
R H Catterall	10	
A L Ochse	10	
A J Bell	7	
N A Quinn	6	
E L Dalton	5	
J P Duminy	2	
H W Taylor	1	

Mr.H.O.Frielinghaus

The Eighth South African Team in the United Kingdom, 1935

The fifteen tourists included six who had toured in 1929 but the captain was a newcomer, H. F. Wade, who performed with great success. This proved to be the tour in which South Africa won their first Test Match in England (at Lord's) and with it the series.

In total they were to play forty-one matches, some thirty-one of them first-class and they were to return home with seventeen victories and two defeats, by Essex and Gloucestershire.

Few were to begrudge the South Africans their success and it appeared that at last they had come of age as a cricketing nation. Their wicket-keeper/batsman H. B. 'Jock' Cameron (Vice-Captain) scored a total of 1,458 runs (av. 41.65) on the tour with three centuries, including 160 in the last match at Scarborough against H. D. G. Leveson-Gower's XI. Regrettably he contracted enteric fever on the return voyage and died three weeks after reaching home at the early age of 30. He was universally acknowledged at the time as second only to W. A. 'Bert' Oldfield, the Australian, as a wicket-keeper.

(standing) **R.J.Williams K.G.Viljoen E.A.B.Rowan D.S.Tomlinson R.J.Crisp A.B.C.Langton A.D.Nourse X.C.Balaskas**

(sitting) **I.J.Siedle C.L.Vincent H.B.Cameron Mr.S.J.Snooke** (Manager) **H.F.Wade** (Captain) **B.Mitchell A.J.Bell E.L.Dalton**

Touring party (15):

* H F Wade (*Natal*) (Captain)
Age 29. Right-handed opening/middle order batsman.

† H B Cameron (*Transvaal*) (Vice-Captain)
Age 29. Right-handed middle order batsman and wicket-keeper.

B Mitchell (*Transvaal*)
Age 26. Stylish right-handed opening batsman, leg-break bowler and good slip fieldsman.

I J Siedle (*Natal*)
Age 32. Right-handed opening batsman.

E L Dalton (*Natal*)
Age 28. Right-handed middle order batsman and leg break bowler.

A J Bell (*Rhodesia*)
Age 29. Right-arm fast-medium bowler and right-handed tail end batsman.

C L Vincent (*Transvaal*)
Age 33. Right-handed lower order batsman and left-arm slow bowler.

X C Balaskas (*Western Province*)
Age 24. Right-handed middle order batsman, leg-break and googly bowler.

R J Crisp (*Western Province*)
Age 24. Right-arm fast medium bowler and right-handed lower order batsman.

A B C Langton (*Transvaal*)
Age 23. Right-handed lower order batsman and right-arm fast/medium pace bowler.

A D Nourse (*Natal*)
Age 24. Sound right-handed middle order batsman and excellent fieldsman.

E A B Rowan (*Transvaal*)
Age 25. Right-handed opening batsman and right-arm medium pace bowler.

D S Tomlinson (*Rhodesia*)
Age 24. Right-handed lower order batsman, leg-break and googly bowler.

K G Viljoen (*Orange Free State*)
Age 25. Right-handed middle order batsman and excellent outfielder.

† R J Williams (*Natal*)
Age 23. Right-handed lower order batsman and wicket-keeper.

Manager: Mr. S J Snooke

Scorer and Baggage-Master: Mr. W H Ferguson

Summary of all matches:

Played 41   Won 23   Lost 2   Drawn 16

Summary of first-class matches:

Played 31   Won 17   Lost 2   Drawn 12

Summary of Test Matches:

Played 5   Won 1   Lost 0   Drawn 4

First Match vs ‡ Reigate Priory played at Reigate on 22 April. South Africans 196 for 8 (I J Siedle 78, C L Vincent 28, J H Paul 2 for 38) beat Reigate Priory 30 (J K Guy 10, A J Bell 3 for 3, D S Tomlinson 3 for 10) by 166 runs.

Second Match vs ‡ R Earle's XI played at Godalming on 25 April. South Africans 156 for 6 dec (B Mitchell 50, A D Nourse 34, A R Gover 3 for 32) drew with R. Earle's XI.

Third Match vs Worcestershire played at County Cricket Ground, New Road, Worcester on 1, 2, and 3 May. South Africans 351 (E L Dalton 91, A D Nourse 74, H B Cameron 68, E A B Rowan 43, R J Crisp 32, Hon. C J Lyttelton 4 for 83) beat Worcestershire 90 (C F Walters 27, R J Crisp 6 for 34, A J Bell 3 for 6) and 95 (Hon. C J Lyttelton 30, A J Bell 5 for 22) by an innings and 166 runs.

Fourth Match vs Leicestershire played at Aylestone Road, Leicester on 4, 6 and 7 May. South Africans 312 (K G Viljoen 93, E A B Rowan 91, I J Siedle 36, G Geary 4 for 62) and 214 for 3 dec (E A B Rowan 89, H F Wade 74, W E Astill 2 for 47) beat Leicestershire 123 (H A Smith 21*, L G Berry 20, R J Crisp 5 for 40, D Tomlinson 3 for 38) and 233 (N F Armstrong 43, F Prentice 40, C S Dempster 35, A B C Langton 5 for 49, D Tomlinson 4 for 63) by 170 runs.

Fifth Match vs Cambridge University played at Fenner's University Cricket Ground, Cambridge on 8, 9 and 10 May. South Africans 485 (H F Wade 161, E A B Rowan 103, A D Nourse 71, E L Dalton 61, J H Cameron 5 for 133, J W T Grimshaw 4 for 104) beat Cambridge University 253 (M Tindall 68, G W Parker 35, N S Hotchkin 33, J W T Grimshaw 28, A B C Langton 5 for 70, D Tomlinson 3 for 62) and 192 (S C Griffith 54, M. Jahangir Khan 26, D Tomlinson 4 for 64, A B C Langton 3 for 41) by an innings and 40 runs.

Sixth Match vs Surrey played at Kennington Oval, London on 11, 13 and 14 May. South Africans 367 (A D Nourse 147, H B Cameron 58, D Tomlinson 43, A B C Langton 40*, P G H Fender 3 for 99, A R Gover 3 for 110) and 280 for 2 dec (A D Nourse 108*, I J Siedle 104*, H F Wade 33, E A B Rowan 31) beat Surrey 266 (L B Fishlock 62, R J Gregory 53, T H Barling 35, A Sandham 31, E W Brooks 26, A B C Langton 3 for 44) and 191 (T H Barling 68, L B Fishlock 42*, E R T Holmes 28, D Tomlinson 4 for 62) by 190 runs.

Seventh Match vs Oxford University played at University Parks, Oxford on 15, 16 and 17 May. South Africans 372 (A D Nourse 148, D Tomlinson 70*, I J Siedle 52, H B Cameron 39, A R Legard 5 for 114) and 369 for 1 (I J Siedle 164*, E A B Rowan 104*, H F Wade 89) drew with Oxford University 429 (N S Mitchell-Innes 168, A Benn 90, D F Walker 83, J W Seamer 38, A J Bell 4 for 129, C L Vincent 4 for 81).

Eighth Match vs M.C.C. played at Lord's Cricket Ground, London on 18, 20 and 21 May. South Africans 297 (I J Siedle 132*, E L Dalton 37, E A B Rowan 35, K G Viljoen 31, I A R Peebles 4 for 59) drew with M.C.C. 144 (W F Price 61, C F Walters 30, C L Vincent 5 for 47, A B C Langton 4 for 80) and 32 for 3.

Ninth Match vs Hampshire played at County Cricket Ground, Northlands Road, Southampton on 22, 23 and 24 May. South Africans 304 (A D Nourse 75, K G Viljoen 66, E L Dalton 59, R J Crisp 45, W L Creese 2 for 17, E H Cadogan 2 for 55) and 248 (H B Cameron 74, E A B Rowan 63, H F Wade 34, E L Dalton 31, O W Herman 4 for 69) beat Hampshire 197 (W G Lowndes 62, C P Mead 27, R J Crisp 5 for 59, C L Vincent 4 for 78) and 245 (J Arnold 79, C P Mead 31, E H Cadogan 27, X C Balaskas 4 for 45) by 110 runs.

Tenth Match vs Middlesex played at Lord's Cricket Ground, London on 25, 27 and 28 May. South Africans 202 (E L Dalton 56, H B Cameron 40, K G Viljoen 27, H G O Owen-Smith 4 for 55, R W V Robins 3 for 39) and 163 (K G Viljoen 40, H B Cameron 36, E A B Rowan 25, J Smith 5 for 40, H G O Owen-Smith 3 for 54) beat Middlesex 192 (H G O Owen-Smith 41, J W Hearne 39, J H Human 36, G C Newman 33, A B C Langton 6 for 53) and 151 (E H Hendren 39, J Hulme 25*, J H Human 20, A B C Langton 5 for 59, R J Crisp 4 for 45) by 22 runs.

Eleventh Match vs Derbyshire played at Rutland Recreation Ground, Ilkeston on 29, 30 and 31 May. South Africans 443 (K G Viljoen 152, H B Cameron 132, A B C Langton 43*, A D Nourse 31, T B Mitchell 5 for 167) and 200 for 4 dec (I J Siedle 98, E L Dalton 41*, E A B Rowan 33, T B Mitchell 3 for 58) beat Derbyshire 236 (G F Hodgkinson 44, G H Pope 38, D Smith 33, E Carrington 33, T S Worthington 32, C L Vincent 4 for 61, A J Bell 3 for 67) and 198 (T S Worthington 49, A V Pope 39*, D Smith 37, A J Bell 4 for 77, D Tomlinson 4 for 63) by 209 runs.

Twelfth Match vs Lancashire played at Old Trafford, Manchester on 1, 3 and 4 June. South Africans 268 (B Mitchell 59, I J Siedle 44, E L Dalton 41, A D Nourse 37, F S Booth 6 for 79) and 142 for 6 (I J Siedle 32, E L Dalton 30, B Mitchell 29, J L Hopwood 3 for 46) drew with Lancashire 128 (J L Hopwood 73*, C L Vincent 4 for 32, A B C Langton 3 for 60).

Thirteenth Match vs Northamptonshire played at County Cricket Ground, Wantage Road, Northampton on 5, 6 and 7 June. South Africans 297 (I J Siedle 65, X C Balaskas 65, E L Dalton 58, E W Clark 4 for 78) beat Northamptonshire 129 (G B Cuthbertson 63*, E W Clark 26, R J Crisp 6 for 50) and 133 (A H Bakewell 26, A L Cox 24, R J Crisp 4 for 35) by an innings and 35 runs.

Fourteenth Match vs Glamorgan played at Arms Park, Cardiff on 8, 10 and 11 June. South Africans 401 (E A B Rowan 153, H F Wade 139, J Mercer 3 for 82) drew with Glamorgan 142 (D E Davies 75*, D Tomlinson 5 for 72) and 245 for 9 (C C Smart 114*, D W Hughes 70*, J Mercer 34, A B C Langton 6 for 66).

Fifteenth Match vs ‡ Club Cricket Conference played at Lord's Cricket Ground, London on 12 and 13 June. Club Cricket Conference 69 (R T Bryan 27, A J Bell 3 for 20, R J Crisp 3 for 24) drew with South Africans 189 for 4 (E A B Rowan 103*, H B Cameron 49, H T O Smith 2 for 38).

Sixteenth Match vs England (First Test Match) played at Trent Bridge, Nottingham on 15, 17 and 18 June.

England

H Sutcliffe	lbw b Langton	61
R E S Wyatt	c Wade b Crisp	149
* W R Hammond	lbw b Vincent	28
N S Mitchell-Innes	lbw b Mitchell	5
M Leyland	c Mitchell b Crisp	69
† L E G Ames	c Viljoen b Vincent	17
J Iddon	c Rowan b Vincent	29
M S Nichols	not out	13
Extras	b 3 lb 10	13
Total	**(7 wickets, declared)**	**384**

R W V Robins, H Verity and W E Bowes did not bat.
Fall 1st inns: 1/118 2/170 3/179 4/318 5/325 6/355 7/384

Bowling		1st inns		
Crisp	18	4	49	2
Langton	39	3	117	1
Vincent	43	9	101	3
Tomlinson	10	0	38	0
Mitchell	22	1	66	1

South Africa

I J Siedle	b Verity	59	c Verity b Nichols	2
B Mitchell	b Nichols	25	not out	8
E A B Rowan	c Ames b Robins	20	not out	6
A D Nourse	c Hammond b Verity	4		
* H F Wade	c Nichols b Verity	18		
† H B Cameron	b Nichols	52		
K G Viljoen	b Nichols	13		
C L Vincent	lbw b Nichols	0		
D S Tomlinson	b Nichols	9		
A B C Langton	not out	0		
R J Crisp	c Robins b Nichols	4		
Extras	b 4 lb 10 nb 2	16	nb 1	1
Total		**220**	**(1 wicket)**	**17**

Fall 1st inns: 1/42 2/98 3/103 4/120 5/174 6/198 7/198 8/215 9/216 10/220
Fall 2nd inns: 1/3

Bowling		1st inns				2nd inns		
Bowes	22	9	31	0	4	3	2	0
Nichols	23.5	9	35	6	5	1	14	1
Verity	41	18	52	3				
Robins	19	4	65	1				
Iddon	4	2	3	0				
Leyland	7	2	18	0				

Umpires: J Hardstaff and A Dolphin

England drew with South Africa.

Seventeenth Match vs Lancashire played at Aigburth Cricket Ground, Liverpool on 19, 20 and 21 June. Lancashire 92 for 6 dec (J L Hopwood 45, C L Vincent 2 for 23, A B C Langton 2 for 23) drew with South Africans 153 for 2 (B Mitchell 82, K G Viljoen 31*).

Eighteenth Match vs Yorkshire played at Bramall Lane, Sheffield on 22, 24 and 25 June. South Africans 263 (I J Siedle 51, H B Cameron 45, B Mitchell 39, E A B Rowan 31, H Fisher 4 for 52, W E Bowes 3 for 58) and 301 for 7 dec (H B Cameron 103*, E A B Rowan 76, I J Siedle 48, W E Bowes 3 for 70) beat Yorkshire 201 (A Mitchell 61, W Barber 28, X C Balaskas 4 for 55, A J Bell 4 for 65) and 235 (A Mitchell 41, C Turner 35, T F Smailes 27, X C Balaskas 8 for 99) by 128 runs.

Nineteenth Match vs ‡ Staffordshire played at Stoke-on-Trent on 26 and 27 June. South Africans 190 (B Mitchell 73, E L Dalton 32, E N Backhouse 5 for 49) beat Staffordshire 60 (L H Crump 12, A B C Langton 4 for 6) and 88 (C C Clarke 24, A J Bell 4 for 38) by an innings and 42 runs.

Twentieth Match vs England (Second Test Match) played at Lord's Cricket Ground, London on 29 June, 1 and 2 July.

South Africa

B Mitchell	lbw b Nichols	30	not out		164
I J Siedle	b Mitchell	6	c Farrimond b Mitchell		13
E A B Rowan	c Farrimond b Verity	40	lbw b Nichols		44
A D Nourse	b Verity	3	b Verity		2
* H F Wade	c Hammond b Langridge	23	b Verity		0
† H B Cameron	b Nichols	90	c Ames b Mitchell		3
E L Dalton	c & b Langridge	19	c Wyatt b Verity		0
X C Balaskas	b Verity	4			
A B C Langton	c Holmes b Hammond	4	(8) c & b Hammond		44
R J Crisp	not out	4			
A J Bell	b Hammond	0			
Extras	b 1 lb 1 w 1 nb 2	5	b 3 lb 5		8
Total		**228**	**(7 wickets, declared)**		**278**

Fall 1st inns: 1/27 2/59 3/62 4/98 5/158 6/187 7/196 8/224 9/228 10/228
Fall 2nd inns: 1/32 2/136 3/158 4/169 5/169 6/177 7/278

Bowling		1st inns				2nd inns		
Nichols	21	5	47	2	18	4	64	1
Wyatt	4	2	9	0	4	2	2	0
Hammond	5.3	3	8	2	14.4	4	26	1
Mitchell	20	3	71	1	33	5	93	2
Verity	28	10	61	3	38	16	56	3
Langridge	13	3	27	2	10	4	19	0
Holmes					4	2	10	0

England

R E S Wyatt	c Nourse b Dalton	53	b Balaskas		16
H Sutcliffe	lbw b Bell	3	lbw b Langton		38
M Leyland	b Balaskas	18	b Crisp		4
* W R Hammond	b Dalton	27	c Cameron b Langton		27
† L E G Ames	b Balaskas	5	lbw b Langton		8
E R T Holmes	c Bell b Balaskas	10	b Langton		8
Jas. Langridge	c Mitchell b Balaskas	27	lbw b Balaskas		17
W Farrimond	b Balaskas	13	b Crisp		13
M S Nichols	c Cameron b Langton	10	not out		7
H Verity	lbw b Langton	17	c Langton b Balaskas		8
T B Mitchell	not out	5	st Cameron b Balaskas		1
Extras	b 4 lb 5 w 1	10	lb 4		4
Total		**198**			**151**

Fall 1st inns: 1/5 2/46 3/100 4/109 5/116 6/121 7/158 8/161 9/177 10/198
Fall 2nd inns: 1/24 2/45 3/89 4/90 5/102 6/111 7/129 8/141 9/149 10/151

Bowling		1st inns				2nd inns		
Crisp	8	1	32	0	15	4	30	2
Bell	6	0	16	1	12	3	21	0
Langton	21.3	3	58	2	11	3	31	4
Balaskas	32	8	49	5	27	8	54	4
Dalton	13	1	33	2				
Mitchell					2	0	11	0

Umpires: E J Smith and F Walden

South Africa beat England by 154 runs.

Twenty-First Match vs Somerset played at Recreation Ground, Bath on 3, 4 and 5 July. South Africans 173 (R J Williams 37, E A B Rowan 36, A W Wellard 4 for 61) and 284 (E L Dalton 78, A D Nourse 71, I J Siedle 33, A W Wellard 4 for 92) beat Somerset 218 (F S Lee 86, J W Lee 29, A W Wellard 29, A B C Langton 6 for 99) and 188 (L Hawkins 48, E F Longrigg 37, F S Lee 32, B Mitchell 5 for 45, A B C Langton 4 for 56) by 51 runs.

X. L. BALASKAS

K. G. VILJOEN

Twenty-Second Match vs Nottinghamshire played at Trent Bridge, Nottingham on 6, 8 and 9 July. Nottinghamshire 312 (J Hardstaff 154, C B Harris 77, B Lilley 26, A J Bell 4 for 66, X C Balaskas 3 for 89) and 312 for 9 (G V Gunn 100*, G F H Heane 60, J Hardstaff 35, B Mitchell 6 for 118) drew with South Africans 512 (H F Wade 151, B Mitchell 142, E L Dalton 77, A D Nourse 47, H Larwood 3 for 97).

Twenty-Third Match vs ‡ Norfolk played at Lakenham Cricket Ground, Norwich on 10 and 11 July. Norfolk 325 (W J Edrich 111, M R Barton 59, F D Cunliffe 55, R C Rought-Rought 25, R J Crisp 4 for 65) and 59 for 3 (M R Barton 39*) drew with South Africans 367 (K G Viljoen 103, I J Siedle 62, E A B Rowan 57, H B Cameron 42, D C Rought-Rought 3 for 58).

Twenty-Fourth Match vs England (Third Test Match) played at Headingley Cricket Ground, Leeds on 13, 15 and 16 July.

England

R E S Wyatt	c Cameron b Crisp	0	c Vincent b Bell		44
D Smith	c Cameron b Vincent	36	b Vincent		57
W Barber	c Bell b Langton	24	c Dalton b Vincent		14
* W R Hammond	lbw b Vincent	63	not out		87
A Mitchell	c Mitchell b Langton	58	c Viljoen b Vincent		72
J Hardstaff	c & b Vincent	10	b Bell		0
† L E G Ames	b Vincent	0	b Bell		13
M S Nichols	lbw b Langton	4	b Vincent		2
J Sims	b Langton	12			
H Verity	c Cameron b Crisp	1			
W E Bowes	not out	0			
Extras	b 2 lb 6	8	b 1 lb 4		5
Total		**216**	**(7 wickets, declared)**		**294**

Fall 1st inns: 1/0 2/52 3/78 4/147 5/177 6/177 7/188 8/215 9/216 10/216
Fall 2nd inns: 1/128 2/139 3/148 4/277 5/277 6/291 7/294

Bowling	1st inns				2nd inns			
Crisp	13.5	3	26	2	11	1	52	0
Bell	16	3	48	0	14	4	38	3
Langton	26	5	59	4	31	8	95	0
Vincent	32	12	45	4	23.3	3	104	4
Mitchell	6	0	30	0				

South Africa

I J Siedle	run out	33	c Hammond b Bowes		21
B Mitchell	lbw b Hammond	8	b Hammond		58
E A B Rowan	c Hammond b Bowes	62	b Bowes		5
K G Viljoen	c Smith b Wyatt	19	b Sims		9
* H F Wade	c Mitchell b Verity	3	not out		32
† H B Cameron	lbw b Nichols	9	st Ames b Barber		49
E L Dalton	b Bowes	4			
C L Vincent	c Barber b Verity	0			
A B C Langton	b Nichols	0			
R J Crisp	c Hammond b Nichols	18			
A J Bell	not out	3			
Extras	b 8 lb 3 nb 1	12	b 14 lb 4 w 1 nb 1		20
Total		**171**	**(5 wickets)**		**194**

Fall 1st inns: 1/21 2/65 3/120 4/123 5/141 6/149 7/150 8/150 9/150 10/171
Fall 2nd inns: 1/53 2/61 3/91 4/111 5/194

Bowling	1st inns				2nd inns			
Bowes	29	5	62	2	19	9	31	2
Nichols	21.4	4	58	3	22	5	65	0
Hammond	12	6	13	1	7	4	10	1
Sims	9	4	20	0	27	13	48	1
Verity	12	9	5	2	13	11	4	0
Wyatt	4	3	1	1	6	2	12	0
Mitchell					1	0	4	0
Barber					0.2	0	0	1

Umpires: J W Hitch and F Chester

England drew with South Africa.

Twenty-Fifth Match vs ‡ Durham played at Ashbrooke Cricket Ground, Sunderland on 17 and 18 July. South Africans 231 (K G Viljoen 85, R J Williams 39, A D Nourse 34, J Latchford 3 for 35, S Ellis 3 for 49, A L Howell 3 for 62) beat Durham 45 (T K Dobson 12, A B C Langton 4 for 14, C L Vincent 4 for 12) and 141 (D C H Townsend 48, S Ellis 24*, A B C Langton 7 for 38) by an innings and 45 runs.

Twenty-Sixth Match vs ‡ Scotland played at Glasgow on 19 and 20 July. Scotland 91 (H Wass 30, R J Crisp 7 for 20) and 126 for 6 (H Wass 38, P A Gibb 33, E L Dalton 2 for 9, D S Tomlinson 2 for 38) drew with South Africans 199 for 5 (E A B Rowan 71, A D Nourse 47*, B Mitchell 45, H F Wade 27, A B Hipkin 2 for 38, A Smith 2 for 46).

Twenty-Seventh Match vs ‡ Scotland played at Forthill, Broughty Ferry, Dundee on 22 and 23 July. South Africans 252 (H B Cameron 67, C L Vincent 59*, R J Williams 35, R A Hollingdale 5 for 39, A D Baxter 3 for 64) beat Scotland 80 (P A Gibb 20, C L Vincent 6 for 19, D S Tomlinson 4 for 26) and 87 (E I S McPherson 25, A J Bell 3 for 17, D S Tomlinson 3 for 36) by an innings and 85 runs.

A. B. C. LANGTON

A J BELL

Twenty-Eighth Match vs ‡ Northumberland played at County Cricket Ground, Jesmond, Newcastle-upon-Tyne on 24 and 25 July. South Africans 323 (A D Nourse 52, E A B Rowan 50, K G Viljoen 41, H B Cameron 37, R J Crisp 36*, B Mitchell 34, Wilson 5 for 103) and 101 for 2 (B Mitchell 43*, J L Allan 2 for 22) beat Northumerland 198 (H C Lee 50, W G Mackay 46, H Robson 28, J A L Paterson 28, R J Crisp 6 for 41) and 222 (H C Lee 64, H Robson 28, J A L Paterson 27, A B C Langton 4 for 44) by 8 wickets.

Twenty-Ninth Match vs England (Fourth Test Match) played at Old Trafford, Manchester on 27, 29 and 30 July.

England

Batsman	Dismissal 1st	Runs	Dismissal 2nd	Runs
D Smith	c Mitchell b Bell	35	lbw b Crisp	0
A H Bakewell	b Crisp	63	b Langton	54
W Barber	c Langton b Bell	1	b Vincent	44
* W R Hammond	b Crisp	29	(7) not out	63
R E S Wyatt	lbw b Crisp	3	(8) not out	15
M Leyland	c Mitchell b Crisp	53	(4) c Mitchell b Vincent	37
R W V Robins	b Bell	108	(5) c Wade b Vincent	14
H Verity	lbw b Langton	16		
M W Tate	c Viljoen b Vincent	34	(6) b Vincent	0
† G Duckworth	c Nourse b Crisp	2		
W E Bowes	not out	0		
Extras	b 2 lb 9 w 1 nb 1	13	b 1 lb 1 w 1 nb 1	4
Total		357	(6 wickets, declared)	231

Fall 1st inns: 1/71 2/77 3/123 4/132 5/141 6/246 7/302 8/338 9/357 10/357
Fall 2nd inns: 1/1 2/90 3/110 4/172 5/200 6/200

Bowling		1st inns				2nd inns		
Crisp	26.1	1	99	5	11	0	43	1
Bell	26	3	90	3	1	0	3	0
Vincent	28	4	85	1	26	6	78	4
Langton	11	0	59	1	25	2	80	1
Mitchell	1	0	11	0				
Dalton					4	0	23	0

South Africa

Batsman	Dismissal 1st	Runs	Dismissal 2nd	Runs
B Mitchell	c Duckworth b Hammond	10	not out	48
E A B Rowan	b Bowes	13	hit wicket b Robins	49
K G Viljoen	c Verity b Bowes	124	lbw b Robins	10
A D Nourse	lbw b Verity	29	not out	53
* H F Wade	lbw b Bowes	16		
† H B Cameron	c Bowes b Tate	53		
E L Dalton	lbw b Robins	47		
C L Vincent	not out	14		
A B C Langton	c Bakewell b Bowes	0		
R J Crisp	c Verity b Bowes	3		
A J Bell	lbw b Tate	1		
Extras	b 3 lb 5	8	b 6 lb 1 w 2	9
Total		318	(2 wickets)	169

Fall 1st inns: 1/21 2/41 3/91 4/124 5/223 6/288 7/311 8/311 9/315 10/318
Fall 2nd inns: 1/67 2/103

Bowling		1st inns				2nd inns		
Bowes	36	7	100	5	15	1	34	0
Tate	22.3	5	67	2	9	2	20	0
Hammond	17	2	49	1	5	0	15	0
Verity	20	4	48	1	20	10	24	0
Robins	10	0	34	1	19	8	31	2
Wyatt	4	1	12	0				
Leyland					12	4	28	0
Bakewell					3	0	8	0

Umpires: F Chester and F Walden

England drew with South Africa.

Thirtieth Match vs Surrey played at Kennington Oval, London on 31 July and 1 August. South Africans 572 (B Mitchell 195, E A B Rowan 171, E L Dalton 89, H F Wade 37, H B Cameron 28, A R Gover 4 for 151, P G H Fender 3 for 151) beat Surrey 183 (L B Fishlock 82, A B C Langton 4 for 85, C L Vincent 4 for 53) and 184 (E R T Holmes 43, L B Fishlock 30, A B C Langton 4 for 50, B Mitchell 4 for 47) by an innings and 205 runs.

Thirty-First Match vs Glamorgan played at St. Helen's Cricket Ground, Swansea on 3, 5 and 6 August. South Africans 309 (B Mitchell 78, H B Cameron 67, E A B Rowan 39, E L Dalton 30, H F Wade 29, C C Smart 3 for 51, D E Davies 3 for 67, J C Clay 3 for 89) and 168 (A D Nourse 52, E A B Rowan 34, J C Clay 6 for 63) beat Glamorgan 227 (R G Duckfield 63, D Davies 26, D E Davies 25, T L Brierley 25, D S Tomlinson 6 for 105) and 154 (M J L Turnbull 39, A H Dyson 30, B Mitchell 4 for 13) by 96 runs.

Thirty-Second Match vs Warwickshire played at Edgbaston Cricket Ground, Birmingham on 7, 8 and 9 August. South Africans 498 (A D Nourse 160, E A B Rowan 102, H B Cameron 73, R J Crisp 38, K G Viljoen 37, C L Vincent 31, K Wilmot 4 for 115, G E Paine 4 for 119) beat Warwickshire 221 (W A Hill 83, T Collin 53, R J Crisp 5 for 31) and 103 (R E S Wyatt 25*, R J Crisp 5 for 36) by an innings and 174 runs.

Thirty-Third Match vs Gloucestershire played at College Ground, Cheltenham on 10, 12 and 13 August. Gloucestershire 279 (R A Sinfield 102, W L Neale 61, W R Hammond 38, X C Balaskas 4 for 101) and 298 (W R Hammond 123, C J Barnett 46, C L Vincent 6 for 90) beat South Africans 289 (K G Viljoen 122, E L Dalton 48, H B Cameron 39, E A B Rowan 31, R A Sinfield 3 for 41, W R Hammond 3 for 48) and 201 (I J Siedle 44, E A B Rowan 39, K G Viljoen 33, R A Sinfield 5 for 31) by 87 runs.

Thirty-Fourth Match vs Essex played at Southchurch Park, Southend-on-Sea on 14, 15 and 16 August. Essex 302 (J A Cutmore 72, N G Wykes 46, R Smith 43, X C Balaskas 3 for 62) and 172 for 3 (M S Nichols 70, J A Cutmore 59*) beat South Africans 250 (E L Dalton 117, I J Siedle 69, R J Williams 29, J W A Stephenson 7 for 66) and 223 (E L Dalton 65, A D Nourse 46, R J Williams 46, A B C Langton 34, M S Nichols 4 for 35) by 7 wickets.

Thirty-Fifth Match vs England (Fifth Test Match) played at Kennington Oval, London on 17, 19 and 20 August.

South Africa

I J Siedle	c Ames b Robins	35	b Bowes	36
B Mitchell	c Ames b Read	128	b Read	9
E A B Rowan	lbw b Robins	0	b Bowes	7
A D Nourse	c Wyatt b Bowes	32	b Read	34
K G Viljoen	c Clay b Read	60	st Ames b Robins	45
† H B Cameron	c Mitchell b Read	8	st Ames b Robins	42
* H F Wade	c Hammond b Bowes	0	not out	40
E L Dalton	c Robins b Read	117	not out	57
C L Vincent	b Robins	5		
A B C Langton	not out	73		
R J Crisp	c Ames b Bowes	0		
Extras	b 6 lb 10 nb 2	18	b 6 lb 9 nb 2	17
Total		**476**	**(6 wickets)**	**287**

Fall 1st inns: 1/116 2/116 3/164 4/234 5/248 6/254 7/312 8/333 9/470 10/476
Fall 2nd inns: 1/16 2/23 3/67 4/112 5/178 6/193

Bowling	1st inns				2nd inns			
Read	35	13	136	4	10	1	64	2
Nichols	23	3	79	0	5	1	20	0
Bowes	40.4	7	112	3	13	2	40	2
Hammond	9	2	25	0				
Clay	14	1	30	0	18	6	45	0
Robins	22	3	73	3	17	1	61	2
Wyatt	2	0	3	0	3	0	25	0
Leyland					7	2	15	0

England

A H Bakewell	c Cameron b Langton	20
A Mitchell	b Crisp	40
R E S Wyatt	c Cameron b Vincent	37
* W R Hammond	st Cameron b Vincent	65
M Leyland	st Cameron b Mitchell	161
† L E G Ames	not out	148
M S Nichols	c Siedle b Langton	30
R W V Robins	not out	10
Extras	b 5 lb 6 nb 2	23
Total	**(6 wickets, declared)**	**534**

J C Clay, W E Bowes and H D Read did not bat.
Fall 1st inns: 1/34 2/98 3/98 4/249 5/428 6/506

Bowling	1st inns			
Crisp	28	0	113	1
Langton	38	5	124	2
Dalton	16	1	50	0
Vincent	42	5	188	2
Mitchell	8	0	36	1

Umpires: F Chester and J Hardstaff

England drew with South Africa.

Thirty-Sixth Match vs ‡ Sir Julien Cahn's XI played at West Bridgford, Nottingham on 22 and 23 August. Sir Julien Cahn's XI 235 (R C Blunt 85, C R Maxwell 41, C S Dempster 30, R J Crisp 4 for 46) drew with South Africans 91 for 0 (A B C Langton 47*, R J Williams 39*).

Thirty-Seventh Match vs Sussex played at County Cricket Ground, Hove on 24, 26 and 27 August. South Africans 218 (E L Dalton 51, A B C Langton 51, A D Nourse 41, E A B Rowan 30, M W Tate 3 for 38, J H Parks 3 for 44) and 156 (C L Vincent 51, M W Tate 3 for 17) drew with Sussex 150 (John G.Langridge 63, B Mitchell 3 for 23, A B C Langton 3 for 32, R J Crisp 3 for 43).

Thirty-Eighth Match vs Kent played at St. Lawrence Cricket Ground, Canterbury on 28 and 29 August. South Africans 311 (E A B Rowan 77, H F Wade 56, A D Nourse 51, B Mitchell 43, K J Viljoen 36, L J Todd 4 for 70, D V P Wright 4 for 124) beat Kent 124 (F E Woolley 31, C L Vincent 7 for 48) and 49 (W H Ashdown 16, R J Crisp 4 for 21, A B C Langton 4 for 18) by an innings and 138 runs.

Thirty-Ninth Match vs An England XI played at Cheriton Road, Folkestone on 31 August, 1 and 2 September. South Africans 311 for 5 dec (K G Viljoen 119, B Mitchell 90, A D Nourse 29, M Jahangir Khan 1 for 16) beat An England XI 96 (H G O Owen-Smith 41, A B C Langton 5 for 38, C L Vincent 4 for 32) and 106 (D Smith 32, C L Vincent 3 for 8, D S Tomlinson 3 for 31, R J Crisp 3 for 43) by an innings and 109 runs.

Fortieth Match vs Minor Counties played at Skegness on 4, 5 and 6 September. South Africans 394 (K G Viljoen 168, E A B Rowan 115, C L Vincent 32, H R W Butterworth 5 for 105) and 21 for 2 (W Smith 2 for 10) beat Minor Counties 190 (G S Butler 84, H R W Butterworth 30, R J Crisp 5 for 60, A B C Langton 3 for 53) and 224 (W J Edrich 79, R J Crisp 4 for 60, A B C Langton 3 for 44) by 8 wickets.

Forty-First Match vs H D G Leveson-Gower's XI played at North Marine Drive, Scarborough on 7, 9 and 10 September. H D G Leveson-Gower's XI 457 (A Mitchell 103, H Sutcliffe 96, R A Sinfield 75, M Leyland 55, R E S Wyatt 49, R J Crisp 4 for 104) and 45 for 1 drew with South Africans 240 (E A B Rowan 75, K G Viljoen 46, B Mitchell 43, M S Nichols 5 for 55) and 382 for 8 dec (H B Cameron 160, A D Nourse 78, A B C Langton 68, W E Bowes 3 for 81).

Test Match batting averages:

	Inns	NO	Runs	HS	Ave
B Mitchell	10	3	488	164*	69.71
E L Dalton	6	1	244	117	48.80
K G Viljoen	7	0	280	124	40.00
H B Cameron	8	0	306	90	38.25
A B C Langton	6	2	121	73*	30.25
E A B Rowan	10	1	246	62	27.33
A D Nourse	7	1	157	53*	26.16
I J Siedle	8	0	205	59	25.62
H F Wade	8	2	132	40*	22.00
R J Crisp	5	1	29	18	7.25
C L Vincent	4	1	19	14*	6.33

Also batted during Tests:

X C Balaskas 4, A J Bell 0, 3* and 1, D S Tomlinson 9.

Test Match bowling averages:

	Overs	Mdns	Runs	Wkts	Ave
X C Balaskas	59	16	103	9	11.44
A J Bell	75	13	216	7	30.85
C L Vincent	194.3	39	601	18	33.38
R J Crisp	131	14	444	13	34.15
A B C Langton	202.3	29	623	15	41.53
E L Dalton	33	2	106	2	53.00
B Mitchell	39	1	154	2	77.00

Also bowled during Tests:

	Overs	Mdns	Runs	Wkts	Ave
D S Tomlinson	10	0	38	0	-

Tour batting averages - all matches:

	Inns	NO	Runs	HS	Ave
K G Viljoen	35	4	1,454	168	46.90
B Mitchell	35	3	1,451	195	45.34
E A B Rowan	46	2	1,948	171	44.27
H B Cameron	38	3	1,458	160	41.65
A D Nourse	46	5	1,681	160*	41.00
I J Siedle	37	3	1,346	164*	39.58
E L Dalton	41	2	1,446	117	37.07
H F Wade	39	3	1,042	161	28.94
A B C Langton	32	7	537	73*	21.48
D S Tomlinson	24	10	282	70*	20.14
R J Williams	11	0	181	46	16.45
R J Crisp	30	6	322	45	13.41
C L Vincent	31	4	362	51	13.40
X C Balaskas	16	2	146	65	10.42
A J Bell	16	8	58	24	7.25

Tour bowling averages - all matches:

	Overs	Mdns	Runs	Wkts	Ave
B Mitchell	206	14	666	35	19.02
R J Crisp	690.5	105	2,096	107	19.58
X C Balaskas	289.5	34	873	42	20.78
C L Vincent	743	187	1,923	92	20.90
A B C Langton	875.5	158	2,434	115	21.16
A J Bell	413.1	77	1,146	52	22.03
D S Tomlinson	361	34	1,380	52	26.53
E L Dalton	122	18	384	7	54.85
E G Viljoen	14	4	35	0	-

Also bowled during the tour:

	Overs	Mdns	Runs	Wkts	Ave
A D Nourse	1	0	3	0	-

Centuries recorded for South Africans during the tour:

E A B Rowan   (6) :   171   vs Surrey (The Oval)
                                    153   vs Glamorgan (Cardiff)
                                    115   vs Minor Counties (Skegness)
                                    104* vs Oxford University (The Parks)
                                    103   vs Cambridge University (Fenner's)
                                    102   vs Warwickshire (Edgbaston)

K G Viljoen   (5) :   168   vs Minor Counties (Skegness)
                                    152   vs Derbyshire (Ilkeston)
                                    124   vs England (Old Trafford) (Fourth Test Match)
                                    122   vs Gloucestershire (Cheltenham)
                                    119* vs An England XI (Folkestone)

B Mitchell   (4) :   195   vs Surrey (The Oval)
                                    164* vs England (Lord's) (Second Test Match)
                                    142   vs Nottinghamshire Trent Bridge)
                                    128   vs England (The Oval) (Fifth Test Match)

A D Nourse   (4) :   160* vs Warwickshire (Edgbaston)
                                    148   vs Oxford University (The Parks)
                                    147   vs Surrey (The Oval)
                                    108* vs Surrey (The Oval)

H B Cameron   (3) :   160   vs H D G Leveson-Gower's XI
                                                                        (Scarborough)
                                    132   vs Derbyshire (Ilkeston)
                                    103* vs Yorkshire (Sheffield)

I J Siedle   (3) :   164* vs Oxford University (The Parks)
                                    132* vs M.C.C. (Lord's)
                                    104* vs Surrey (The Oval)

H F Wade   (3) :   161   vs Cambridge University (Fenner's)
                                    151   vs Nottinghamshire (Trent Bridge)
                                    139   vs Glamorgan (Cardiff)

E L Dalton   (2) :   117   vs Essex (Southend-on-Sea)
                                    117   vs England (The Oval) (Fifth Test Match)

Fielding:

	Catches	Stumpings
H B Cameron	35	20
B Mitchell	33	
A D Nourse	26	
A B C Langton	24	
R J Williams	17	7
C L Vincent	22	
H F Wade	22	
E L Dalton	21	
R J Crisp	19	
K G Viljoen	18	
A J Bell	14	
E A B Rowan	11	
D S Tomlinson	11	
I J Siedle	9	
X C Balaskas	8	

The Ninth South African Team in the United Kingdom, 1947

The ninth South African team set sail for England on 3rd April and arrived at Southampton on 18th April. It was twelve years since the South Africans had visited England during which the Second World War had prevented international cricket for some eight years. It was not surprising therefore that the touring party should have a high average age and rely on players who had been in their prime around 1939. The party was made up of seventeen players but still did not include Eric Rowan nor R. R. Phillips who had finished second in the Currie Cup batting averages.

They were captained by Alan Melville who England had first met on their tour to South Africa in 1938-39. Of the party three members, B. Mitchell, A. D. Nourse and K. G. Viljoen, had toured in 1935, but they lacked a truly fast bowler.

After so many years away from Test Cricket it was not surprising that they failed to gain a win and in fact lost three of the five Tests. However, Bruce Mitchell not only became the second South African to hit two hundreds in a Test (at The Oval) but also equalled Alan Melville's record score of 189 by a South African against England.

They won fourteen of their twenty-eight first-class games and lost only five (three of which were Tests). Of some significance was the fact that they were plagued by the Middlesex 'twins'. D. C. S. Compton scored six centuries against the tourists out of his record total of eighteen during the summer while W. J. Edrich scored three of his twelve centuries against South Africa. Few tourists have ever had to face such an onslaught.

(standing) **T.A.Harris D.M.Ovenstone D.W.Begbie V.I.Smith L.Tuckett J.B.Plimsoll L.W.Payn J.D.Lindsay G.M.Fullerton**

(sitting) **O.C.Dawson D.V.Dyer B.Mitchell A.Melville** (Captain)
Mr.A.S.Frames (Manager) **A.D.Nourse K.G.Viljoen N.B.F.Mann A.M.B.Rowan**

Touring party (17):

* A Melville (*Oxford University, Sussex and Transvaal*) (Captain)
Age 37. Right-handed batsman.

A D Nourse (*Natal*) (Vice-Captain)
Age 36. Sound right-handed middle order batsman and excellent fieldsman.

B Mitchell (*Transvaal*)
Age 38. Right-handed opening batsman, effective leg-break bowler and specialist slip fieldsman.

K G Viljoen (*Transvaal*)
Age 37. Right-handed middle order batsman and fine outfielder.

T A Harris (*Transvaal*)
Age 30. Right-handed batsman.

O C Dawson (*Natal*)
Age 27. Right-handed batsman and right-arm medium pace bowler.

† G M Fullerton (*Transvaal*)
Age 24. Right-handed batsman and wicket-keeper.

D W Begbie (*Transvaal*)
Age 32. Right-hand batsman and leg-break bowler.

D V Dyer (*Natal*)
Age 33. Right-handed opening batsman.

A M B Rowan (*Transvaal*)
Age 26. Right-handed batsman and right-arm off-break bowler.

N B F Mann (*Eastern Province*)
Age 26. Left-arm medium pace bowler.

† D M Ovenstone (*Western Province*)
Age 25. Right-handed batsman and wicket-keeper.

L W Payn (*Natal*)
Age 32. Left-arm leg-break bowler.

L Tuckett (*Orange Free State*)
Age 28. Right-arm fast-medium bowler.

J B Plimsoll (*Western Province*)
Age 29. Left-arm medium pace bowler.

† J D Lindsay (*North Eastern Transvaal*)
Age 37. Wicket-keeper and right-handed batsman.

V I Smith (*Natal*)
Age 22. Right-handed batsman and right-arm leg-break bowler.

Manager: Mr. A S Frames

Scorer/Baggage-Master: Mr. W H Ferguson

Summary of all matches:

Played 34   Won 16   Lost 6   Drawn 12

Summary of first-class matches:

Played 28   Won 14   Lost 5   Drawn 9

Summary of Test Matches:

Played 5   Won 0   Lost 3   Drawn 2

First Match vs Worcestershire played at County Cricket Ground, New Road, Worcester on 30 April, 1 and 2 May. Worcestershire 202 (R E Bird 79, R O Jenkins 27, A F T White 25, H Yarnold 25, A M B Rowan 5 for 59, N B F Mann 3 for 40) and 111 (E Cooper 22, A M B Rowan 5 for 34, N B F Mann 5 for 36) beat South Africans 167 (A M B Rowan 28, D V Dyer 26, K G Viljoen 26, R T D Perks 5 for 66, P F Jackson 4 for 63) and 107 (R Howorth 6 for 38, P F Jackson 4 for 53) by 39 runs.

Second Match vs Leicestershire played at County Cricket Ground, Grace Road, Leicester on 3 and 5 May. South Africans 216 (A Melville 104, D W Begbie 33, B Mitchell 25, G Lester 6 for 42, J E Walsh 3 for 71) and 35 for 0 (B Mitchell 29*) beat Leicestershire 128 (F T Prentice 28, G Watson 27, L Tuckett 5 for 27) and 121 (L G Berry 45*, L Tuckett 4 for 32) by 10 wickets.

Third Match vs Cambridge University played at Fenner's University Cricket Ground, Cambridge on 7, 8 and 9 May. South Africans 370 (K G Viljoen 128, D W Begbie 80, A Melville 35, A D Nourse 32, T E Bailey 5 for 70) beat Cambridge University 116 (J Pepper 37, N M Mischler 27, J B Plimsoll 4 for 35) and 101 (G L Willatt 27, V I Smith 7 for 40) by an innings and 153 runs.

Fourth Match vs Surrey played at Kennington Oval, London on 10, 12 and 13. South Africans 83 (E A Watts 5 for 31) and 311 (A Melville 122, O C Dawson 75, D V Dyer 45, A V Bedser 6 for 65) beat Surrey 112 (L B Fishlock 41, L Tuckett 7 for 63) and 167 (E A Watts 33, R J Gregory 29, A J McIntyre 29, N B F Mann 4 for 17) by 115 runs.

Fifth Match vs Hampshire played at County Cricket Ground, Northlands Road, Southampton on 14, 15 and 16 May. Hampshire 300 for 6 dec (J Arnold 138, G Hill 58*, N H Rogers 45, D W Begbie 2 for 33) and 79 for 7 (J Bailey 29*, A M B Rowan 4 for 31) drew with South Africans 315 (G M Fullerton 82, T A Harris 71, A D Nourse 54, L W Payn 32, O W Herman 4 for 46).

Sixth Match vs M.C.C. played at Lord's Cricket Ground, London on 17, 19 and 20 May. M.C.C. 230 (T C Dodds 80, D Brookes 54, H A Pawson 34, L Tuckett 6 for 64, A M B Rowan 3 for 61) and 253 for 4 dec (D C S Compton 97, D Brookes 77, M P Donnelly 31*, T C Dodds 25, A M B Rowan 2 for 72) beat South Africans 127 (A D Nourse 29, A W H Mallett 5 for 55, J W Martin 4 for 55) and 198 (B Mitchell 103*, A Melville 40, D V Dyer 30, C Cook 6 for 44, A V Bedser 3 for 46) by 158 runs.

Seventh Match vs Oxford University played at University Parks, Oxford on 21, 22 and 23 May. Oxford University 303 for 9 dec (W G Keighley 105, M P Donnelly 45, N C F Bloy 45*, B H Travers 30, J B Plimsoll 3 for 73, A M B

Rowan 3 for 74) and 19 for 2 drew with South Africans 510 for 6 dec (K G Viljoen 110*, A D Nourse 101, A Melville 84, B Mitchell 72, T A Harris 68, D W Begbie 25, H B Robinson 3 for 151).

Eighth Match vs Glamorgan played at Arms Park, Cardiff on 24, 26 and 27 May. South Africans 479 for 8 dec (B Mitchell 113, A M B Rowan 100*, N B F Mann 97, D W Begbie 39, A Melville 29, D V Dyer 28, A Porter 2 for 68, W Wooller 2 for 92) beat Glamorgan 128 (W Wooller 30*, L Tuckett 5 for 48) and 220 (M Robinson 83, A Watkins 37, W Wooller 37, A M B Rowan 4 for 59, N B F Mann 3 for 50) by an innings and 131 runs.

Ninth Match vs Combined Services played at United Services Officers Sports Ground, Portsmouth on 28, 29 and 30 May. South Africans 259 (B Mitchell 108, O C Dawson 57, D M Ovenstone 42, D W Begbie 29, Capt. J H C Deighton 4 for 88) and 86 for 3 (O/Cadet J N Bartlett 2 for 33) beat Combined Services 182 (Sub/Lt. J G Dewes 68, Maj. W M F White 35, J B Plimsoll 6 for 53) and 162 (S/Ldr. W F Roberts 52, S/Ldr. A C Shirreff 35, N B F Mann 5 for 48) by 7 wickets.

Tenth Match vs Middlesex played at Lord's Cricket Ground, London on 31 May, 2 and 3 June. South Africans 424 (B Mitchell 109, K G Viljoen 104, A D Nourse 92, A M B Rowan 36, A Melville 25, L Tuckett 25*, J M Sims 4 for 148, J A Young 4 for 52) and 217 (T A Harris 76, A Melville 42, N B F Mann 30, J M Sims 6 for 89) drew with Middlesex 316 for 8 dec (D C S Compton 154, W J Edrich 67, L H Compton 32, A M B Rowan 4 for 130) and 226 for 6 (W J Edrich 133*, D C S Compton 34, N B F Mann 2 for 38).

Eleventh Match vs Northamptonshire played at County Cricket Ground, Wantage Road, Northampton on 4 and 5 June. South Africans 319 (T A Harris 67, O C Dawson 62, K G Viljoen 47, D W Begbie 29, L A Smith 4 for 55) beat Northamptonshire 103 (D Brookes 27, D J W Bridge 25*, J B Plimsoll 6 for 40, O C Dawson 4 for 37) and 184 (L A Smith 55, A W Childs-Clarke 32*, J B Plimsoll 5 for 90, O C Dawson 4 for 71) by an innings and 32 runs.

D.W.Begbie

J.B.Plimsoll

Twelfth Match vs England (First Test Match) played at Trent Bridge, Nottingham on 7, 9, 10 and 11 June.

South Africa

* A Melville	b Martin	189	not out		104
B Mitchell	b Bedser	14	c Evans b Bedser		4
K G Viljoen	lbw b Edrich	10	not out		51
A D Nourse	b Hollies	149			
O C Dawson	st Evans b Hollies	48			
T A Harris	c Hutton b Hollies	60			
A M B Rowan	not out	34			
L Tuckett	lbw b Hollies	0			
N B F Mann	b Bedser	8			
† J D Lindsay	b Bedser	0			
V I Smith	c Yardley b Hollies	1			
Extras	b 7 lb 12 w 1	20	b 1 w 5 nb 1		7
Total		**533**	**(1 wicket)**		**166**

Fall 1st inns: 1/23 2/44 3/363 4/384 5/450 6/505 7/505 8/528 9/530 10/533
Fall 2nd inns: 1/21

Bowling		1st inns				2nd inns	
Martin	36	4	111	1	9	2	18	0
Bedser	57.1	14	106	3	14	3	31	1
Edrich	20	8	56	1	4	0	8	0
Hollies	55.2	16	123	5	9	1	33	0
Cook	21	4	87	0	9	0	40	0
Yardley	5	0	24	0				
Compton	2	1	6	0	4	0	14	0
Hutton					2	0	15	0

England

L Hutton	lbw b Rowan	17	b Tuckett		9
C Washbrook	lbw b Tuckett	25	c Lindsay b Rowan		59
W J Edrich	b Smith	57	b Smith		50
D C S Compton	c Mitchell b Tuckett	65	c Mitchell b Mann		163
H E Dollery	b Dawson	9	c & b Dawson		17
* N W D Yardley	lbw b Tuckett	22	c Tuckett b Dawson		99
† T G Evans	st Lindsay b Smith	2	c & b Smith		74
A V Bedser	c Melville b Smith	7	c Harris b Smith		2
C Cook	b Tuckett	0	c Dawson b Smith		4
J W Martin	c Lindsay b Tuckett	0	(11) b Rowan		26
W E Hollies	not out	0	(10) not out		18
Extras	b 1 lb 2 w 1	4	b 15 lb 13 w 2		30
Total		**208**			**551**

Fall 1st inns: 1/40 2/48 3/154 4/165 5/198 6/198 7/207 8/208 9/208 10/208
Fall 2nd inns: 1/20 2/116 3/133 4/170 5/407 6/434 7/472 8/499 9/500 10/551

Bowling		1st inns				2nd inns	
Tuckett	37	9	68	5	47	12	127	1
Dawson	13	2	35	1	25	7	57	2
Rowan	16	6	45	1	43.2	8	100	2
Mann	20	13	10	0	60	22	94	1
Smith	27.1	10	46	3	51	15	143	4

Umpires: A R Coleman and J Smart

England drew with South Africa.

Thirteenth Match vs Somerset played at County Cricket Ground, Taunton on 14, 16 and 17 June. South Africans 368 for 8 dec (B Mitchell 72, A D Nourse 65, D W Begbie 62, K G Viljoen 54*, D V Dyer 39, O C Dawson 33, A W Wellard 2 for 74, M F Tremlett 2 for 92) beat Somerset 170 (M Coope 64, W T Luckes 47*, J B Plimsoll 4 for 70, O C Dawson 4 for 41) and 155 (J Lawrence 49, J B Plimsoll 4 for 41, O C Dawson 3 for 28) by an innings and 43 runs.

Fourteenth Match vs England (Second Test Match) played at Lord's Cricket Ground, London on 21, 23, 24 and 25 June.

England

L Hutton	b Rowan	18	not out	13
C Washbrook	c Tuckett b Dawson	65	not out	13
W J Edrich	b Mann	189		
D C S Compton	c Rowan b Tuckett	208		
C J Barnett	b Tuckett	33		
* N W D Yardley	c Rowan b Tuckett	5		
† T G Evans	b Tuckett	16		
G H Pope	not out	8		
A V Bedser	b Tuckett	0		
Extras	b 2 lb 10	12		
Total	**(8 wickets, declared)**	**554**	**(no wicket)**	**26**

D V P Wright and W E Hollies did not bat.
Fall 1st inns: 1/75 2/96 3/466 4/515 5/526 6/541 7/554 8/554

Bowling		1st inns				2nd inns		
Tuckett	47	8	115	5	3	0	4	0
Dawson	33	11	81	1	6	2	6	0
Mann	53	16	99	1	3.1	1	16	0
Rowan	65	11	174	1				
Smith	17	2	73	0				

South Africa

* A Melville	c Bedser b Hollies	117	b Edrich	8
B Mitchell	st Evans b Compton	46	c Edrich b Wright	80
K G Viljoen	b Wright	1	b Edrich	6
A D Nourse	lbw b Wright	61	b Edrich	58
O C Dawson	c Barnett b Hollies	36	c Edrich b Compton	33
T A Harris	st Evans b Compton	30	c Yardley b Compton	3
A M B Rowan	b Wright	8	not out	38
L Tuckett	b Wright	5	lbw b Wright	9
N B F Mann	b Wright	4	b Wright	5
† J D Lindsay	not out	7	c Yardley b Wright	5
V I Smith	c Edrich b Pope	11	c Edrich b Wright	0
Extras	lb 1	1	b 3 lb 4	7
Total		**327**		**252**

Fall 1st inns: 1/95 2/104 3/222 4/230 5/290 6/300 7/302 8/308 9/309 10/327
Fall 2nd inns: 1/16 2/28 3/120 4/192 5/192 6/201 7/224 8/236 9/252 10/252

Bowling		1st inns				2nd inns		
Edrich	9	1	22	0	13	5	31	3
Bedser	26	1	76	0	14	6	20	0
Pope	19.2	5	49	1	17	7	36	0
Wright	39	10	95	5	32.2	6	80	5
Hollies	28	10	52	2	20	7	32	0
Compton	21	11	32	2	32	10	46	2

Umpires: H G Baldwin and D Davies

England beat South Africa by 10 wickets.

Fifteenth Match vs Nottinghamshire played at Trent Bridge, Nottingham on 28 and 30 June and 1 July. Nottinghamshire 324 (W W Keeton 90, F W Stocks 73, R T Simpson 46, J B Plimsoll 4 for 60) and 164 for 6 (C B Harris 51, R T Simpson 51, L W Payn 3 for 41) drew with South Africans 365 (B Mitchell 97, D V Dyer 62, G M Fullerton 57, N B F Mann 41, D W Begbie 34, T A Harris 32, A Jepson 5 for 115).

Sixteenth Match vs ‡ Northumberland played at County Cricket Ground, Jesmond, Newcastle-Upon-Tyne on 2 and 3 July. South Africans 347 (K G Viljoen 130, A M B Rowan 49, D W Begbie 38, D V Dyer 37, O C Dawson 33, A D Nourse 28, L F Townsend 3 for 75, H Elsdon 3 for 81) beat Northumberland 182 (J H G Deighton 73*, J B Plimsoll 5 for 62, L W Payn 3 for 27) and 133 (J H G Deighton 49*, J B Plimsoll 6 for 49) by an innings and 32 runs.

L.W.Payn

O.C.Dawson

Seventeenth Match vs England (Third Test Match) played at Old Trafford, Manchester on 5, 7, 8 and 9 July.

South Africa

* A Melville	c Hutton b Gladwin	17	b Edrich	59
D V Dyer	b Edrich	62	b Gladwin	1
B Mitchell	run out	80	c Hutton b Compton	6
A D Nourse	c Yardley b Cranston	23	b Edrich	115
K G Viljoen	c Compton b Edrich	93	c Hutton b Wright	32
O C Dawson	b Cranston	1	b Edrich	9
A M B Rowan	lbw b Hollies	13	c Evans b Wright	0
L Tuckett	b Edrich	13	lbw b Edrich	17
N B F Mann	c Hollies b Gladwin	8	c Barnett b Wright	9
† J D Lindsay	not out	9	b Hollies	0
J B Plimsoll	c Evans b Edrich	8	not out	8
Extras	b 3 lb 9	12	b 5 lb 5 nb 1	11
Total		**339**		**267**

Fall 1st inns: 1/32 2/125 3/163 4/214 5/215 6/260 7/287 8/298 9/327 10/339
Fall 2nd inns: 1/12 2/42 3/96 4/217 5/225 6/228 7/232 8/244 9/244 10/267

Bowling		1st inns				2nd inns		
Edrich	35.1	9	95	4	22.4	4	77	4
Gladwin	50	24	58	2	16	6	28	1
Cranston	34	12	64	2				
Barnett	8	3	11	0	5	1	12	0
Wright	9	1	30	0	10	2	32	3
Hollies	23	9	42	1	14	4	49	1
Compton	7	1	27	0	17	2	58	1

England

L Hutton	c Lindsay b Plimsoll	12	c Dawson b Mann	24
C Washbrook	c Nourse b Tuckett	29	c Lindsay b Dawson	40
W J Edrich	b Tuckett	191	not out	22
D C S Compton	c Tuckett b Dawson	115	hit wicket b Mann	6
C J Barnett	c sub (Harris) b Mann	5	not out	19
* N W D Yardley	c Melville b Plimsoll	41		
K Cranston	c Dawson b Rowan	23		
† T G Evans	b Tuckett	27		
C Gladwin	b Tuckett	16		
D V P Wright	not out	4		
W E Hollies	c Nourse b Plimsoll	5		
Extras	b 2 lb 7 nb 1	10	b 9 lb 8 nb 2	19
Total		**478**	**(3 wickets)**	**130**

Fall 1st inns: 1/40 2/48 3/276 4/289 5/363 6/415 7/439 8/466 9/471 10/478
Fall 2nd inns: 1/63 2/80 3/103

Bowling		1st inns				2nd inns		
Tuckett	50	9	148	4	5	0	26	0
Plimsoll	35.3	9	128	3	4	0	15	0
Rowan	17	1	63	1	4	0	13	0
Mann	35	12	85	1	14	8	19	2
Dawson	14	2	44	1	9.5	2	38	1

Umpires: F Chester and A R Coleman

England beat South Africa by 7 wickets.

Eighteenth Match vs ‡ Gentlemen of Ireland played at Dublin on 10 and 11 July. Gentlemen of Ireland 102 (E A Ingham 22, A M B Rowan 9 for 39) drew with South Africans 167 for 7 (A Melville 58*, A M B Rowan 39, T A Harris 38, E A Ingham 4 for 42).

Nineteenth Match vs ‡ Gentlemen of Ireland played at Belfast on 12 July. South Africans 218 (V I Smith 64*, D V Dyer 34, B Mitchell 33, D W Begbie 31, G M Fullerton 27, J C Boucher 4 for 80) beat Gentlemen of Ireland 32 (A M B Rowan 7 for 10, L Tuckett 3 for 17) and 61 (E A Ingham 14, A M B Rowan 5 for 14, L W Payn 3 for 17) by an innings and 125 runs.

Twentieth Match vs ‡ Gentlemen of Ireland played at Belfast on 14 July. Ireland 202 (Rev. R J Barnes 57, E D R Shearer 43, J C Boucher 24, L Tuckett 4 for 23) beat South Africans 114 (B Mitchell 24, J C Boucher 7 for 37) by 6 wickets.

K.G.Viljoen

D.V.Dyer

Twenty-First Match vs Derbyshire played at County Cricket Ground, Derby on 16, 17 and 18 July. South Africans 172 (N B F Mann 45, O C Dawson 30, G M Fullerton 28, G H Pope 5 for 60, W H Copson 3 for 38) and 85 for 7 (G M Fullerton 23*, G H Pope 5 for 36) beat Derbyshire 224 (A C Revill 60, C S Elliott 56, R M Watson 25*, V I Smith 7 for 65) and 32 (C S Elliott 18, V I Smith 6 for 1, J B Plimsoll 3 for 13) by 3 wickets.

Twenty-Second Match vs Yorkshire played at Bramall Lane, Sheffield on 19, 21 and 22 July. South Africans 279 (G M Fullerton 50, B Mitchell 47, K G Viljoen 39, O C Dawson 38, A M B Rowan 38, A Melville 28, W E Bowes 4 for 36, E P Robinson 3 for 86) and 147 for 3 (G M Fullerton 42, D V Dyer 41*, A Melville 36, J H Wardle 3 for 59) drew with Yorkshire 308 (L Hutton 137, W G Keighley 51, G A Smithson 35, V I Smith 5 for 105, A M B Rowan 4 for 39).

Twenty-Third Match vs ‡ Scotland played at Paisley on 23 and 24 July. South Africans 278 for 4 dec (G M Fullerton 129, D W Begbie 74, K G Viljoen 32, R S Hodge 3 for 69) drew with Scotland 177 (J Aitchison 106*, H F Sheppard 39, L W Payn 3 for 44, V I Smith 3 for 72) and 104 for 5 (W Nichol 41*, W A Edwards 29*, L Tuckett 4 for 15).

Twenty-Fourth Match vs England (Fourth Test Match) played at Headingley Cricket Ground, Leeds on 26, 28 and 29 July.

South Africa

* A Melville	b Edrich	0	c Compton b Young		30
D V Dyer	c Evans b Wright	9	c Yardley b Edrich		2
B Mitchell	b Butler	53	b Young		5
A D Nourse	b Butler	51	lbw b Butler		57
K G Viljoen	b Wright	5	lbw b Butler		29
O C Dawson	c Young b Butler	5	b Butler		17
† G M Fullerton	c Cranston b Edrich	13	lbw b Cranston		13
A M B Rowan	c Yardley b Edrich	0	not out		21
L Tuckett	c Edrich b Cranston	29	c Evans b Cranston		0
N B F Mann	c Evans b Butler	3	b Cranston		0
J B Plimsoll	not out	0	b Cranston		0
Extras	lb 5 nb 2	7	b 4 lb 6		10
Total		**175**			**184**

Fall 1st inns: 1/1 2/23 3/113 4/121 5/125 6/130 7/131 8/158 9/175 10/175
Fall 2nd inns: 1/6 2/16 3/59 4/130 5/139 6/156 7/184 8/184 9/184 10/184

Bowling	1st inns				2nd inns			
Butler	28	15	34	4	24	9	32	3
Edrich	17	4	46	3	14	2	35	1
Young	17	5	31	0	19	7	54	2
Wright	20	9	24	2	14	7	31	0
Cranston	11.1	3	24	1	7	3	12	4
Compton	4	0	9	0	2	0	10	0

England

L Hutton	run out	100	not out	32
C Washbrook	b Mann	75	not out	15
W J Edrich	c Melville b Mann	43		
D C S Compton	c Mitchell b Mann	30		
C J Barnett	c Tuckett b Rowan	6		
* N W D Yardley	c Nourse b Smith	36		
K Cranston	c Melville b Mann	3		
† T G Evans	not out	6		
J A Young	not out	0		
Extras	b 8 lb 8 nb 2	18		
Total	**(7 wickets, declared)**	**317**	**(no wicket)**	**47**

D V P Wright and H J Butler did not bat.
Fall 1st inns: 1/141 2/218 3/241 4/253 5/289 6/306 7/316

Bowling	1st inns				2nd inns			
Tuckett	18	4	48	0	6	1	12	0
Dawson	4	0	12	0	4	1	13	0
Mann	50	20	68	4	3.4	0	17	0
Smith	36	9	82	1				
Mitchell	46	12	89	1	2	1	5	0

Umpires: F Chester and J J Hills

England beat South Africa by 10 wickets.

Twenty-Fifth Match vs Glamorgan played at St. Helen's Cricket Ground, Swansea on 2, 4 and 5 August. South Africans 260 (T A Harris 100, O C Dawson 40, A Melville 39, K G Viljoen 31, J C Clay 5 for 76) and 188 (K G Viljoen 38, L W Payn 28, J C Clay 6 for 86) beat Glamorgan 197 (A Porter 39, A H Dyson 38, A M B Rowan 6 for 53) and 211 (A Watkins 75, H G Davies 37*, M Robinson 32, G Lavis 25, O C Dawson 5 for 50, A M B Rowan 4 for 92) by 40 runs.

Twenty-Sixth Match vs Warwickshire played at Edgbaston Cricket Ground, Birmingham on 6, 7 and 8 August. South Africans 520 for 7 dec (A D Nourse 205*, K G Viljoen 113, B Mitchell 51, G M Fullerton 29, A M B Rowan 27*, N B F Mann 27, T A Harris 26, C W Grove 2 for 86) beat Warwickshire 330 (P Cramner 101, W A Hill 73, H E Dollery 38, V H D Cannings 27*, N B F Mann 5 for 109, V I Smith 4 for 85) and 76 (P Cramner 38, L Tuckett 5 for 30, O C Dawson 5 for 42) by an innings and 114 runs.

T.A.Harris

J.D.Lindsay

Twenty-Seventh Match vs Lancashire played at Old Trafford, Manchester on 9, 11 and 12 August. Lancashire 218 (C Washbrook 128, K Cranston 27, L Tuckett 4 for 66, O C Dawson 4 for 88) and 233 for 8 dec (C Washbrook 57, G A Edrich 43, A Wharton 32, J T Ikin 31, O C Dawson 3 for 70) drew with South Africans 338 (B Mitchell 131, A Melville 52, G M Fullerton 43, L Tuckett 37*, K Cranston 5 for 69, J Bowes 4 for 103) and 30 for 0.

Twenty-Eighth Match vs Gloucestershire played at College Ground, Cheltenham on 13, 14 and 15 August. South Africans 225 (D V Dyer 74, T A Harris 36, G M Fullerton 35*, T W Goddard 3 for 73, L M Cranfield 3 for 42) and 248 (G M Fullerton 70, N B F Mann 63, A M B Rowan 32, C Cook 4 for 80) beat Gloucestershire 185 (J F Crapp 58, B O Allen 52, G M Emmett 29, A M B Rowan 4 for 40) and 155 (W L Neale 43, C J Barnett 41, J F Crapp 25, A M B Rowan 7 for 47) by 133 runs.

Twenty-Ninth Match vs England (Fifth Test Match) played at Kennington Oval, London on 16, 18, 19 and 20 August.

England

L Hutton	b Mann	83	c Tuckett b Mann	36
C Washbrook	lbw b Mann	32	c Fullerton b Roawn	43
J D Robertson	c Melville b Smith	4	b Rowan	30
D C S Compton	c Tuckett b Rowan	53	c Nourse b Dawson	113
* N W D Yardley	b Mann	59	c sub (Begbie) b Mann	11
K Cranston	st Fullerton b Rowan	45	c Mitchell b Rowan	0
R Howorth	c Fullerton b Rowan	23	not out	45
† T G Evans	run out	45	not out	39
C Gladwin	not out	51		
D V P Wright	b Mann	14		
W H Copson	b Dawson	6		
Extras	b 4 lb 7 nb 1	12	b 6 w 2	8
Total		**427**	**(6 wickets, declared)**	**325**

Fall 1st inns: 1/63 2/80 3/178 4/178 5/271 6/290 7/322 8/358 9/408 10/427
Fall 2nd inns: 1/73 2/89 3/158 4/179 5/180 6/267

Bowling	1st inns				2nd inns			
Tuckett	32	6	82	0	7	0	34	0
Dawson	35	5	80	1	15	1	59	1
Mann	64	28	93	4	27	7	102	2
Rowan	38	9	92	3	25	1	95	3
Smith	21	0	68	1	3	0	27	0

South Africa

B Mitchell	c Evans b Copson	120	not out	189
D V Dyer	c Gladwin b Howorth	18	lbw b Wright	4
K G Viljoen	c Evans b Wright	10	st Evans b Howorth	33
A D Nourse	c Yardley b Howorth	10	b Howorth	97
* A Melville	lbw b Cranston	39	c Evans b Cranston	6
O C Dawson	lbw b Wright	55	c Howorth b Cranston	0
† G M Fullerton	c Howorth b Cranston	6	c Evans b Howorth	14
A M B Rowan	b Howorth	0		
N B F Mann	b Copson	36	(8) c Hutton b Wright	10
L Tuckett	not out	0	(9) not out	40
V I Smith	lbw b Copson	0		
Extras	b 3 lb 2 w 1 nb 2	8	b 12 lb 12 w 4	30
Total		**302**	**(7 wickets)**	**423**

Fall 1st inns: 1/47 2/62 3/78 4/164 5/243 6/253 7/254 8/293 9/302 10/302
Fall 2nd inns: 1/8 2/48 3/232 4/247 5/249 6/266 7/314

Bowling	1st inns				2nd inns			
Copson	27	13	46	3	30	11	66	0
Gladwin	16	2	39	0	16	5	33	0
Wright	29	7	89	2	30	8	103	2
Howorth	39	16	64	3	37	12	85	3
Compton	11	4	31	0	4	0	30	0
Cranston	9	2	25	2	21	3	61	2
Hutton					2	0	14	0
Yardley					1	0	1	0

Umpires: J Smart and H G Baldwin

England drew with South Africa.

Thirtieth Match vs Essex played at Southchurch Park, Southend-On-Sea on 23, 25 and 26 August. South Africans 400 (D W Begbie 132, A Melville 84, A M B Rowan 58*, A D Nourse 36, D M Ovenstone 36, T P B Smith 6 for 158, R Smith 3 for 121) and 85 for 2 (D W Dyer 42*, T E Bailey 2 for 21) beat Essex 380 (H P Crabtree 117, S J Cray 98, D R Wilcox 73, T C Dodds 37, J B Plimsoll 3 for 86, A M B Rowan 3 for 108) and 102 (D R Wilcox 24*, J B Plimsoll 7 for 47) by 8 wickets.

Thirty-First Match vs Kent played at St. Lawrence Cricket Ground, Canterbury on 27, 28 and 29 August. South Africans 410 (K G Viljoen 104, O C Dawson 87, B Mitchell 46, G M Fullerton 46, A Melville 38, A M B Rowan 35, N B F Mann 26*, D V P Wright 5 for 124) and 227 for 7 dec (B Mitchell 57, K G Viljoen 35, O C Dawson 32*, A D Nourse 31, N W Harding 3 for 58) beat Kent 318 (J G W Davies 80, T G Evans 61, B H Valentine 55, A E Fagg 44, R R Dovey 26, N B F Mann 6 for 132) and 231 (L J Todd 41, A E Fagg 34, R R Dovey 31*, J G W Davies 26, N B F Mann 7 for 95) by 88 runs.

Thirty-Second Match vs Sussex played at County Cricket Ground, Hove on 30 August, 1 and 2 September. Sussex 415 for 5 dec (H W Parks 140, G Cox 132, H T Bartlett 66*, John G Langridge 57, L Tuckett 3 for 112) and 281 (H W Parks 60, James Langridge 55, John G Langridge 40, P Carey 37, H T Bartlett 28, S C Griffith 25, L Tuckett 3 for 34, J B Plimsoll 3 for 86) drew with South Africans 555 for 6 dec (K G Viljoen 201, A Melville 114*, T A Harris 71, D V Dyer 54, B Mitchell 41, N B F Mann 33*, A M B Rowan 30, C Oakes 2 for 51) and 45 for 0.

Thirty-Third Match vs South of England played at Central Cricket Ground, Hastings on 3, 4 and 5 September. South Africans 510 for 8 dec (O C Dawson 166*, B Mitchell 145, K G Viljoen 50, G M Fullerton 46, A D Nourse 27, R T D Perks 2 for 51) and 31 for 1 beat South of England 341 for 9 dec (D C S Compton 101, W J Edrich 64, J D B Robertson 55, H T Bartlett 46, R W V Robins 33, A M B Rowan 5 for 108, N B F Mann 4 for 97) and 199 (W J Edrich 54, B H Valentine 33, D C S Compton 30, N B F Mann 5 for 71, A M B Rowan 5 for 83) by 9 wickets.

Thirty-Fourth Match vs ‡ Club Cricket Conference played at Woodbridge Road, Guildford on 6 September. South Africans 402 for 1 dec (T A Harris 229*, G M Fullerton 94, D W Begbie 59*) drew with Club Cricket Conference 313 for 4 (A C L Bennett 156, P G Wreford 50).

Thirty-Fifth Match vs ‡ H D G Leveson-Gower's XI to be played at North Marine Drive, Scarborough was cancelled owing to shipping conditions which compelled the team to return home earlier than originally scheduled.

Test Match batting averages:

	Inns	NO	Runs	HS	Ave
A D Nourse	9	0	621	149	69.00
B Mitchell	10	1	597	189*	66.33
A Melville	10	1	569	189	63.22
T A Harris	3	0	93	60	31.00
K G Viljoen	10	1	270	93	30.00
A M B Rowan	8	3	114	38*	22.80
O C Dawson	9	0	204	55	22.66
D V Dyer	6	0	96	62	16.00
J B Plimsoll	2	1	16	8*	16.00
L Tuckett	9	2	87	40*	12.42
N B F Mann	9	0	109	36	12.11
G M Fullerton	4	0	46	14	11.50
J D Lindsay	5	2	21	9*	7.00
V I Smith	6	1	12	11	2.40

Test Match bowling averages:

	Overs	Mdns	Runs	Wkts	Ave
N B F Mann	329.5	127	603	15	40.20
L Tuckett	252	44	664	15	44.26
J B Plimsoll	39.3	9	143	3	47.66
V I Smith	155.1	35	439	9	48.77
O C Dawson	158.5	33	425	8	53.12
A M B Rowan	274.2	48	671	12	55.91
B Mitchell	2	1	5	0	-

Tour batting averages - all matches:

	Inns	NO	Runs	HS	Ave
B Mitchell	37	4	2,014	189*	61.03
K G Viljoen	33	4	1,441	201	49.68
A D Nourse	36	2	1,453	205*	42.73
A Melville	40	2	1,547	189	40.71
T A Harris	20	1	701	100	36.89
O C Dawson	35	4	1,002	166*	32.32
G M Fullerton	26	4	698	82	31.72
D W Begbie	21	1	612	132	30.60
D V Dyer	28	2	673	74	25.88
A M B Rowan	33	9	607	100*	25.29
N B F Mann	32	3	591	97	20.37
D M Ovenstone	14	0	184	42	13.14
L W Payn	10	1	102	32	11.33
L Tuckett	25	4	226	40*	10.76
J B Plimsoll	18	6	127	17*	10.58
J D Lindsay	16	6	104	17	10.40
V I Smith	24	11	89	18*	6.84

Tour bowling averages - all matches:

	Overs	Mdns	Runs	Wkts	Ave
K G Viljoen	1.4	0	11	1	11.00
V I Smith	549.3	151	1,344	58	23.17
J B Plimsoll	750.4	215	1,586	68	23.32
A M B Rowan	1,075.4	263	2,547	102	24.97
N B F Mann	954	350	1,869	74	25.25
L Tuckett	724	150	1,779	69	25.78
O C Dawson	601.3	146	1,408	54	26.07
D W Begbie	105.3	21	322	12	26.83
L W Payn	253.4	85	571	17	33.58
B Mitchell	22	3	101	2	50.50

Centuries recorded for South Africans during the tour:

B Mitchell	(8) :	120 vs England (The Oval) (Fifth Test Match)
		189* vs England (The Oval) (Fifth Test Match)
		145 vs South of England (Hastings)
		131 vs Lancashire (Old Trafford)
		113 vs Glamorgan (Cardiff)
		109 vs Middlesex (Lord's)
		108 vs Combined Services (Portsmouth)
		103* vs M.C.C. (Lord's)
A Melville	(6) :	189 vs England (Trent Bridge) (First Test Match)
		104* vs England (Trent Bridge) (First Test Match)
		122 vs Surrey (The Oval)
		117 vs England (Lord's) (Second Test Match)
		114* vs Sussex (Hove)
		104 vs Leicestershire (Grace Road, Leicester)
K G Viljoen	(6) :	201 vs Sussex (Hove)
		128 vs Cambridge University (Fenner's)
		113 vs Warwickshire (Edgbaston)
		110* vs Oxford University (Oxford)
		104 vs Middlesex (Lord's)
		104 vs Kent (Canterbury)
A D Nourse	(4) :	205* vs Warwickshire (Edgbaston)
		149 vs England (Trent Bridge) (First Test Match)
		115 vs England (Old Trafford) (Third Test Match)
		101 vs Oxford University (The Parks)
D W Begbie	(1) :	132 vs Essex (Southend-On-Sea)
O C Dawson	(1) :	16* vs South of England (Hastings)
T A Harris	(1) :	100 vs Glamorgan (Swansea)
A M B Rowan	(1) :	100* vs Glamorgan (Cardiff)

Fielding:

	Catches	Stumpings
B Mitchell	32	
D M Ovenstone	22	7
A D Nourse	26	
J D Lindsay	18	7
G M Fullerton	17	7
A Melville	21	
O C Dawson	20	
L Tuckett	14	
D V Dyer	12	
A M B Rowan	11	
V I Smith	11	
D W Begbie	8	
T A Harris	7	
K G Viljoen	7	
N B F Mann	5	
L W Payn	4	
J B Plimsoll	4	

B.Mitchell

The Tenth South African Team in the United Kingdom, 1951

Despite the lapse of four years the 1951 tourists were to prove no more successful than their predecessors of 1947 of whom only Nourse, as captain, A. M. B. Rowan and G. M. Fullerton remained. Three of those to receive their initiation in international cricket on this tour, Jackie McGlew, Roy McLean and John Waite, were finally to earn a total of over 120 Test caps between them.

They were not helped by Nourse sustaining a broken thumb in the fifth match at Gloucester when fielding a fierce drive by T. W. Graveney, an injury which was to restrict his appearances. He finally amassed 673 runs in 18 matches of which 208 runs were scored in the First Test at Trent Bridge less than three weeks after the injury. Athol Rowan suffered a damaged knee which led to Hugh Tayfield flying in to join the tourists. Michael Melle also had to undergo an operation and N. B. F. 'Tufty' Mann had to retire from the tour before the end with an illness which was to end his life less than a year later at the premature age of 31.

(standing) **D.J.McGlew J.H.B.Waite J.E.Cheetham C.B.van Ryneveld C.N.McCarthy R.A.McLean P.N.F.Mansell M.G.Melle W.R.Endean**

(sitting) **A.M.B.Rowan G.W.A.Chubb E.A.B.Rowan Mr.S.J.Pegler** (Manager) **A.D.Nourse** (Captain) **N.B.F.Mann G.M.Fullerton**

Touring party (16):

* A D Nourse (*Natal*) (Captain)
Age 40. Sound right-handed middle order batsman and excellent fieldsman.

E A B Rowan (*Transvaal*) (Vice-Captain)
Age 41. Right-handed opening batsman.

J E Cheetham (*Western Province*)
Age 31. Right-handed batsman and fine fieldsman.

D J McGlew (*Natal*)
Age 22. Right-handed batsman.

† J H B Waite (*Eastern Province*)
Age 21. Right-handed batsman and wicket-keeper.

G M Fullerton (*Transvaal*)
Age 28. Right-handed batsman.

R A McLean (*Natal*)
Age 20. Right-handed batsman and fine fieldsman.

C B van Ryneveld (*Oxford University/Western Province*)
Age 23, Right-handed leg-spin bowler, right-handed batsman and fine outfielder.

A M B Rowan (*Transvaal*)
Age 30. Right-arm off-spin bowler, useful right-handed batsman and excellent fielder.

P N F Mansell (*Rhodesia*)
Age 31. Right-arm leg-spin and googly bowler, right-handed batsman and brilliant slip fieldsman.

† W R Endean (*Transvaal*)
Age 27. Right-handed middle order batsman and wicket-keeper.

H J Tayfield (*Natal/Rhodesia*)
Age 23. Right-handed batsman and right-arm off-break bowler.

N B F Mann (*Eastern Province*)
Age 30. Right-handed hard hitting batsman and left-arm slow bowler.

G W A Chubb (*Transvaal*)
Age 40. Right-arm medium-fast bowler.

M G Melle (*Transvaal*)
Age 21. Right-handed attacking batsman and right-arm fast seam bowler.

C N McCarthy (*Natal*)
Age 22. Right-arm fast bowler and improving fieldsman.

Manager: Mr. S J Pegler

Scorer/Baggage-Master: Mr. W H Ferguson

Summary of all matches:

Played 38   Won 10   Lost 5   Drawn 23   Abandoned 1

Summary of first-class matches:

Played 30   Won 5   Lost 5   Drawn 20

Summary of Test Matches:

Played 5   Won 1   Lost 3   Drawn 1

First Match vs ‡ D G Clark's XI played at Mote Park, Maidstone on 25 April. D G Clark's XI 199 for 4 dec (A E Fagg 74, G H G Doggart 56) drew with South Africans 191 for 5 (G M Fullerton 118*, C B van Ryneveld 43*).

Second Match vs ‡ Union Castle played at Lee on 27 April. South Africans 177 for 6 dec (G M Fullerton 65, E A B Rowan 64) drew with Union Castle.

Third Match vs ‡ Club Cricket Conference to be played at Wardown Park, Luton on 28 April was abandoned without a ball being bowled due to snow.

Fourth Match vs Worcestershire played at County Ground, New Road, Worcester on 2, 3 and 4 May. Worcestershire 192 (R E Bird 70*, R E S Wyatt 25, R Howorth 25, A M B Rowan 4 for 49) and 50 for 6 (E Cooper 23, A M B Rowan 3 for 7) drew with South Africans 157 (N B F Mann 49, A M B Rowan 44, C B van Ryneveld 29, R T D Perks 4 for 36).

Fifth Match vs Yorkshire played at Park Avenue, Bradford on 5, 7 and 8 May. Yorkshire 214 for 4 dec (H Halliday 67, L Hutton 58, F A Lowson 42, J V Wilson 28, A M B Rowan 3 for 94) drew with South Africans 76 (J H B Waite 31, R Appleyard 6 for 38, J H Wardle 3 for 25) and 86 for 9 (J H B Waite 17, F S Trueman 5 for 19, J H Wardle 4 for 32).

Sixth Match vs Cambridge University played at Fenner's University Cricket Ground, Cambridge on 9, 10 and 11 May. Cambridge University 188 (D S Sheppard 71, P B H May 33, M H Stevenson 25, C B van Ryneveld 5 for 62, N B F Mann 4 for 34) drew with South Africans 283 for 4 (E A B Rowan 104*, G M Fullerton 72, R A McLean 51, C B van Ryneveld 40*).

Seventh Match vs Glamorgan played at Arms Park, Cardiff on 12, 14 and 15 May. South Africans 330 (D J McGlew 110, E A B Rowan 59, R A McLean 42, A D Nourse 32, D J Shepherd 4 for 66) beat Glamorgan 130 (A J Watkins 43, G W A Chubb 5 for 21, C N McCarthy 3 for 22) and 186 (H G Davies 80, W G A Parkhouse 25, A M B Rowan 5 for 42, C N McCarthy 3 for 49) by an innings and 14 runs.

Eighth Match vs Gloucestershire played at County Cricket Ground, Nevil Road, Bristol on 16, 17 and 18 May. South Africans 388 for 9 dec (J E Cheetham 92, D J McGlew 90, J H B Waite 62, A D Nourse 38, P N F Mansell 37*, G E Lambert 5 for 78) and 15 for 1 drew with Gloucestershire 207 (D M Young 87, T W Graveney 37, C A Milton 36, G M Emmett 28, C N McCarthy 6 for 56, M G Melle 3 for 44) and 322 for 4 dec (T W Graveney 93, D M Young 68, J F Crapp 64, C A Milton 46* N B F Mann 2 for 66).

Ninth Match vs M.C.C. played at Lord's Cricket Ground, London on 19, 21 and 22 May. South Africans 190 (C B van Ryneveld 56, E A B Rowan 26, W R Endean 26, R Tattersall 8 for 51) and 97 for 2 (J H B Waite 36, E A B Rowan 30) drew with M.C.C. 271 (D C S Compton 147, J D B Robertson 51, F R Brown 33, N B F Mann 4 for 67).

Tenth Match vs Oxford University played at the University Parks, Oxford on 23, 24 and 25 May. South Africans 300 for 5 dec (E A B Rowan 147, J E Cheetham 89, R A McLean 39, R V Divecha 3 for 102) and 62 for 0 (J H B Waite 44*) drew with Oxford University 159 (D B Carr 36, C E Winn 36, D Lewis 29, M G Melle 5 for 37, G W A Chubb 3 for 36) and 50 for 0 (M B Hofmeyr 32*).

Eleventh Match vs Nottinghamshire played at Trent Bridge, Nottingham on 26, 28 and 29 May. South Africans 304 (A M B Rowan 98, E A B Rowan 55, J E Cheetham 38, N B F Mann 35, H J Butler 5 for 63, P F Harvey 3 for 89) and 176 for 2 (E A B Rowan 95, G M Fullerton 54*) drew with Nottinghamshire 297 (J Hardstaff 151, C B Harris 57, C J Poole 39, C N McCarthy 5 for 67, G W A Chubb 3 for 70).

Twelfth Match vs Essex played at Valentine's Park, Ilford on 30, 31 May and 1 June. South Africans 312 for 9 dec (J H B Waite 128, H J Tayfield 68, A M B Rowan 40, N B F Mann 40, K C Preston 4 for 77, T P B Smith 3 for 77) and 286 for 5 dec (G M Fullerton 167, D J McGlew 56, D J Insole 2 for 38) drew with Essex 319 for 7 dec (T C Dodds 138, D J Insole 60, R Horsfall 35, P A Gibb 30, N B F Mann 3 for 70) and 255 for 5 (R Smith 147, R Horsfall 47, T P B Smith 25, M G Melle 3 for 77).

Thirteenth Match vs Surrey played at Kennington Oval, London on 2, 4 and 5 June. South Africans 209 (C B van Ryneveld 60, A D Nourse 45, W R Endean 37, J E Cheetham 20, W S Surridge 3 for 63) and 358 for 8 dec (D J McGlew 99, W R Endean 72, J E Cheetham 68, C B van Ryneveld 39, G A R Lock 4 for 87) drew with Surrey 246 (L B Fishlock 62, A J McIntyre 57, M R Barton 46, T Clark 27, M G Melle 4 for 66) and 95 for 4 (T Clark 40).

Fourteenth Match vs England (First Test Match) played at Trent Bridge, Nottingham on 7, 8, 9, 11 and 12 June.

South Africa

	1st innings		2nd innings	
E A B Rowan	c Evans b Brown	17	c Ikin b Bedser	11
† J H B Waite	run out	76	c Ikin b Tattersall	5
D J McGlew	b Brown	40	st Evans b Bedser	5
* A D Nourse	run out	208	absent hurt	0
J E Cheetham	c Ikin b Bedser	31	b Bedser	28
G M Fullerton	c Compton b Tattersall	54	c Brown b Tattersall	13
C B van Ryneveld	lbw b Bedser	32	c Hutton b Bedser	22
A M B Rowan	b Bedser	2	c Evans b Bedser	5
N B F Mann	c Tattersall b Wardle	1	b Tattersall	2
G W A Chubb	not out	0	not out	11
C N McCarthy	not out	1	b Bedser	5
Extras	b 3 lb 17 nb 1	21	b 4 lb 9 nb 1	14
Total	(9 wickets, declared)	483		121

Fall 1st inns: 1/31 2/107 3/189 4/273 5/394 6/465 7/467 8/476 9/482
Fall 2nd inns: 1/12 2/20 3/24 4/52 5/87 6/98 7/103 8/106 9/121 10/121

Bowling	1st inns				2nd inns			
Bedser	63	18	122	3	22.4	8	37	6
Bailey	45	13	102	0	2	0	10	0
Brown	34	11	74	2				
Tattersall	47	20	80	1	23	6	56	3
Wardle	49	21	77	1	4	3	4	0
Compton	2	0	7	0				

England

	1st innings		2nd innings	
L Hutton	c Waite b A M B Rowan	63	c & b A M B Rowan	11
J T Ikin	c McCarthy b Chubb	1	b Mann	33
R T Simpson	c Waite b McCarthy	137	c & b A M B Rowan	7
D C S Compton	c Waite b McCarthy	112	lbw b A M B Rowan	5
W Watson	lbw b McCarthy	57	lbw b Mann	5
* F R Brown	c Fullerton b Chubb	29	c McCarthy b A M B Rowan	7
† T G Evans	c sub b Chubb	5	c van Ryneveld b Mann	0
J H Wardle	c Fullerton b Chubb	5	c sub b A M B Rowan	30
T E Bailey	c Fullerton b McCarthy	3	c Waite b Mann	11
A V Bedser	not out	0	b McCarthy	0
R Tattersall	did not bat		not out	0
Extras	b 4 lb 3	7	lb 5	5
Total	(9 wickets, declared)	419		114

Fall 1st inns: 1/4 2/148 3/234 4/375 5/382 6/395 7/410 8/419 9/419
Fall 2nd inns: 1/23 2/41 3/57 4/63 5/67 6/80 7/83 8/84 9/110 10/114

Bowling	1st inns				2nd inns			
McCarthy	48	10	104	4	8	1	8	1
Chubb	46.2	12	146	4	6	2	9	0
A M B Rowan	46	10	101	1	27.2	4	68	5
Mann	20	5	51	0	24	16	24	4
van Ryneveld	3	0	10	0				

Umpires: F Chester and H G Baldwin

South Africa beat England by 71 runs.

Fifteenth Match vs Northamptonshire played at County Cricket Ground, Wantage Road, Northampton on 13, 14 and 15 June. Northamptonshire 426 for 6 dec (L Livingston 201, F Jakeman 131, C N McCarthy 2 for 75) drew with South Africans 212 (W R Endean 57, E A B Rowan 39, D J McGlew 32, N B F Mann 29*, G E Tribe 6 for 53, F R Brown 3 for 51) and 418 for 6 (E A B Rowan 202*, R A McLean 68, G M Fullerton 53, D J McGlew 38).

Sixteenth Match vs Lancashire played at Old Trafford, Manchester on 16, 18 and 19 June. South Africans 403 for 7 dec (J E Cheetham 127, J H B Waite 122, E A B Rowan 66, C B van Ryneveld 38, A Wharton 3 for 99) and 60 for 4 (C B van Ryneveld 38*) drew with Lancashire 412 (G A Edrich 121, A Wharton 98, J T Ikin 64, K Grieves 36, M J Hilton 31, H J Tayfield 5 for 84).

C. B. VAN RYNEVELD

Seventeenth Match vs England (Second Test Match) played at Lord's Cricket Ground, London on 21, 22 and 23 June.

England

L Hutton	lbw b McCarthy	12	not out		12
J T Ikin	b Mann	51	not out		4
R T Simpson	lbw b McCarthy	26			
D C S Compton	lbw b McCarthy	79			
W Watson	c McCarthy b Chubb	79			
* F R Brown	b Chubb	1			
† T G Evans	c Fullerton b McCarthy	0			
J H Wardle	lbw b Chubb	18			
A V Bedser	not out	26			
J B Statham	b Chubb	1			
R Tattersall	b Chubb	1			
Extras	b 8 lb 9	17			
Total		**311**	**(no wicket)**		**16**

Fall 1st inns: 1/20 2/89 3/103 4/225 5/226 6/231 7/265 8/299 9/301 10/311

Bowling		1st inns			2nd inns		
McCarthy	23	2	76	4			
Chubb	34.4	9	77	5			
A M B Rowan	13	1	63	0			
Mann	32	12	51	1			
van Ryneveld	5	0	27	0			
Nourse					2	0	9	0
E A B Rowan					1.5	0	7	0

South Africa

E A B Rowan	c Ikin b Tattersall	24	c Ikin b Statham	10
† J H B Waite	c Hutton b Wardle	15	c Compton b Tattersall	17
D J McGlew	c Evans b Tattersall	3	b Tattersall	2
* A D Nourse	c Watson b Tattersall	20	lbw b Wardle	3
J E Cheetham	c Hutton b Tattersall	15	b Statham	54
G M Fullerton	b Tattersall	12	lbw b Bedser	60
C B van Ryneveld	lbw b Wardle	0	c Ikin b Tattersall	18
A M B Rowan	c Ikin b Tattersall	3	c Brown b Bedser	10
N B F Mann	c Brown b Tattersall	14	c Brown b Tattersall	13
G W A Chubb	c Tattersall b Wardle	5	b Tattersall	3
C N McCarthy	not out	1	not out	2
Extras	lb 3	3	b 11 lb 8	19
Total		**115**		**211**

Fall 1st inns: 1/25 2/38 3/47 4/72 5/88 6/91 7/91 8/103 5/112 10/115
Fall 2nd inns: 1/21 2/29 3/32 4/58 5/152 6/160 7/178 8/196 9/200 10/211

Bowling		1st inns				2nd inns		
Bedser	8	5	7	0	24	8	53	2
Statham	6	3	7	0	18	6	33	2
Tattersall	28	10	52	7	32.2	14	49	5
Wardle	22.5	10	46	3	20	5	44	1
Compton					2	0	13	0

Umpires: F S Lee and H Elliott

England beat South Africa by 10 wickets.

Eighteenth Match vs Combined Services played at United Services Officers Sports Ground, Portsmouth on 27, 28 and 29 June. South Africans 499 for 5 dec (J H B Waite 139, J E Cheetham 133, G M Fullerton 69, A D Nourse 61, D J McGlew 47, R A McLean 43*, St. A J Underwood 2 for 101) drew with Combined Services 235 (Sgmn. D B Close 66, AC1 J M Parks 51, AC1 F J Titmus 30, Cmdr. R J L Hammond 28, N B F Mann 3 for 16, H J Tayfield 3 for 44) and 256 for 4 (Sgmn. D B Close 135*, Lt-Cmdr. J E Manners 75, AC1 J M Parks 38, G W A Chubb 2 for 34).

Nineteenth Match vs Yorkshire played at Bramall Lane, Sheffield on 30 June, 2 and 3 July. South Africans 454 for 8 dec (C B van Ryneveld 150, R A McLean 88, G M Fullerton 63, J H B Waite 57, J P Whitehead 4 for 103) drew with Yorkshire 579 (L Hutton 156, F A Lowson 115, J V Wilson 84, N W D Yardley 57, W Watson 34, D V Brennan 33*, J P Whitehead 23, G W A Chubb 3 for 141, H J Tayfield 3 for 135).

A.M.B.Rowan

E.A.B.Rowan

Twentieth Match vs England (Third Test Match) played at Old Trafford, Manchester on 5, 6, 7, 9 and 10 July.

South Africa

E A B Rowan	c Brown b Bedser	0	c Ikin b Laker	57
† J H B Waite	c Ikin b Bedser	1	b Statham	0
C B van Ryneveld	lbw b Tattersall	40	b Laker	7
* A D Nourse	c Ikin b Bedser	29	c Evans b Tattersall	20
J E Cheetham	c Hutton b Bedser	20	b Bedser	46
G M Fullerton	c Hutton b Bedser	0	c Tattersall b Laker	10
R A McLean	b Laker	20	c Ikin b Bedser	19
A M B Rowan	b Statham	17	lbw b Bedser	3
N B F Mann	b Bedser	0	b Bedser	4
G W A Chubb	not out	15	b Bedser	1
C N McCarthy	c Ikin b Bedser	0	not out	0
Extras	lb 14 nb 2	16	b 13 lb 10 nb 1	24
Total		**158**		**191**

Fall 1st inns: 1/0 2/13 3/66 4/87 5/88 6/105 7/129 8/132 9/143 10/158
Fall 2nd inns: 1/4 2/19 3/60 4/145 5/155 6/168 7/181 8/185 9/190 10/191

Bowling	1st inns				2nd inns			
Bedser	32.3	10	58	7	24.2	8	54	5
Statham	7	2	8	1	17	3	30	1
Laker	27	7	47	1	19	3	42	3
Tattersall	18	6	29	1	18	3	41	1

England

L Hutton	c van Ryneveld b A M B Rowan	27	not out	98
J T Ikin	c Cheetham b Chubb	22	b Mann	38
R T Simpson	st Waite b Mann	11	not out	4
T W Graveney	b A M B Rowan	15		
W Watson	b Chubb	21		
* F R Brown	c van Ryneveld b A M B Rowan	42		
† T G Evans	c Waite b Chubb	2		
J C Laker	c Nourse b Chubb	27		
A V Bedser	not out	30		
J B Statham	c Cheetham b Chubb	1		
R Tattersall	c Cheetham b Chubb	1		
Extras	b 4 lb 8	12	lb 1 nb 1	2
Total		**211**	**(1 wicket)**	**142**

Fall 1st inns: 1/22 2/58 3/70 4/91 5/127 6/147 7/147 8/200 9/207 10/211
Fall 2nd inns: 1/121

Bowling	1st inns				2nd inns			
McCarthy	14	4	36	0	19	4	46	0
Chubb	26.2	7	51	6	23	6	72	0
A M B Rowan	29	4	75	3	7	1	17	0
Mann	16	5	37	1	2.3	1	5	1

Umpires: F S Lee and H G Baldwin

England beat South Africa by 9 wickets.

Twenty-First Match vs ‡ Scotland played at Hamilton Crescent, Glasgow on 11 and 12 July. Scotland 115 (J Aitchison 55, W Nichol 25, A M B Rowan 4 for 21) drew with South Africans 110 for 3 (R A McLean 40, E A B Rowan 35, S J Thomson 2 for 10).

Twenty-Second Match vs ‡ Ireland played at Belfast on 13 and 14 July. South Africans 145 (C B van Ryneveld 37*, D J McGlew 29, J C Boucher 4 for 43, J Bowden 3 for 38) and 61 for 2 (R A McLean 35*) beat Ireland 159 (J S Pollock 50, G Wilson 29, N B F Mann 4 for 48, A M B Rowan 3 for 49) and 46 (T McCloy 17, A M B Rowan 7 for 23, N B F Mann 3 for 15) by 8 wickets.

Twenty-Third Match vs ‡ Ireland played at Dublin on 16 and 17 July. South Africans 312 for 4 dec (R A McLean 107, E A B Rowan 85, P N F Mansell 85, J Bowden 2 for 62) beat Ireland 110 (E A Ingham 50*, H J Tayfield 4 for 32, C B van Ryneveld 4 for 60) and 130 (S F Bergin 79*, L Armstrong 22, N B F Mann 6 for 37, C N McCarthy 3 for 14) by an innings and 72 runs.

N.B.F.Mann

Twenty-Fourth Match vs Derbyshire played at County Cricket Ground, Derby on 18, 19 and 20 July. South Africans 382 for 9 dec (J H B Waite 99, E A B Rowan 74, P N F Mansell 51, A D Nourse 46, A M B Rowan 37, D J McGlew 31, C Gladwin 4 for 72) and 82 for 2 (J H B Waite 38) beat Derbyshire 258 (A C Revill 74, A Hamer 65, C Gladwin 39, C N McCarthy 3 for 61) and 205 (G L Willatt 50, T A Hall 34*, A Hamer 33, C S Elliott 32, N B F Mann 3 for 32) by 8 wickets.

Twenty-Fifth Match vs Leicestershire played at County Cricket Ground, Grace Road, Leicester on 21, 23 and 24 July. South Africans 235 (E A B Rowan 61, C B van Ryneveld 61, R A McLean 47, C H Palmer 5 for 46, J Sperry 3 for 58) and 168 for 4 (E A B Rowan 115*, R A McLean 25) beat Leicestershire 267 (M Tompkin 64, V Munden 44, L G Berry 38, C H Palmer 37, G Lester 31, G W A Chubb 3 for 48, H J Tayfield 3 for 55) and 134 for 6 dec (C H Palmer 43, L G Berry 31, N B F Mann 3 for 16) by 6 wickets.

Twenty-Sixth Match vs England (Fourth Test Match) played at Headingley Cricket Ground, Leeds on 26, 27, 28, 30 and 31 July.

South Africa

E A B Rowan	c Bedser b Brown	236	not out	60
† J H B Waite	lbw b Bedser	13	not out	25
C B van Ryneveld	c & b Hilton	83		
* A D Nourse	lbw b Brown	13		
J E Cheetham	b Bedser	7		
R A McLean	run out	67		
P N F Mansell	c Tattersall b Hilton	90		
A M B Rowan	b Brown	9		
N B F Mann	b Tattersall	2		
G W A Chubb	c Lowson b Hilton	11		
C N McCarthy	not out	0		
Extras	b 1 lb 6	7	lb 2	2
Total		**538**	**(no wicket)**	**87**

Fall 1st inns: 1/40 2/238 3/267 4/286 5/392 6/480 7/498 8/505 9/538 10/538

Bowling		1st inns				2nd inns		
Bedser	58	14	113	2	4	1	5	0
Bailey	17	4	48	0	1	0	8	0
Brown	38	10	107	3	11	2	26	0
Tattersall	60	23	83	1	16	9	13	0
Hilton	61.3	18	176	3	10	5	17	0
Compton	1	0	4	0	7	1	16	0

England

L Hutton	b van Ryneveld	100
P A Lowson	c Mansell b A M B Rowan	58
P B H May	b A M B Rowan	138
D C S Compton	lbw b A M B Rowan	25
W Watson	b Chubb	32
T E Bailey	b Mann	95
* F R Brown	c E A B Rowan b A M B Rowan	2
A V Bedser	b Mann	8
† D V Brennan	b Mann	16
R Tattersall	c E A B Rowan b A M B Rowan	4
M J Hilton	not out	9
Extras	b 10 lb 7 nb 1	18
Total		**505**

Fall 1st inns: 1/99 2/228 3/266 4/345 5/387 6/391 7/400 8/432 9/435 10/505

Bowling		1st inns		
McCarthy	41	10	81	0
Chubb	43	12	99	1
A M B Rowan	68	17	174	5
Mann	60.5	23	96	3
Mansell	4	0	11	0
van Ryneveld	8	0	26	1

Umpires: H Elliott and D Davies

England drew with South Africa.

Twenty-Seventh Match vs Somerset played at County Cricket Ground, Taunton on 1, 2 and 3 August. South Africans 235 (D J McGlew 68, P N F Mansell 62, J E Cheetham 36, J Lawrence 3 for 67, Khan Mohammad 3 for 74) and 180 (J E Cheetham 62, A D Nourse 31, G M Fullerton 20, E P Robinson 5 for 59, H L Hazell 3 for 66) beat Somerset 305 (S S Rogers 107*, H T F Buse 46, M F Tremlett 41, E Hill 34, H L Hazell 29, M G Melle 3 for 59, G W A Chubb 3 for 99) and 86 (F L Angell 18, J Lawrence 18, G W A Chubb 5 for 21, N B F Mann 4 for 30) by 24 runs.

Twenty-Eighth Match vs Glamorgan played at St. Helen's Cricket Ground, Swansea on 4 and 6 August. Glamorgan 111 (B L Muncer 30, A J Watkins 26, P N F Mansell 5 for 37, A M B Rowan 4 for 45) and 147 (W Wooller 46, J Pleass 29, A M B Rowan 4 for 42, P N F Mansell 4 for 73) beat South Africans 111 (A M B Rowan 49, B L Muncer 7 for 45, W Wooller 3 for 41) and 83 (W R Endean 35, J McConnon 6 for 27, B L Muncer 4 for 16) by 64 runs.

G.M.Fullerton

Twenty-Ninth Match vs Warwickshire played at Edgbaston Cricket Ground, Birmingham on 8, 9 and 10 August. Warwickshire 230 (D D Taylor 73, H E Dollery 52, A V Wolton 27, A M B Rowan 8 for 106) and 201 for 7 dec (D D Taylor 69, R E Hitchcock 28, A V Wolton 28, G W A Chubb 3 for 87) drew with South Africans 77 (G W A Chubb 24*, C W Grove 4 for 31, R Weeks 3 for 23) and 290 for 6 (J E Cheetham 116*, R A McLean 80, P N F Mansell 48, C W Grove 3 for 72).

Thirtieth Match vs Sussex played at County Cricket Ground, Hove on 11, 13 and 14 August. Sussex 213 (D S Shepphard 100, G H G Doggart 60, John G Langridge 26, C N McCarthy 8 for 36) and 15 for 0 drew with South Africans 314 (D J McGlew 80, G M Fullerton 65, H J Tayfield 36, A D Nourse 28, J E Cheetham 25, E A B Rowan 23, James Langridge 2 for 13).

Thirty-First Match vs England (Fifth Test Match) played at Kennington Oval, London on 16, 17 and 18 August.

South Africa

E A B Rowan	c Hutton b Brown	55	lbw b Laker		45
† W R Endean	c Brown b Laker	31	lbw b Laker		7
C B van Ryneveld	st Brennan b Laker	10	lbw b Laker		5
* A D Nourse	lbw b Brown	4	b Laker		4
J E Cheetham	lbw b Laker	0	c Hutton b Tattersall		18
R A McLean	c May b Laker	14	c Lowson b Laker		18
P N F Mansell	b Tattersall	8	lbw b Laker		0
A M B Rowan	c Laker b Bedser	41	not out		15
G W A Chubb	b Bedser	10	c Hutton b Bedser		7
M G Melle	b Shackleton	5	b Laker		17
C N McCarthy	not out	4	b Bedser		0
Extras	b 11 lb 8 nb 1	20	b 11 lb 7		18
Total		**202**			**154**

Fall 1st inns: 1/66 2/106 3/106 4/106 5/126 6/131 7/146 8/175 9/186 10/202
Fall 2nd inns: 1/15 2/35 3/57 4/84 5/106 6/111 7/116 8/130 9/153 10/154

Bowling		1st inns			2nd inns		
Bedser	19.3	6	36	2	19.5	6	32	3
Shackleton	15	5	20	1	10	2	19	0
Tattersall	14	7	26	1	5	1	10	1
Laker	37	12	64	4	28	8	55	6
Brown	20	10	31	2	13	5	20	0
Compton	1	0	5	0			

England

L Hutton	lbw b A M B Rowan	28	obstructing the field		27
F A Lowson	c Endean b Melle	0	c van Ryneveld b A M B Rowan		37
P B H May	b Chubb	33	c E A B Rowan b A M B Rowan		0
D C S Compton	b McCarthy	73	c van Ryneveld b Chubb		18
W Watson	run out	31	c Endean b Chubb		15
* F R Brown	c van Ryneveld b A M B Rowan	1	lbw b Chubb		40
J C Laker	b Chubb	6	not out		13
D Shackleton	c van Ryneveld b Melle	14	not out		5
A V Bedser	c Endean b Melle	2			
† D V Brennan	lbw b Melle	0			
R Tattersall	not out	0			
Extras	lb 4 nb 2	6	b 5 lb 3 nb 1		9
Total		**194**	**(6 wickets)**		**164**

Fall 1st inns: 1/2 2/51 3/79 4/128 5/134 6/145 7/173 8/189 9/190 10/194
Fall 2nd inns: 1/53 2/53 3/84 4/90 5/132 6/151

Bowling		1st inns			2nd inns		
McCarthy	17	0	45	1	7	0	17	0
Melle	10	6	9	4	3	0	8	0
A M B Rowan	27	9	44	2	24.1	2	77	2
Chubb	30	5	70	2	28	10	53	3
van Ryneveld	3	0	20	0			

Umpires: F Chester and D Davies

England beat South Africa by 4 wickets.

Thirty-Second Match vs Hampshire played at County Cricket Ground, Northlands Road, Southampton on 22, 23 and 24 August. Hampshire 180 (N H Rogers 37, J R Gray 28, A W H Rayment 26, G Hill 26, M G Melle 4 for 39) and 243 for 4 dec (N H Rogers 118, N McCorkell 31, A W H Rayment 26, G W A Chubb 2 for 34) drew with South Africans 251 (D J McGlew 114, R A McLean 22, H J Tayfield 22, C J Knott 3 for 61, D Shackleton 3 for 62, V H D Cannings 3 for 81) and 151 for 7 (C B van Ryneveld 65, D J McGlew 20, C J Knott 2 for 30, V H D Cannings 2 for 28, D Shackleton 2 for 32).

Thirty-Third Match vs Middlesex played at Lord's Cricket Ground, London on 25, 27 and 28 August. South Africans 297 (G M Fullerton 89*, E A B Rowan 36, P N F Mansell 36, J E Cheetham 32, R A McLean 26, D C S Compton 3 for 93, J A Young 3 for 45) drew with Middlesex 136 for 2 (J D B Robertson 70*, J G Dewes 32, D C S Compton 28*)

Thirty-Fourth Match vs Kent played at St. Lawrence Cricket Ground, Canterbury on 29, 30 and 31 August. Kent 163 (M C Cowdrey 71, T G Evans 25, C B van Ryneveld 5 for 53) drew with South Africans 201 for 4 (J E Cheetham 80*, G M Fullerton 52*, W R Endean 41, D V P Wright 3 for 56).

Thirty-Fifth Match vs An England XI played at Central Cricket Ground, Hastings on 1, 3 and 4 September. An England XI 208 for 9 dec (D C S Compton 84, T C Dodds 43, John G Langridge 25, C N McCarthy 4 for 31) drew with South Africans 285 (R A McLean 88, G M Fullerton 61, D J McGlew 45, J A Young 6 for 106, R O Jenkins 3 for 85).

Thirty-Sixth Match vs ‡ Minor Counties played at Lakenham Cricket Ground, Norwich on 5 and 6 September. South Africans 318 for 8 dec (J E Cheetham 114*, E A B Rowan 73, D J McGlew 40, H J Tayfield 36, B Shardlow 3 for 80, A Coxon 3 for 102) beat Minor Counties 182 (B H Belle 48, J H Hastie 29, A G Coomb 23, M G Melle 6 for 51) and 113 (J F Mendl 39, P N F Mansell 5 for 24, H J Tayfield 4 for 26) by an innings and 23 runs.

Thirty-Seventh Match vs T N Pearce's XI played at North Marine Drive, Scarborough on 8, 10 and 11 September. T N Pearce's XI 101 (J E Walsh 23, G W A Chubb 4 for 16, P N F Mansell 3 for 43) and 248 (L Hutton 91, F R Brown 39, R T Simpson 34, M G Melle 6 for 71) beat South Africans 95 (D J McGlew 64, T L Pritchard 4 for 38, A V Bedser 3 for 22) and 245 (C B van Ryneveld 61, H J Tayfield 38, E A B Rowan 36, P N F Mansell 31, G M Fullerton 27, A V Bedser 5 for 44) by 9 runs.

Thirty-Eighth Match vs ‡ Dutch Team played at Haarlem, Netherlands on 15 September. South Africans 154 beat Dutch Team 55 (M G Melle 8 for 18) and 60 (P N F Mansell 4 for 24, H J Tayfield 4 for 19) by an innings and 39 runs.

Thirty-Ninth Match vs ‡ Dutch Team played at Haarlem, Netherlands on 16 September. South Africans 291 (E A B Rowan 106, D J McGlew 106) beat Dutch Team 127 (C B van Ryneveld 4 for 22) by 164 runs.

Test Match batting averages:

	Inns	NO	Runs	HS	Ave
E A B Rowan	10	1	515	236	57.22
A D Nourse	8	0	301	208	37.62
P N F Mansell	3	0	98	90	32.66
R A McLean	5	0	138	67	27.60
G M Fullerton	6	0	149	60	24.83
J E Cheetham	9	0	219	54	24.33
C B van Ryneveld	9	0	217	83	24.11
J H B Waite	8	1	152	76	21.71
A M B Rowan	9	1	105	41	13.12
D J McGlew	4	0	50	40	12.50
G W A Chubb	9	3	63	15*	10.50
N B F Mann	7	0	36	14	5.14
C N McCarthy	9	6	13	5	4.33

Also batted during Tests:

W R Endean 31, 7; M G Melle 5, 17.

Test Match bowling averages:

	Overs	Mdns	Runs	Wkts	Ave
N B F Mann	155.2	62	264	10	26.40
G W C Chubb	237.2	63	577	21	27.47
A M B Rowan	241.3	48	619	18	34.44
C N McCarthy	177	31	83	1	83.00

Also bowled during Tests:

	Overs	Mdns	Runs	Wkts	Ave
P N F Mansell	4	0	11	0	-
M G Melle	13	6	17	4	4.25
A D Nourse	2	0	9	0	-
E A B Rowan	1.5	0	7	0	-

Tour batting averages - all matches:

	Inns	NO	Runs	HS	Ave
E A B Rowan	41	4	1,852	236	50.05
J E Cheetham	33	5	1,196	133*	42.71
D J McGlew	29	3	1,002	114*	38.53
J H B Waite	32	2	1,011	139	33.70
G M Fullerton	40	4	1,129	167	31.36
R A McLean	31	2	887	88	30.58
C B van Ryneveld	35	2	983	150	29.78
A D Nourse	28	2	673	208	25.88
A M B Rowan	22	4	432	98	24.00
P N F Mansell	27	4	504	90	21.91

W R Endean	32	3	527	72	18.17
H J Tayfield	22	4	304	68	16.88
N B F Mann	26	5	316	49*	15.04
G W A Chubb	27	8	190	24*	10.00
M G Melle	18	7	96	20	8.72
C N McCarthy	22	12	20	5	2.00

Tour bowling averages - all matches:

	Overs	Mdns	Runs	Wkts	Ave
M G Melle	358	79	1,014	50	20.98
C N McCarthy	617.1	140	1,414	59	23.96
G W A Chubb	809.4	211	2,005	76	26.38
N B F Mann	647.3	246	1,161	44	26.38
A M B Rowan	566	134	1,409	53	26.58
C B van Ryneveld	283	56	814	24	33.91
P N F Mansell	408.1	80	1,103	31	35.58
H J Tayfield	434.3	116	1,060	29	36.55
G M Fullerton	31	12	83	2	41.50

Also bowled during the tour:

J E Cheetham	1	0	3	0	-
D J McGlew	2	1	4	1	4.00
A D Nourse	2	0	9	0	-
E A B Rowan	4.5	0	19	0	-

Centuries recorded for South Africans during the tour:

E A B Rowan	(5) :	236	vs England (Headingley) (Fourth Test Match)
		202*	vs Northamptonshire (Northampton)
		147	vs Oxford University (The Parks)
		115*	vs Leicestershire (Grace Road, Leicester)
		104*	vs Cambridge University (Cambridge)
J E Cheetham	(3) :	133*	vs Combined Services (Portsmouth)
		127	vs Lancashire (Old Trafford)
		116*	vs Warwickshire (Edgbaston)
J H B Waite	(3) :	139	vs Combined Services (Portsmouth)
		128	vs Essex (Ilford)
		122	vs Lancashire (Old Trafford)
D J McGlew	(2) :	114*	vs Hampshire (Southampton)
		110	vs Glamorgan (Cardiff)
G M Fullerton	(1) :	167	vs Essex (Ilford)
R A McLean	(1) :	107	vs Ireland (Dublin)
A D Nourse	(1) :	208	vs England (Trent Bridge) (First Test Match)
C B van Ryneveld	(1) :	150	vs Yorkshire (Sheffield)

Fielding:

	Catches	*Stumpings*
W R Endean	22	4
P N F Mansell	21	
J H B Waite	15	5
C B van Ryneveld	19	
G M Fullerton	15	
E A B Rowan	15	
J E Cheetham	14	
R A McLean	13	
A D Nourse	11	
H J Tayfield	11	
M G Melle	10	
C N McCarthy	8	
N B F Mann	7	
G W A Chubb	6	
A M B Rowan	4	
D J McGlew	3	

A.D.Nourse

The Eleventh South African Team in the United Kingdom, 1955

The 1955 tourists were considered at the time to be probably the finest group of South African cricketers to visit these shores. Certainly they surpassed their predecessors in winning two Tests (at Old Trafford and Headingley) and in total they lost only four of their games (three of the Tests and the game with Worcestershire) out of the twenty-eight first-class matches played.

Captained by Jack Cheetham, who had toured England in 1951 with seven of the others, they were managed by K. G. Viljoen who had played on two previous tours to England (1935 and 1947).

While four batsman scored over 1,000 runs, Jackie McGlew scored 1,871 runs (av. 58.46) including six centuries, and Hugh Tayfield took a total of 143 wickets (av. 15.75), nearly twice as many as any of the other bowlers. The tourists were also much admired at all times for their excellent fielding.

(standing) H.J.Keith V.I.Smith T.L.Goddard P.L.Winslow P.S.Heine N.A.T.Adcock
C.A.R.Duckworth E.R.H.Fuller Mr.M.McLennan (Scorer)

(sitting) P.N.F.Mansell R.A.McLean W.R.Endean J.E.Cheetham (Captain)
Mr.K.G.Viljoen (Manager) D.J.McGlew H.J.Tayfield J.H.B.Waite A.R.A.Murray

Touring party (16):

* J E Cheetham (*Western Province*) (Captain)
Age 35. Right-handed batsman and fine fieldsman.

D J McGlew (*Natal*) (Vice-Captain)
Age 26. Right-handed batsman.

† J H B Waite (*Eastern Province*)
Age 25. Right-handed batsman and wicket-keeper.

R A McLean (*Natal*)
Age 24. Right-handed batsman and fine fieldsman.

P N F Mansell (*Rhodesia*)
Age 35. Right-arm leg-spin and googly bowler, right-handed batsman and brilliant slip fieldsman.

† W R Endean (*Transvaal*)
Age 31. Right-handed middle order batsman and wicket-keeper.

H J Tayfield (*Natal*)
Age 26. Right-handed batsman and right-arm off-break bowler.

T L Goddard (*Natal*)
Age 23. Left-handed opening batsman, left-arm fast and spin bowler and excellent fieldsman.

H J Keith (*Natal*)
Age 27. Left-handed batsman and left-arm slow bowler.

† C A R Duckworth (*Rhodesia*)
Age 22. Right-handed batsman and reserve wicket-keeper.

P L Winslow (*Transvaal*)
Age 26. Right-handed aggressive batsman.

P S Heine (*Orange Free State*)
Age 26. Right-arm fast-medium opening bowler and right-handed forceful batsman.

A R A Murray (*Eastern Province*)
Age 33. Right-handed batsman, right-arm fast-medium/stock bowler and excellent fieldsman.

E R H Fuller (*Western Province*)
Age 23. Right-handed batsman, right-arm fast-medium bowler and fine fielder.

V I Smith (*Natal*)
Age 30. Right-arm leg-spin bowler and right-handed batsman.

N A T Adcock (*Transvaal*)
Age 24. Right-arm fast bowler and right-handed late order batsman.

Manager: Mr. K G Viljoen

Scorer: Mr. M McLennan

Summary of all matches:

Played 31   Won 16   Lost 4   Drawn 11

Summary of first-class matches:

Played 28   Won 15   Lost 4   Drawn 9

Summary of Test Matches:

Played 5   Won 2   Lost 3   Drawn 0

First Match vs Worcestershire played at County Cricket Ground, New Road, Worcester on 7, 9 and 10 May. Worcestershire 260 (L Outschoorn 80, D Kenyon 58, R T D Perks 41, G Dews 39, H J Tayfield 5 for 93) and 209 (G Dews 52, J P Whitehead 51*, D Kenyon 32, H J Tayfield 5 for 81) beat South Africans 209 (T L Goddard 47, P L Winslow 37, J H B Waite 36, W R Endean 32, R Berry 5 for 60) and 143 (D J McGlew 46, T L Goddard 23, M J Horton 9 for 56) by 117 runs.

Second Match vs Derbyshire played at County Cricket Ground, Derby on 11, 12 and 13 May. Derbyshire 179 (A Hamer 47, J M Kelly 24, H J Tayfield 4 for 61) and 100 for 4 (J M Kelly 35*, H L Johnson 30*, N A T Adcock 3 for 20) drew with South Africans 113 (D J McGlew 23, J H B Waite 19, C Gladwin 3 for 26, H L Jackson 3 for 37, D C Morgan 3 for 40).

Third Match vs Nottinghamshire played at Trent Bridge, Nottingham on 14, 16 and 17 May. South Africans 272 (D J McGlew 88, W R Endean 78, J H B Waite 30, B Dooland 5 for 94, K Smales 3 for 55) and 54 for 0 (D J McGlew 24*, T L Goddard 24*) drew with Nottinghamshire 231 (R T Simpson 57, F W Stocks 54, C J Poole 25, A Jepson 23, H J Tayfield 5 for 95, V I Smith 5 for 70).

Fourth Match vs Cambridge University at Fenner's University Cricket Ground, Cambridge on 18, 19 and 20 May. South Africans 268 (D J McGlew 85, J H B Waite 78, W R Endean 24, J E Cheetham 23, S Singh 5 for 73) drew with Cambridge University 67 (R O'Brien 25, D R W Silk 15, H J Tayfield 4 for 31, V I Smith 3 for 9) and 154 for 8 (D R W Silk 54, G Goonesena 31, S Singh 20, J F Pretlove 19*, H J Tayfield 4 for 51, E R H Fuller 3 for 24).

Fifth Match vs M.C.C. at Lord's Cricket Ground, London on 21, 23 and 24 May. South Africans 185 for 9 dec (J E Cheetham 38, P L Winslow 25, H J Keith 21, W R Endean 20, H J Tayfield 20*, F J Titmus 2 for 27, T E Bailey 2 for 29) and 184 (R A McLean 85, J E Cheetham 29, J H B Waite 27, F J Titmus 8 for 43) beat M.C.C. 87 (D C S Compton 25, T E Bailey 19, J M Parks 15, V I Smith 3 for 21) and 189 (T W Graveney 34, J M Parks 30, P J Loader 29*, V I Smith 4 for 76) by 93 runs.

Sixth Match vs Oxford University played at Christ Church Cricket Ground, Iffley Road, Oxford on 25, 26 and 27 May. South Africans 434 for 8 dec (T L Goddard 121, R A McLean 67, D J McGlew 66, P L Winslow 60, A R A Murray 36*, J B Philips 3 for 87, D C P R Jowett 3 for 101) beat Cambridge University 90 (J P Fellows-Smith 28, A C Walton 22, P S Heine 5 for 31, V I Smith 3 for 13) and 207 (J P Fellows-Smith 40, M J K Smith 33, G P S Delisle 32, A C Walton 21, H J Keith 4 for 60) by an innings and 137 runs.

Seventh Match vs Glamorgan played at Arms Park, Cardiff on 28, 30 and 31 May. Glamorgan 234 (W G A Parkhouse 62, B Hedges 58, A J Watkins 37, W E Jones 27, E R H Fuller 4 for 46) and 73 for 4 (W G A Parkhouse 29*, E R H Fuller 3 for 27) drew with South Africans 156 (D J McGlew 53, P L Winslow 36, T L Goddard 26, J E McConnon 6 for 49).

J. H. B. WAITE

Eighth Match vs Essex played at Castle Park, Colchester on 1, 2 and 3 June. South Africans 503 for 4 dec (D J McGlew 118, R A McLean 101*, P N F Mansell 99, H J Keith 94, W R Endean 64, W T Greensmith 1 for 70) drew with Essex 350 (D J Insole 129, T E Bailey 107, R Horsfall 42, R Smith 24, V I Smith 3 for 138) and 89 for 5 (D J Insole 22*, T C Dodds 21, A R A Murray 1 for 14).

Ninth Match vs Lancashire played at Old Trafford, Manchester on 4, 6 and 7 June. South Africans 154 (P L Winslow 61, R A McLean 35, A Wharton 4 for 26) and 232 for 4 (P N F Mansell 79, W R Endean 51, J E Cheetham 45, R A McLean 34*, F Goodwin 3 for 47) drew with Lancashire 201 (K Grieves 77, J T Ikin 35, J Jordan 29, H J Tayfield 4 for 27, T L Goddard 3 for 41, N A T Adcock 3 for 53).

Tenth Match vs England (First Test Match) played at Trent Bridge, Nottingham on 9, 10, 11 and 13 June.

England

D Kenyon	lbw b Goddard	87
T W Graveney	c Waite b Adcock	42
* P B H May	c McGlew b Smith	83
D C S Compton	lbw b Adcock	27
K F Barrington	c Waite b Fuller	0
T E Bailey	lbw b Goddard	49
† T G Evans	c Goddard b Fuller	12
J H Wardle	lbw b Tayfield	2
F H Tyson	c McLean b Tayfield	0
J B Statham	c Waite b Fuller	20
R Appleyard	not out	0
Extras	b 6 lb 6	12
Total		**334**

Fall 1st inns: 1/91 2/166 3/228 4/233 5/252 6/285 7/294 8/298 9/334 10/334

Bowling	1st inns			
Adcock	36	9	74	2
Goddard	36.4	18	61	2
Fuller	29	5	59	3
Tayfield	37	11	66	2
Smith	30	9	62	1

South Africa

D J McGlew	c Evans b Wardle	68	c May b Bailey	51
T L Goddard	lbw b Statham	12	run out	32
† J H B Waite	run out	0	c Compton b Tyson	3
W R Endean	lbw b Tyson	0	c Graveney b Bailey	6
R A McLean	b Tyson	13	c Graveney b Tyson	16
P L Winslow	c May b Appleyard	2	b Tyson	3
* J E Cheetham	c Graveney b Wardle	54	b Tyson	5
H J Tayfield	c Bailey b Appleyard	11	b Tyson	0
E R H Fuller	b Wardle	15	c Evans b Wardle	6
V I Smith	c May b Wardle	0	not out	2
N A T Adcock	not out	1	b Tyson	6
Extras	b 1 lb 2 nb 2	5	b 8 lb 4 w 4 nb 2	18
Total		**181**		**148**

Fall 1st inns: 1/15 2/17 3/19 4/35 5/55 6/149 7/156 8/174 9/180 10/181
Fall 2nd inns: 1/73 2/83 3/101 4/108 5/131 6/132 7/132 8/135 9/141 10/148

Bowling	1st inns				2nd inns			
Statham	25	5	47	1	10	4	16	0
Tyson	24	5	51	2	21.3	7	28	6
Bailey	5	2	8	0	17	8	21	2
Appleyard	28	9	46	2	19	4	32	0
Wardle	32	23	24	4	29	17	33	1

Umpires: F S Lee and T J Bartley

England beat South Africa by an innings and 5 runs.

Eleventh Match vs Somerset played at County Cricket Ground, Taunton on 15, 16 and 17 June. South Africans 270 for 9 dec (J E Cheetham 87*, H J Keith 49, H J Tayfield 44, J H B Waite 42, Yawar Saeed 5 for 61, B Lobb 4 for 72) beat Somerset 68 (Yawar Saeed 24, J Lawrence 14, P S Heine 3 for 33) and 170 (Yawar Saeed 43, G G Tordoff 41*, P S Heine 7 for 58, H J Tayfield 2 for 32) by an innings and 32 runs.

Twelfth Match vs Sussex played at County Cricket Ground, Hove on 18, 20 and 21 June. South Africans 308 for 7 dec (R A McLean 129, D J McGlew 69, W R Endean 38*, A E James 3 for 95) and 143 for 1 (W R Endean 73*, J H B Waite 53*) beat Sussex 352 for 6 dec (J M Parks 118, D S Sheppard 104, K G Suttle 44*, E R H Fuller 3 for 86) and 97 (J M Parks 45, R T Webb 17, E R H Fuller 7 for 61) by 9 wickets.

D. J. McGLEW

V.I.Smith

Thirteenth Match vs England (Second Test Match) played at Lord's Cricket Ground, London on 23, 24, 25 and 27 June.

England

D Kenyon	b Adcock	1	lbw b Goddard	2
T W Graveney	c Waite b Heine	15	c Heine b Goddard	60
* P B H May	c Tayfield b Heine	0	hit wicket b Heine	112
D C S Compton	c Keith b Heine	20	c Mansell b Goddard	69
K F Barrington	b Heine	34	c McLean b Tayfield	18
T E Bailey	lbw b Goddard	13	c Adcock b Tayfield	22
† T G Evans	c Waite b Heine	20	c & b Tayfield	14
F J Titmus	lbw b Goddard	4	c Waite b Adcock	16
J H Wardle	c Tayfield b Goddard	20	c Heine b Tayfield	4
J B Statham	c McLean b Goddard	0	b Tayfield	11
F S Trueman	not out	2	not out	6
Extras	b 2 lb 2	4	b 15 lb 2 nb 2	19
Total		**133**		**353**

Fall 1st ins: 1/7 2/8 3/30 4/45 5/82 6/98 7/111 8/111 9/111 10/133
Fall 2nd inns: 1/9 2/141 3/237 4/277 5/285 6/302 7/306 8/336 9/336 10/353

Bowling	1st inns				2nd inns			
Heine	25	7	60	5	29	5	87	1
Adcock	8	3	10	1	25	5	64	1
Goddard	21.2	8	59	4	55	23	96	3
Tayfield					38.5	12	80	5
Mansell					2	0	7	0

South Africa

D J McGlew	c Evans b Statham	0	lbw b Statham	0
T L Goddard	c Evans b Trueman	0	c Evans b Statham	10
* J E Cheetham	lbw b Bailey	13	retired hurt	3
W R Endean	lbw b Wardle	48	c Evans b Statham	28
R A McLean	b Statham	142	b Statham	8
† J H B Waite	c Evans b Trueman	8	lbw b Statham	9
H J Keith	c Titmus b Wardle	57	c Graveney b Statham	5
P N F Mansell	c Graveney b Wardle	2	c Kenyon b Wardle	16
H J Tayfield	b Titmus	21	c Evans b Statham	3
P S Heine	st Evans b Wardle	2	c Kenyon b Wardle	14
N A T Adcock	not out	0	not out	0
Extras	b 6 lb 1 nb 4	11	b 9 lb 5 nb 1	15
Total		**304**		**111**

Fall 1st inns: 1/0 2/7 3/51 4/101 5/138 6/247 7/259 8/302 9/304 10/304
Fall 2nd inns: 1/0 2/17 3/40 4/54 5/63 6/75 7/78 8/111 9/111 10/111

Bowling	1st inns				2nd inns			
Statham	27	9	49	2	29	12	39	7
Trueman	16	2	73	2	19	2	39	0
Bailey	16	2	56	1				
Wardle	29	10	65	4	9.4	4	18	2
Titmus	14	3	50	1				

Umpires: F Chester and L H Gray

England beat South Africa by 71 runs.

Fourteenth Match vs Northamptonshire played at County Cricket Ground, Wantage Road, Northampton on 29, 30 June and 1 July. South Africans 409 (C A R Duckworth 158, P N F Mansell 88, T L Goddard 70, G E Tribe 5 for 81) and 80 for 1 dec (A R A Murray 46, C A R Duckworth 30*) drew with Northamptonshire 271 (R Subba Row 70, D Brookes 64, D W Barrick 42, T L Goddard 4 for 20) and 133 for 4 (R Subba Row 59, G E Tribe 24*, N A T Adcock 2 for 30).

Fifteenth Match vs Yorkshire played at Bramall Lane, Sheffield on 2, 4 and 5 July. South Africans 209 (D J McGlew 51, T L Goddard 42, R A McLean 41, R Illingworth 4 for 21, J H Wardle 4 for 72) and 360 (H J Tayfield 65, P L Winslow 51, D J McGlew 47, J H B Waite 39, E R H Fuller 38, C A R Duckworth 35, J H Wardle 5 for 105, D B Close 3 for 67) beat Yorkshire 198 (W Watson 51, F A Lowson 50, J V Wilson 23, H J Tayfield 4 for 94, P S Heine 3 for 60) and 178 (J H Wardle 74, D B Close 29, H J Tayfield 4 for 58, T L Goddard 3 for 32) by 193 runs.

H. J. TAYFIELD

R. A. McLEAN

Sixteenth Match vs England (Third Test Match) played at Old Trafford, Manchester on 7, 8, 9, 11 and 12 July.

England

D Kenyon	c Waite b Heine	5	c Waite b Heine		1
T W Graveney	c Tayfield b Adcock	0	b Adcock		1
* P B H May	c Mansell b Goddard	34	b Mansell		117
D C S Compton	c Waite b Adcock	158	c Mansell b Heine		71
M C Cowdrey	c Mansell b Tayfield	1	c Goddard b Heine		50
T E Bailey	c Waite b Adcock	44	not out		38
F J Titmus	lbw b Heine	0	c Mansell b Adcock		19
† T G Evans	c Keith b Heine	0	c McLean b Tayfield		36
G A R Lock	not out	19	c McGlew b Adcock		17
F H Tyson	b Goddard	2	b Heine		8
A V Bedser	lbw b Goddard	1	c Waite b Heine		3
Extras	b 13 lb 6 w 1	20	b 13 lb 5 w 2		20
Total		**284**			**381**

Fall 1st inns: 1/2 2/22 3/70 4/75 5/219 6/234 7/242 8/271 9/280 10/284
Fall 2nd inns: 1/2 2/2 3/126 4/234 5/270 6/274 7/304 8/325 9/333 10/381

Bowling	1st inns				2nd inns			
Heine	24	4	71	3	32	8	86	5
Adcock	25	5	52	3	28	12	48	3
Tayfield	35	15	57	1	51.5	21	102	1
Goddard	27	10	52	3	47	21	92	0
Mansell	6	2	13	0	15	3	33	1
Keith	6	1	19	0				

South Africa

* D J McGlew	not out	104	b Tyson		48
T L Goddard	c Graveney b Tyson	62	c May b Bedser		8
H J Keith	c Graveney b Bailey	38	b Bedser		0
P N F Mansell	lbw b Lock	7	lbw b Tyson		4
W R Endean	c Evans b Lock	5	c Titmus b Lock		2
R A McLean	b Tyson	3	run out		50
† J H B Waite	c Kenyon b Bedser	113	not out		10
P L Winslow	lbw b Bedser	108	b Tyson		16
H J Tayfield	b Tyson	28	not out		1
P S Heine	not out	22			
Extras	b 15 lb 12 w 1 nb 3	31	b 2 lb 2 w 1 nb 1		6
Total	**(8 wickets, declared)**	**521**	**(7 wickets)**		**145**

N A T Adcock did not bat.
Fall 1st inns: 1/147 2/171 3/179 4/182 5/245 6/416 7/457 8/494
Fall 2nd inns: 1/18 2/23 3/95 4/112 5/129 6/132 7/135

Bowling	1st inns				2nd inns			
Bedser	31	2	92	2	10	1	61	2
Tyson	44	5	124	3	13.3	2	55	3
Bailey	37	8	102	1				
Lock	64	24	121	2	7	2	23	1
Titmus	19	7	51	0				

Umpires: F S Lee and D Davies

South Africa beat England by 3 wickets.

Seventeenth Match vs Surrey played at Kennington Oval, London on 16, 18 and 19 July. South Africans 244 (R A McLean 151, W R Endean 32, P J Loader 4 for 46, A V Bedser 3 for 48) and 170 (J H B Waite 41, J C Laker 5 for 56, P J Loader 3 for 58) beat Surrey 140 (P B H May 60, B Constable 34, H J Tayfield 5 for 22) and 192 (T H Clark 58, P B H May 43, K F Barrington 34, H J Tayfield 8 for 76) by 82 runs.

Eighteenth Match vs England (Fourth Test Match) played at Headingley Cricket Ground, Leeds on 21, 22, 23, 25 and 26 July.

South Africa

* D J McGlew	c McIntyre b Loader	23	c May b Wardle	133
T L Goddard	b Loader	9	c McIntyre b Wardle	74
H J Keith	c McIntyre b Loader	0	b Wardle	73
P N F Mansell	b Bailey	0	lbw b Bailey	1
R A McLean	c May b Loader	41	c Lowson b Wardle	3
† J H B Waite	run out	2	c McIntyre b Lock	32
P L Winslow	b Statham	8	c Lock b Statham	19
W R Endean	b Statham	41	not out	116
H J Tayfield	not out	25	lbw b Statham	14
P S Heine	b Lock	14	b Bailey	10
N A T Adcock	lbw b Statham	0	b Bailey	6
Extras	lb 4 nb 4	8	b 8 lb 6 w 1 nb 4	19
Total		**171**		**500**

Fall 1st inns: 1/33 2/33 3/34 4/34 5/38 6/63 7/98 8/154 9/170 10/171
Fall 2nd inns: 1/176 2/265 3/269 4/303 5/311 6/387 7/400 8/439 9/468 10/500

Bowling		1st inns				2nd inns		
Statham	20.2	7	35	3	40	10	129	2
Loader	19	7	52	4	29	9	67	0
Bailey	16	7	23	1	40.5	11	97	3
Wardle	9	1	33	0	57	22	100	4
Lock	6	1	20	1	32	13	88	1

England

T E Bailey	lbw b Heine	9	c & b Tayfield	8
F A Lowson	lbw b Goddard	5	b Goddard	0
* P B H May	b Tayfield	47	lbw b Tayfield	97
G A R Lock	lbw b Goddard	17	c Mansell b Goddard	7
D C S Compton	c Mansell b Tayfield	61	c Waite b Goddard	26
T W Graveney	lbw b Heine	10	c McLean b Tayfield	36
D J Insole	b Heine	3	c Keith b Goddard	47
† A J McIntyre	lbw b Heine	3	c Heine b Tayfield	4
J H Wardle	c Goddard b Tayfield	24	c Heine b Tayfield	21
J B Statham	b Tayfield	4	hit wicket b Goddard	3
P J Loader	not out	0	not out	0
Extras	b 5 lb 2 w 1	8	b 1 lb 6	7
Total		**191**		**256**

Fall 1st inns: 1/15 2/23 3/53 4/117 5/152 6/152 7/161 8/186 9/191 10/191
Fall 2nd inns: 1/3 2/59 3/160 4/204 5/210 6/215 7/239 8/246 9/256 10/256

Bowling		1st inns				2nd inns		
Heine	29.5	11	70	4	14	2	33	0
Adcock	4	3	4	0				
Goddard	25	12	39	2	62	37	69	5
Tayfield	31	14	70	4	47.1	15	94	5
Mansell					19	2	53	0

Umpires: F Chester and T J Bartley

South Africa beat England by 224 runs.

Nineteenth Match vs ‡ Minor Counties played at Stoke-on-Trent on 27 and 28 July. Minor Counties 233 (K Taylor 57, D J Smith 39, H D Fairclough 38, D E V Padgett 33, E Leadbeater 30*, V I Smith 5 for 71, H J Tayfield 4 for 71) and 180 for 8 (D E V Padgett 59, K Taylor 32, V I Smith 4 for 51) drew with South Africans 302 (A R A Murray 100, W R Endean 66, P L Winslow 40, J H B Waite 37, F Taylor 4 for 88).

Twentieth Match vs Glamorgan played at St. Helen's Cricket Ground, Swansea on 30 July, 1 and 2 August. South Africans 225 (J E Cheetham 46, D J McGlew 36, C A R Duckworth 32, P N F Mansell 29, H D Davies 5 for 32) and 230 (P N F Mansell 61, J H B Waite 31, A J Watkins 4 for 73, J S Pressdee 4 for 46) beat Glamorgan 64 (P B Clift 16, P S Heine 5 for 26) and 165 (W E Jones 50, A J Watkins 23, H J Tayfield 6 for 35) by 226 runs.

Twenty-First Match vs Warwickshire played at Edgbaston Cricket Ground, Birmingham on 3, 4 and 5 August. South Africans 382 for 9 dec (W R Endean 98, D J McGlew 84, T L Goddard 71, R A McLean 64, W E Hollies 4 for 100, R G Thompson 3 for 67) and 8 for 0 beat Warwickshire 188 (F C Gardner 58, H E Dollery 33, N F Horner 26, E R H Fuller 7 for 60) and 201 (A Townsend 36, A V Wolton 33, R T Spooner 28, P N F Mansell 4 for 52, V I Smith 3 for 39) by 10 wickets.

Twenty-Second Match vs Gloucestershire played at College Ground, Cheltenham on 6, 8 and 9 August. Gloucestershire 184 (C A Milton 58, J F Crapp 28, D M Young 26, J B Mortimore 26*, V I Smith 5 for 75, A R A Murray 3 for 22) and 226 (T W Graveney 98, J F Crapp 46, E R H Fuller 4 for 60, T L Goddard 3 for 33) drew with South Africans 197 (T L Goddard 93, A R A Murray 51, W R Endean 28, B D Wells 4 for 39, J B Mortimore 4 for 42) and 108 for 3 (R A McLean 50*).

Twenty-Third Match vs Leicestershire played at County Cricket Ground, Grace Road, Leicester on 10, 11 and 12 August. South Africans 463 for 6 dec (D J McGlew 161, H J Keith 100, T L Goddard 61, P N F Mansell 53*, W R Endean 41, V S Munden 3 for 83) beat Leicestershire 208 (C H Palmer 68, M J K Smith 36, R A Diment 31, H J Tayfield 5 for 56) and 138 (G Lester 36, M J K Smith 28, P N F Mansell 6 for 52, H J Tayfield 3 for 28) by an innings and 117 runs.

Twenty-Fourth Match vs England (Fifth Test Match) played at Kennington Oval, London on 13, 15, 16 and 17 August.

England

J T Ikin	c Waite b Heine	17	c Goddard b Heine	0
D B Close	c Mansell b Goddard	32	b Goddard	15
* P B H May	c Goddard b Fuller	3	not out	89
D C S Compton	c Waite b Goddard	30	c Waite b Fuller	30
W Watson	c Mansell b Tayfield	25	b Fuller	3
T W Graveney	c Fuller b Goddard	13	b Tayfield	42
T E Bailey	c Heine b Tayfield	0	lbw b Tayfield	1
† R T Spooner	b Tayfield	0	b Tayfield	0
J C Laker	c & b Goddard	2	b Tayfield	12
G A R Lock	c McLean b Goddard	18	lbw b Heine	1
J B Statham	not out	4	lbw b Tayfield	0
Extras	b 2 lb 5	7	b 4 lb 6 nb 1	11
Total		**151**		**204**

Fall 1st inns: 1/51 2/59 3/69 4/105 5/117 6/117 7/118 8/123 9/130 10/151
Fall 2nd inns: 1/5 2/30 3/95 4/157 5/165 6/166 7/170 8/188 9197/ 10/204

Bowling		1st inns				2nd inns	
Heine	21	3	43	1	25	6	44	2
Goddard	22.4	9	31	5	19	10	29	1
Fuller	27	11	31	1	20	3	36	2
Tayfield	19	7	39	3	53.4	29	60	5
Mansell					6	0	24	0

South Africa

D J McGlew	c Spooner b Statham	30	lbw b Lock	19
T L Goddard	lbw b Bailey	8	c Graveney b Lock	20
H J Keith	b Lock	5	c May b Lock	0
W R Endean	c Ikin b Lock	0	lbw b Laker	0
R A McLean	b Lock	1	lbw b Laker	0
† J H B Waite	c Lock b Laker	28	b Laker	60
* J E Cheetham	not out	12	lbw b Laker	9
P N F Mansell	lbw b Laker	6	c Watson b Lock	9
H J Tayfield	b Statham	4	not out	10
E R H Fuller	c Spooner b Lock	5	run out	16
P S Heine	run out	5	c Graveney b Laker	7
Extras	lb 7 nb 1	8	lb 1	1
Total		**112**		**151**

Fall 1st inns: 1/22 2/29 3/31 4/33 5/77 6/77 7/86 8/91 9/98 10/112
Fall 2nd inns: 1/28 2/28 3/29 4/33 5/59 6/88 7/118 8/118 9/144 10/151

Bowling		1st inns				2nd inns	
Statham	15	3	31	2	11	4	17	0
Bailey	5	1	6	1	6	1	15	0
Lock	22	11	39	4	33	14	62	4
Laker	23	13	28	2	37.4	18	56	5

Umpires: D Davies and T J Bartley

England beat South Africa by 92 runs.

Twenty-Fifth Match vs Hampshire played at County Cricket Ground, Northlands Road, Southampton on 20, 22 and 23 August. South Africans 259 (D J McGlew 81, R A McLean 75, P S Heine 58, D Shackleton 4 for 66, M D Burden 4 for 68) and 302 for 7 dec (P L Winslow 87, T L Goddard 77, P S Heine 54, W R Endean 46, P J Sainsbury 3 for 111) beat Hampshire 166 (D Shackleton 50, L Harrison 43, R E Marshall 37, H J Tayfield 6 for 86) and 120 (R E Marshall 38, H M Barnard 29, H J Tayfield 8 for 40) by 275 runs.

Twenty-Sixth Match vs Kent played at St. Lawrence Cricket Ground, Canterbury on 24, 25 and 26 August. South Africans 467 for 8 dec (D J McGlew 161, J E Cheetham 112, P L Winslow 57, J H B Waite 41, A Dixon 4 for 122) and 25 for 2 beat Kent 175 (R C Wilson 70, P N F Mansell 4 for 40, N A T Adcock 3 for 39) and 314 (P Hearn 79, A E Fagg 64, A H Phebey 48, J Pettiford 35, H J Tayfield 5 for 76, A R A Murray 3 for 50) by 8 wickets.

Twenty-Seventh Match vs Middlesex played at Lord's Cricket Ground, London on 27, 29 and 30 August. South Africans 254 (W R Endean 75, T L Goddard 56, P Heine 30, R A McLean 26, F J Titmus 6 for 63, J A Young 3 for 62) and 187 (R A McLean 58, W R Endean 39, F J Titmus 5 for 54, J A Young 3 for 62) beat Middlesex 108 (J D B Robertson 44, P S Heine 7 for 60) and 98 (W J Edrich 25, V I Smith 5 for 27) by 235 runs.

Twenty-Eighth Match vs An England XI played at Central Cricket Ground, Hastings on 31 August, 1 and 2 September. South Africans 165 (H J Keith 60, R A McLean 30, W Wooller 4 for 38) and 287 for 9 dec (R A McLean 79, D J McGlew 47, J E Cheetham 41*, T L Goddard 32, J B Statham 4 for 43) drew with An England XI 218 (R T Spooner 50, D M Young 45, W Wooller 31, H J Tayfield 4 for 68) and 77 for 7 (D M Young 26, A R A Murray 3 for 19).

Twenty-Ninth Match vs ‡ Durham played at Ashbrooke Cricket Ground, Sunderland on 3 and 5 September. South Africans 543 (P N F Mansell 148, P L Winslow 133, H J Keith 65, W R Endean 61, A R A Murray 36, C A R Duckworth 33, K Williamson 4 for 99) beat Durham 111 (D W Hardy 45, H D Bell 28, R Aspinall 28, V I Smith 5 for 29, A R A Murray 3 for 36) and 108 (D W Hardy 23, V I Smith 5 for 44) by an innings and 324 runs.

Thirtieth Match vs T N Pearce's XI played at North Marine Drive, Scarborough on 7, 8 and 9 September. South Africans 354 (W R Endean 138*, J E Cheetham 52, T L Goddard 29, D B Close 3 for 94) and 211 for 6 (D J McGlew 75, T L Goddard 44, J H B Waite 36*, D B Close 3 for 58) beat T N Pearce's XI 236 (W J Edrich 42, T W Graveney 37, J V Wilson 34, D B Close 33, T L Goddard 5 for 30, A R A Murray 3 for 53) and 328 for 9 dec (T W Graveney 159, D B Close 45, T E Bailey 37, J H Wardle 28, D C S Compton 27, H J Tayfield 4 for 93) by 4 wickets.

Thirty-First Match vs ‡ Cumberland and Westmorland played at Carlisle on 10 September. South Africans 332 (R A McLean 83, H J Keith 63) drew with Cumberland and Westmorland 104 for 8 (J Dennis 44).

Test Match batting averages:

	Inns	NO	Runs	HS	Ave
D J McGlew	10	1	476	133	52.88
J H B Waite	10	1	265	113	29.44
R A McLean	10	0	277	142	27.70
W R Endean	10	1	246	116*	27.33
P L Winslow	6	0	156	108	26.00
J E Cheetham	6	2	96	54	24.00
T L Goddard	10	0	235	74	23.50
H J Keith	8	0	178	73	22.25
H J Tayfield	10	3	117	28	16.71
P S Heine	7	1	74	22*	12.33
E R H Fuller	4	0	42	16	10.50
P N F Mansell	8	0	45	16	5.62
N A T Adcock	6	3	13	6	4.33

Test Match bowling averages:

	Overs	Mdns	Runs	Wkts	Ave
E R H Fuller	76	19	126	6	21.00
T L Goddard	315.4	148	528	25	21.12
H J Tayfield	313.3	124	568	26	21.84
P S Heine	199.5	46	494	21	23.52
N A T Adcock	126	37	252	10	25.20

Also bowled during Tests:

H J Keith	6	1	19	0	-
V I Smith	30	9	62	1	62.00
P N F Mansell	48	7	130	1	130.00

Tour batting averages - all matches:

	Inns	NO	Runs	HS	Ave
D J McGlew	34	2	1,871	161	58.46
R A McLean	41	3	1,448	151	38.10
J E Cheetham	30	8	765	112	34.77
W R Endean	40	4	1,242	138*	34.50
T L Goddard	39	1	1,163	121	30.60
J H B Waite	39	3	930	113	25.83
P N F Mansell	27	3	611	99	25.45
H J Keith	29	1	682	100	24.35
C A R Duckworth	19	4	362	158	24.13
P L Winslow	34	2	758	108	23.68
P S Heine	25	6	361	58	19.00
A R A Murray	20	3	275	51	16.17
H J Tayfield	35	9	392	65	15.07
E R H Fuller	23	2	223	38	10.61
V I Smith	15	8	44	10	6.28
N A T Adcock	11	5	18	6	3.00

Tour bowling averages - all matches:

	Overs	Mdns	Runs	Wkts	Ave
H J Tayfield	1,170.5	461	2,253	143	15.75
A R A Murray	321.4	150	575	31	18.54
E R H Fuller	486.1	145	956	49	19.51
P S Heine	653.1	175	1,470	74	19.86
V I Smith	383.3	111	1,030	49	21.02
T L Goddard	810	352	1,311	60	21.85
P N F Mansell	336.4	95	771	29	26.58
N A T Adcock	364	84	914	34	26.88
H J Keith	138	60	276	8	34.50

Also bowled during the tour:

J E Cheetham	1	0	3	0	-
W R Endean	1	0	1	1	1.00
D J McGlew	1	0	4	0	-
R A McLean	2	0	2	0	-

Centuries recorded for South Africans during the tour:

D J McGlew	(5) :	161	vs Kent (Canterbury)
		161	vs Leicestershire (Grace Road, Leicester)
		133	vs England (Headingley) (Fourth Test Match)
		118	vs Essex (Colchester)
		104*	vs England (Old Trafford) (Third Test Match)
R A McLean	(4) :	151	vs Surrey (The Oval)
		142	vs England (Lord's) (Second Test Match)
		129	vs Sussex (Hove)
		101*	vs Essex (Colchester)
W R Endean	(2) :	138*	vs T N Pearce's XI (Scarborough)
		116*	vs England (Headingley) (Fourth Test Match)
P L Winslow	(2) :	133	vs Durham (Sunderland)
		108	vs England (Old Trafford) (Third Test Match)
J E Cheetham	(1) :	112	vs Kent (Canterbury)
C A R Duckworth	(1) :	158	vs Northamptonshire (Northampton)
T L Goddard	(1) :	121	vs Oxford University (Christ Church, Oxford)
H J Keith	(1) :	100	vs Leicestershire (Grace Road, Leicester)
P N F Mansell	(1) :	148	vs Durham (Sunderland)
A R A Murray	(1) :	100	vs Minor Counties (Stoke-on-Trent)
J H B Waite	(1) :	113	vs England (Old Trafford) (Third Test Match)

Fielding:

	Catches	Stumpings
J H B Waite	55	10
P N F Mansell	27	
C A R Duckworth	16	5
T L Goddard	21	
H J Tayfield	21	
R A McLean	18	
H J Keith	17	
W R Endean	16	
P L Winslow	15	
P S Heine	14	
J E Cheetham	13	
E R H Fuller	11	
A R A Murray	8	
N A T Adcock	6	
D J McGlew	4	
V I Smith	2	

The Twelfth South African Team in the United Kingdom, 1960

Managed by Dudley Nourse who had toured England on three previous occasions (1935, 1947 and 1951) the tourists brought seven of the 1955 side including Jackie McGlew who was now the captain. In addition two other players had good experience of England, Syd O'Linn (Kent) and John Fellows-Smith (Oxford University and Northamptonshire).

The tourists were to experience many problems and proved disappointing despite winning fourteen of their thirty first-class matches and losing only five. Faced firstly with the attentions of anti-apartheid demonstrators, the Test series was soon lost as England won the first three matches — McGlew in fact lost the toss on all five occasions that the England captain, M.C. Cowdrey, spun the coin !

They then became embroiled in a controversy regarding the legitimacy of the bowling action of Geoff Griffin who in the match against the M.C.C. at Lord's in May became the first overseas tourist to be no-balled for throwing. In the end he only played in two Test Matches and sixteen other matches taking a total of 26 wickets. However four batsman made over a 1,000 runs and both Tayfield and Adcock took over 100 wickets each.

A far better team than their record suggests, they were admired for their impeccable behaviour on and off the field.

(back row) **J.E.Pothecary H.J.Tayfield A.H.McKinnon P.R.Carlstein Mr.M.McLennan** (Scorer) **J.P.Fellows-Smith N.A.T.Adcock C.A.R.Duckworth A.J.Pithey S.O'Linn**

(front row) **G.M.Griffin R.A.McLean D.J.McGlew** (Captain) **Mr.A.D.Nourse** (Manager) **T.L.Goddard J.H.B.Waite C.Wesley**

Touring party (15):

* D J McGlew (*Natal*) (Captain)
Age 31. Right-handed batsman.

T L Goddard (*Natal*) (Vice-Captain)
Age 28. Left-handed opening batsman, left-arm fast and spin bowler and excellent fieldsman.

† J H B Waite (*Eastern Province*)
Age 30. Right-handed batsman and wicket-keeper.

R A McLean (*Natal*)
Age 29. Right-handed batsman and fine fieldsman.

H J Tayfield (*Natal*)
Age 32. Right-handed batsman and right-arm off-break bowler.

† C A R Duckworth (*Rhodesia*)
Age 27. Right-handed batsman and reserve wicket-keeper.

N A T Adcock (*Transvaal*)
Age 29. Right-arm fast bowler and right-handed late order batsman.

S O'Linn (*Transvaal/Kent*)
Age 33. Left-handed batsman and reserve wicket-keeper.

J P Fellows-Smith (*Transvaal/Oxford University/Northamptonshire*)
Age 28. Aggressive right-handed batsman and right-arm medium pace bowler.

P R Carlstein (*Transvaal*)
Age 21. Right-handed batsman and fine fielder.

A J Pithey (*Rhodesia*)
Age 26. Right-handed opening batsman.

C Wesley (*Natal*)
Age 22. Aggressive left-handed batsman and fine outfielder.

G M Griffin (*Natal*)
Age 20. Useful right-handed batsman and right-arm fast bowler.

J E Pothecary (*Western Province*)
Age 26. Right-handed batsman and right-arm medium pace bowler.

A H McKinnon (*Eastern Province*)
Age 28. Aggressive right-handed batsman and left-arm slow bowler.

Manager: Mr. A D Nourse

Scorer: Mr. M McLennan

Summary of all matches:

Played 31   Won 15   Lost 5   Drawn 11   Abandoned 1

Summary of first-class matches:

Played 30   Won 14   Lost 5   Drawn 11   Abandoned 1

Summary of Test Matches:

Played 5   Lost 3   Drawn 2

First Match vs ‡ The Duke of Norfolk's XI played at Arundel Castle on 30 April. South Africans 224 for 5 (D J McGlew 72, R A McLean 54) beat The Duke of Norfolk's XI 220 for 8 dec (F J Titmus 56*, H J Tayfield 5 for 102) by 5 wickets.

Second Match vs Worcestershire played at County Cricket Ground, New Road, Worcester on 4, 5 and 6 May. South Africans 365 for 6 dec (R A McLean 207, A J Pithey 76, S O'Linn 33, J A Flavell 3 for 78) and 144 for 1 dec (D J McGlew 63*, T L Goddard 63) beat Worcestershire 235 (D W Richardson 72, M J Horton 43, L J Coldwell 28*, J E Pothecary 4 for 55, H J Tayfield 3 for 59) and 141 (M J Horton 49, D W Richardson 33, A H McKinnon 7 for 42) by 133 runs.

Third Match vs Derbyshire played at County Cricket Ground, Derby on 7, 9 and 10 May. South Africans 343 for 8 dec (A J Pithey 96, D J McGlew 93, S O'Linn 73, H L Jackson 4 for 69) beat Derbyshire 108 (G O Dawkes 29, N A T Adcock 4 for 30, G M Griffin 3 for 17) and 211 (I W Hall 67, H L Johnson 44, N A T Adcock 6 for 44, H J Tayfield 2 for 40) by an innings and 24 runs.

Fourth Match vs Oxford University at The University Parks, Oxford on 11, 12 and 13 May. Oxford University 77 for 4 (J Burki 32* G M Griffin 2 for 21) drew with South Africans.

Fifth Match vs Essex played at Valentine's Park, Ilford on 14, 16 and 17 May. South Africans 287 (J P Fellows-Smith 109, P R Carlstein 36, S O'Linn 29, T L Goddard 28, H J Tayfield 26, T E Bailey 7 for 81) and 86 for 4 (C Wesley 27*, P R Carlstein 25*, T E Bailey 2 for 19) beat Essex 98 (J Milner 29, H J Tayfield 5 for 43, N A T Adcock 3 for 15) and 274 (D J Insole 105, G J Smith 50, W T Greensmith 31*, N A T Adcock 4 for 30, T L Goddard 3 for 10) by 6 wickets.

Sixth Match vs Cambridge University played at Fenner's University Cricket Ground, Cambridge on 18, 19 and 20 May. South Africans 145 (J H B Waite 43*, S O'Linn 37, C Wesley 29, J B Brodie 5 for 47) and 128 for 3 (D J McGlew 54*, R A McLean 40, P R Carlstein 26*) beat Cambridge University 192 (R M Prideaux 64, A R Lewis 55, C B Howland 35, J E Pothecary 4 for 79, N A T Adcock 3 for 35) and 80 (R M Prideaux 30, N A T Adcock 6 for 26, A H McKinnon 3 for 12) by 7 wickets.

Seventh Match vs M.C.C. played at Lord's Cricket Ground, London on 21, 23 and 24 May. M.C.C. 208 (P H Walker 57, M C Cowdrey 37, J H Edrich 36, G M Griffin 3 for 47, T L Goddard 3 for 64) and 137 for 9 dec (M C Cowdrey 38, H J Tayfield 4 for 33) drew with South Africans 149 (J H B Waite 50, P H Walker 3 for 36, R Illingworth 3 for 46) and 126 for 7 (T L Goddard 56, R W Barber 3 for 33).

Eighth Match vs Northamptonshire played at County Cricket Ground, Wantage Road, Northampton on 25, 26 and 27 May. Northamptonshire 363 (R Subba Row 108, M E J C Norman 75, B L Reynolds 44, P D Watts 44, F H Tyson 30, H J Tayfield 6 for 123, N A T Adcock 3 for 56) and 203 for 6 (D W Barrick 46, M E J C Norman 44, B L Reynolds 38, F H Tyson 29, N A T Adcock 2 for 39) beat

South Africans 461 for 3 dec (T L Goddard 186*, R A McLean 180, D J McGlew 52, P R Carlstein 34*, P D Watts 2 for 128) and 101 for 8 dec (C A R Duckworth 51*, F H Tyson 3 for 20, J S Manning 3 for 31) by 4 wickets.

Ninth Match vs Nottinghamshire played at Trent Bridge, Nottingham on 28, 30 and 31 May. Nottinghamshire 280 (R T Simpson 63, H M Winfield 58, N Hill 51, J D Springall 34, T L Goddard 5 for 71, G M Griffin 3 for 60) and 193 for 4 (N Hill 48, M Hill 45, J D Springall 42*, G Millman 27*, R T Simpson 27, T L Goddard 2 for 37, H J Tayfield 2 for 59) drew with South Africans 433 (P R Carlstein 80, S O'Linn 72, D J McGlew 68, T L Goddard 68, A J Pithey 59, J H B Waite 34, J Cotton 5 for 69).

T. L. GODDARD

Tenth Match vs ‡ Minor Counties played at Longton, Stoke-on-Trent on 1 and 2 June. South Africans 373 (D J McGlew 124, C Wesley 90, C A R Duckworth 59, J H B Waite 41, J T Ikin 6 for 79, J Birkenshaw 3 for 61) and 20 for 1 beat Minor Counties 220 (R Collins 96, J T Ikin 41, J Birkenshaw 33, N A T Adcock 5 for 37) and 170 (N H Moore 59, I Lomax 34, N A T Adcock 5 for 31, H J Tayfield 3 for 46) by 9 wickets.

Eleventh Match vs Glamorgan played at Arms Park, Cardiff on 4 and 6 June. South Africans 358 for 3 dec (D J McGlew 151, T L Goddard 146, J H B Waite 39*, J B Evans 3 for 63) beat Glamorgan 87 (P M Walker 19, J P Fellows-Smith 6 for 37, T L Goddard 4 for 31) and 138 (W G A Parkhouse 67, A Jones 28, H J Tayfield 5 for 44, A H McKinnon 4 for 17) by an innings and 133 runs.

Twelfth Match vs England (First Test Match) played at Edgbaston Cricket Ground, Birmingham on 9, 10, 11, 13 and 14 June.

England

G Pullar	c McLean b Goddard	37	not out	1
* M C Cowdrey	c Waite b Adcock	3	b Adcock	0
E R Dexter	b Tayfield	52	b Adcock	26
R Subba Row	c Waite b Griffin	56	c Waite b Tayfield	32
M J K Smith	c Waite b Adcock	54	c O'Linn b Tayfield	28
† J M Parks	c Waite b Adcock	35	b Griffin	4
R Illingworth	b Tayfield	1	c Waite b Adcock	16
R W Barber	lbw b Adcock	5	c McLean b Tayfield	4
P M Walker	c Goddard b Adcock	9	c Goddard b Griffin	37
F S Trueman	b Tayfield	11	b Tayfield	25
J B Statham	not out	14	c McLean b Griffin	22
Extras	b 4 lb 9 nb 2	15	b 2 lb 4 nb 2	8
Total		**292**		**203**

Fall 1st inns: 1/19 2/80 3/100 4/196 5/225 6/234 7/255 8/262 9/275 10/292
Fall 2nd inns: 1/0 2/42 3/69 4/74 5/112 6/112 7/118 8/163 9/202 10/203

Bowling	1st inns				2nd inns			
Adcock	41.5	14	62	5	28	8	57	3
Griffin	21	3	61	1	21	4	44	3
Goddard	33	17	47	1	10	5	32	0
Tayfield	50	19	93	3	27	12	62	4
Fellows-Smith	5	1	14	0				

South Africa

* D J McGlew	c Parks b Trueman	11	c Parks b Statham	5
T L Goddard	c Smith b Statham	10	c Walker b Statham	0
A J Pithey	lbw b Statham	6	b Illingworth	17
R A McLean	c Statham b Trueman	21	lbw b Trueman	68
† J H B Waite	b Illingworth	58	not out	56
P R Carlstein	lbw b Trueman	4	b Trueman	10
S O'Linn	c Cowdrey b Illingworth	42	lbw b Barber	12
J P Fellows-Smith	lbw b Illingworth	18	lbw b Illingworth	5
G M Griffin	b Trueman	6	c Walker b Trueman	14
H J Tayfield	run out	6	b Illingworth	3
N A T Adcock	not out	1	b Statham	7
Extras	b 2 nb 1	3	b 7 lb 5	12
Total		**186**		**209**

Fall 1st inns: 1/11 2/21 3/40 4/52 5/61 6/146 7/168 8/179 9/179 10/186
Fall 2nd inns: 1/4 2/5 3/58 4/120 5/132 6/156 7/161 8/167 9/200 10/209

Bowling	1st inns				2nd inns			
Statham	28	8	67	2	18	5	41	3
Trueman	24.5	4	58	4	22	4	58	3
Dexter	1	0	4	0	6	4	4	0
Barber	6	0	26	0	10	2	29	1
Illingworth	17	11	15	3	24	6	57	3
Walker	6	1	13	0	4	2	8	0

Umpires: John G Langridge and W E Phillipson

England beat South Africa by 100 runs.

Thirteenth Match vs Somerset played at County Cricket Ground, Taunton on 15, 16 and 17 July. South Africans 365 (D J McGlew 73, S O'Linn 69, J H B Waite 58, H J Tayfield 45*, T L Goddard 39, C L McCool 3 for 59, A Whitehead 3 for 91) beat Somerset 122 (G G Atkinson 31, W E Alley 26, A H McKinnon 6 for 50, H J Tayfield 3 for 34) and 220 (W E Alley 72, C L McCool 33, P J Eele 29, R Virgin 27, B A Langford 27, A H McKinnon 6 for 69, H J Tayfield 3 for 74) by an innings and 23 runs.

Fourteenth Match vs Hampshire played at County Cricket Ground, Northlands Road, Southampton on 18, 20 and 21 June. South Africans 507 (P R Carlstein 151, C Wesley 84, G M Griffin 65*, D J McGlew 62, J P Fellows-Smith 57, H J Tayfield 37, D W White 5 for 134) and 37 for 1 beat Hampshire 195 (D O Baldry 70, H M Barnard 29, H J Tayfield 5 for 66) and 346 (H Horton 117, H M Barnard 77, J R Gray 51, R E Marshall 43, H J Tayfield 6 for 78) by 9 wickets.

S.O'Linn

Fifteenth Match vs England (Second Test Match) played at Lord's Cricket Ground, London on 23, 24, 25 and 27 June.

England

* M C Cowdrey	c McLean b Griffin	4
R Subba Row	lbw b Adcock	90
E R Dexter	c McLean b Adcock	56
K F Barrington	lbw b Goddard	24
M J K Smith	c Waite b Griffin	99
† J M Parks	c Fellows-Smith	
	b Adcock	3
P M Walker	b Griffin	52
R Illingworth	not out	0
F S Trueman	b Griffin	0
J B Statham	not out	2
Extras	b 6 lb 14 w 1 nb 11	32
Total	**(8 wickets, declared)**	**362**

A.E.Moss did not bat
Fall 1st inns: 1/7 2/103 3/165 4/220 5/227 6/347 7/360 8/360

Bowling		1st inns		
Adcock	36	11	70	3
Griffin	30	7	87	4
Goddard	31	6	96	1
Tayfield	26	9	64	0
Fellows-Smith	5	0	13	0

South Africa

* D J McGlew	lbw b Statham	15	b Statham	17
T L Goddard	b Statham	19	c Parks b Statham	24
S O'Linn	c Walker b Moss	18	lbw b Trueman	8
R A McLean	c Cowdrey b Statham	15	c Parks b Trueman	13
† J H B Waite	c Parks b Statham	3	lbw b Statham	0
P R Carlstein	c Cowdrey b Moss	12	c Parks b Moss	6
C Wesley	c Parks b Statham	11	b Dexter	35
J P Fellows-Smith	c Parks b Moss	29	not out	27
H J Tayfield	c Smith b Moss	12	b Dexter	4
G M Griffin	b Statham	5	b Statham	0
N A T Adcock	not out	8	b Statham	2
Extras	lb 4 nb 1	5	nb 1	1
Total		**152**		**137**

Fall 1st inns: 1/33 2/48 3/56 4/69 5/78 6/88 7/112 8/132 9/138 10/152
Fall 2nd inns: 1/26 2/49 3/49 4/50 5/63 6/72 7/126 8/132 9/133 10/137

Bowling		1st inns				2nd inns		
Statham	20	5	63	6	21	6	34	5
Trueman	13	2	49	0	17	5	44	2
Moss	10.3	0	35	4	14	1	41	1
Illingworth					1	1	0	0
Dexter					4	0	17	2

Umpires: F S Lee and J S Buller

England beat South Africa by an innings and 73 runs.

Exhibition Match vs England played at Lord's Cricket Ground, London on 27 June. South Africa 145 for 7 beat England 142 by 3 wickets.

Sixteenth Match vs Gloucestershire played at County Cricket Ground, Bristol on 29 and 30 June. Gloucestershire 81 (D A Allen 23, H J Tayfield 3 for 20, T L Goddard 2 for 6) and 87 for 7 (R B Nichols 35*, N A T Adcock 4 for 31) beat South Africans 116 (H J Tayfield 24, J B Mortimore 5 for 52, D R Smith 3 for 45) and 49 (P R Carlstein 24, D A'Court 6 for 25, D R Smith 4 for 20) by 3 wickets.

Seventeenth Match vs Lancashire played at Old Trafford, Manchester on 2, 4 and 5 July. Lancashire 351 for 6 dec (K Grieves 104, J D Bond 100*, R Collins 75, J Dyson 46, J E Pothecary 2 for 67, T L Goddard 2 for 68) and 72 for 2 (R W Barber 39*, J Dyson 28, T L Goddard 2 for 22) drew with South Africans 233 (G M Griffin 65*, R A McLean 56, T L Goddard 41, J B Statham 4 for 33, T Greenhough 2 for 18).

D.J.McGlew

J.H.B.Waite

Eighteenth Match vs England (Third Test Match) played at Trent Bridge, Nottingham on 7, 8, 9 and 11 July.

England

R Subba Row	b Tayfield	30	not out		16
* M C Cowdrey	c Fellows-Smith b Goddard	67	lbw b Goddard		27
E R Dexter	b Adcock	3	c Adcock b Goddard		0
K F Barrington	c O'Linn b Goddard	80	not out		1
M J K Smith	lbw b Goddard	0			
† J M Parks	run out	16			
R Illingworth	c & b Tayfield	37			
P M Walker	c O'Linn b Tayfield	30			
F S Trueman	b Goddard	15			
J B Statham	b Goddard	2			
A E Moss	not out	3			
Extras	b 2 lb 2	4	b 4 lb 1		5
Total		**287**	**(2 wickets)**		**49**

Fall 1st inns: 1/57 2/82 3/129 4/154 6/229 7/241 8/261 9/267 10/287
Fall 2nd inns: 1/48 2/48

Bowling		1st inns				2nd inns		
Adcock	30	2	86	1	7.4	2	16	0
Pothecary	20	5	42	0	2	0	15	0
Fellows-Smith	5	0	17	0				
Goddard	42	17	80	5	5	1	13	2
Tayfield	28.3	11	58	3				

South Africa

* D J McGlew	c Parks b Trueman	0	run out		45
T L Goddard	run out	16	b Trueman		0
S O'Linn	c Walker b Trueman	1	c Cowdrey b Moss		98
R A McLean	b Statham	11	c Parks b Trueman		0
P R Carlstein	c Walker b Statham	2	c Cowdrey b Statham		19
C Wesley	c Subba Row b Statham	0	c Parks b Statham		0
J P Fellows-Smith	not out	31	c Illingworth b Trueman		15
† J H B Waite	c Trueman b Moss	1	lbw b Moss		60
H J Tayfield	b Trueman	11	c Parks b Moss		6
J E Pothecary	b Trueman	7	c Parks b Trueman		3
N A T Adcock	b Trueman	0	not out		1
Extras	b 4 lb 4	8			
Total		**88**			**247**

Fall 1st inns: 1/0 2/12 3/13 4/33 5/33 6/44 7/49 8/68 9/82 10/88
Fall 2nd inns: 1/1 2/23 3/23 4/91 5/122 6/122 7/231 8/242 9/245 10/247

Bowling		1st inns				2nd inns		
Trueman	14.3	6	27	5	22	3	77	4
Statham	14	5	27	3	26	3	71	2
Moss	10	3	26	1	15.4	3	36	3
Illingworth					19	9	33	0
Barrington					3	1	5	0
Dexter					6	2	12	0
Walker					3	0	13	0

Umpires: F S Lee and C S Elliott

England beat South Africa by 8 wickets.

Nineteenth Match vs Leicestershire played at County Cricket Ground, Grace Road, Leicester on 13, 14 and 15 July. Leicestershire 287 for 3 dec (M R Hallam 164, H D Bird 104, J E Pothecary 2 for 44) and 117 for 8 dec (W Watson 33*, H D Bird 23, T L Goddard 6 for 29) drew with South Africans 235 (C Wesley 90, D J McGlew 35, J S Savage 3 for 70) and 158 for 4 (P R Carlstein 75, R A McLean 53, R L Pratt 3 for 50).

Twentieth Match vs Middlesex played at Lord's Cricket Ground, London on 16, 18 and 19 July. Middlesex 191 (P H Parfitt 60, R A White 50, S E Russell 31, N A T Adcock 4 for 35, H J Tayfield 4 for 47) and 102 for 4 (J T Murray 39, H J Tayfield 3 for 24) drew with South Africans 397 for 6 dec (T L Goddard 142, P R Carlstein 68, R A McLean 65, A J Pithey 57, F J Titmus 3 for 70).

N. A. T. ADCOCK

N.A.T.Adcock

A.J.Pithey

Twenty-First Match vs England (Fourth Test Match) played at Old Trafford, Manchester on 21, 22, 23, 25 and 26 July.

England

G Pullar	b Pothecary	12	c & b Pothecary		9
R Subba Row	lbw b Adcock	27			
E R Dexter	b Pothecary	38	(2) c McLean b Pothecary		22
* M C Cowdrey	c Waite b Adcock	20	(3) b Adcock		25
K F Barrington	b Goddard	76	(4) c Waite b Goddard		35
D E V Padgett	c Wesley b Pothecary	5	(5) c Waite b Adcock		2
† J M Parks	lbw b Goddard	36	(6) c & b Goddard		20
R Illingworth	not out	22	(7) c McLean b Adcock		5
D A Allen	lbw b Goddard	0	(8) not out		14
F S Trueman	c Tayfield b Adcock	10	(9) not out		14
J B Statham	b Adcock	0			
Extras	b 8 lb 6	14	b 1 lb 5 nb 1		7
Total		**260**	**(7 wickets, declared)**		**153**

Fall 1st inns: 1/27 2/85 3/108 4/113 5/134 6/197 7/239 8/239 9/260 10/260
Fall 2nd inns: 1/23 2/41 3/63 4/65 5/71 6/101 7/134

Bowling		1st inns				2nd inns		
Adcock	23	5	66	4	27	9	59	3
Pothecary	28	3	85	3	32	10	61	2
Goddard	24	16	26	3	16	5	26	2
Tayfield	18	3	69	0				

South Africa

* D J McGlew	c Subba Row b Trueman	32	not out	26
T L Goddard	c Parks b Statham	8	not out	16
A J Pithey	c Parks b Statham	7		
P R Carlstein	b Trueman	11		
R A McLean	b Allen	109		
† J H B Waite	b Statham	11		
S O'Linn	c sub b Allen	27		
C Wesley	c Trueman b Allen	3		
H J Tayfield	c Trueman b Allen	4		
J E Pothecary	b Trueman	12		
N A T Adcock	not out	0		
Extras	b 1 lb 4	5	b 3 nb 1	4
Total		**229**	**(no wicket)**	**46**

Fall 1st inns: 1/25 2/33 3/57 4/62 5/92 6/194 7/198 8/202 9/225 10/229

Bowling		1st inns				2nd inns		
Statham	22	11	32	3	4	2	3	0
Trueman	20	2	58	3	6	1	10	0
Dexter	17	5	41	0				
Allen	19.5	6	58	4	7	4	5	0
Illingworth	11	2	35	0	5	3	6	0
Pullar					1	0	6	0
Padgett					2	0	8	0
Cowdrey					1	0	4	0

Umpires N Oldfield and John G Langridge

England drew with South Africa.

Twenty-Second Match vs Surrey played at Kennington Oval, London on 27, 28 and 29 July. South Africans 338 for 6 dec (J H B Waite 125, R A McLean 53, A J Pithey 46, S O'Linn 43*, J P Fellows-Smith 43, G A R Lock 3 for 85) and 67 for 4 dec (J P Fellows-Smith 28, D Gibson 2 for 40) drew with Surrey 223 for 7 dec (E A Bedser 67*, M J Stewart 53, N A T Adcock 5 for 66) and 53 for 2.

Twenty-Third Match vs Glamorgan played at St. Helen's Cricket Ground, Swansea on 30 July, 1 and 2 August. South Africans 151 (S O'Linn 39, J H B Waite 34, D J Shepherd 8 for 45) and 130 for 1 (D J McGlew 76*, J P Fellows-Smith 32*) beat Glamorgan 111 (D J Ward 24, H J Tayfield 7 for 51) and 169 for 9 dec (A J Watkins 41, W G A Parkhouse 39, B Hedges 29, H J Tayfield 5 for 90) by 9 wickets.

Twenty-Fourth Match vs Warwickshire played at Edgbaston Cricket Ground, Birmingham on 3, 4 and 5 August. South Africans 185 (S O'Linn 61, J E Pothecary 36*, J D Bannister 4 for 80, R G Thompson 4 for 60) and 244 for 5 dec (S O'Linn 120*, R A McLean 55, R G Thompson 2 for 22) drew with Warwickshire 149 (N F Horner 35, H J Tayfield 6 for 66) and 135 for 5 (A Townsend 43*, M J K Smith 29, H J Tayfield 3 for 62).

Twenty-Fifth Match vs Yorkshire played at Bramall Lane, Sheffield on 6, 8 and 9 August. Yorkshire 198 (D E V Padgett 63, P J Sharpe 53, K Taylor 41, J E Pothecary 4 for 68, N A T Adcock 3 for 40) and 140 for 9 dec (J V Wilson 34*, P J Sharpe 32, J E Pothecary 4 for 52) drew with South Africans 103 (D J McGlew 26, J H B Waite 25, R Illingworth 5 for 26) and 91 for 4 (P R Carlstein 33*, M J Cowan 2 for 24).

Twenty-Sixth Match vs Sussex to be played at County Cricket Ground, Hove on 10, 11 and 12 August abandoned without a ball being bowled.

Twenty-Seventh Match vs Kent played at St. Lawrence Cricket Ground, Canterbury on 13, 15 and 16 August. South Africans 271 for 9 dec (J P Fellows-Smith 56, T L Goddard 51, C A R Duckworth 45, R A McLean 31, S O'Linn 27, P H Jones 5 for 50) and 236 for 9 dec (J P Fellows-Smith 50, T L Goddard 41, D J McGlew 38, P R Carlstein 29, A L Dixon 3 for 73, P H Jones 3 for 97) beat Kent 192 (P H Jones 71, R C Wilson 31, A H McKinnon 7 for 73) and 155 (P E Richardson 54, R C Wilson 28, A H McKinnon 4 for 62, H J Tayfield 3 for 51) by 160 runs.

Twenty-Eighth Match vs England (Fifth Test Match) played at Kennington Oval, London on 18, 19, 20, 22 and 23 August.

England

G Pullar	c Goddard b Pothecary	59	st Waite b McKinnon	175	
* M C Cowdrey	b Adcock	11	lbw b Goddard	155	
E R Dexter	b Adcock	28	b Tayfield	16	
K F Barrington	lbw b Pothecary	1	c Carlstein b McKinnon	10	
M J K Smith	b Adcock	0	c Goddard b Tayfield	11	
D E V Padgett	c Waite b Pothecary	13	run out	31	
† J M Parks	c Waite b Pothecary	23	c Waite b Adcock	17	
D A Allen	lbw b Adcock	0	not out	12	
F S Trueman	lbw b Adcock	0	b Goddard	24	
J B Statham	not out	13	c Pothecary b Goddard	4	
T Greenhough	b Adcock	2			
Extras	b 3 lb 2	5	b 14 lb 9 w 1	24	
Total		**155**	**(9 wickets, declared)**	**479**	

Fall 1st inns: 1/27 2/89 3/91 4/96 5/107 6/125 7/130 8/130 9/142 10/155
Fall 2nd inns: 1/290 2/339 3/362 4/373 5/387 6/412 7/447 8/475 9/479

Bowling		1st inns				2nd inns		
Adcock	31.3	10	65	6	38	8	106	1
Pothecary	29	9	58	4	27	5	93	0
Goddard	14	6	25	0	27	6	69	3
McKinnon	2	1	2	0	24	7	62	2
Tayfield					37	14	108	2
Fellows-Smith					4	0	17	0

South Africa

* D J McGlew	c Smith b Greenhough	22	c Allen b Statham	16	
T L Goddard	c Cowdrey b Statham	99	c Cowdrey b Statham	28	
J P Fellows-Smith	c Smith b Dexter	35	c Parks b Trueman	6	
R A McLean	lbw b Dexter	0	(5) not out	32	
† J H B Waite	c Trueman b Dexter	77	(6) not out	1	
S O'Linn	b Trueman	55			
P R Carlstein	b Greenhough	42	(4) lbw b Trueman	13	
J E Pothecary	run out	4			
H J Tayfield	not out	46			
A H McKinnon	run out	22			
N A T Adcock	b Trueman	1			
Extras	b 6 lb 7 nb 3	16	w 1	1	
Total		**419**	**(4 wickets)**	**97**	

Fall 1st inns: 1/44 2/107 3/107 4/222 5/252 6/326 7/330 8/374 9/412 10/419
Fall 2nd inns: 1/21 2/30 3/30 4/89

Bowling		1st inns				2nd inns		
Trueman	31.1	4	93	2	10	0	34	2
Statham	38	8	96	1	12	1	57	2
Dexter	30	5	79	3	0.2	0	0	0
Greenhough	44	17	99	2	5	2	3	0
Allen	28	15	36	0	2	1	2	0

Umpires: W E Phillipson and C S Elliott

England drew with South Africa.

Twenty-Ninth Match vs Combined Services played at United Services Officers Ground, Portsmouth on 27, 29 and 30 August. South Africans 239 (C Wesley 64, C A R Duckworth 28, B E Stead 6 for 68) and 201 for 3 dec (T L Goddard 116, J P Fellows-Smith 57, P J Phelan 2 for 47) beat Combined Services 103 (P J Phelan 26, H J Tayfield 8 for 51) and 110 (D S Williams 37, N A T Adcock 5 for 32) by 227 runs.

Thirtieth Match vs A E R Gilligan's XI played at Central Cricket Ground, Hastings on 31 August, 1 and 2 September. South Africans 238 (A J Pithey 70, C Wesley 61, C A R Duckworth 27, D C Morgan 4 for 39, G A R Lock 3 for 70) and 314 (R A McLean 110, J E Pothecary 68, S O'Linn 27, H L Jackson 3 for 40, G A R Lock 3 for 83) beat A E R Gilligan's XI 261 (R B Kanhai 62, D C Morgan 59, M E J C Norman 53, S Jayasinghe 31, H J Tayfield 4 for 107) and 178 (M E J C Norman 47, D W Barrick 34, D C Morgan 25, T L Goddard 3 for 36, H J Tayfield 3 for 74) by 113 runs.

Thirty-First Match vs Lancashire played at Stanley Park, Blackpool on 3 and 5 September. South Africans 198 (R A McLean 62, C A R Duckworth 50, D J McGlew 36, J P Fellows-Smith 26, J B Statham 4 for 25) and 66 for 5 (J P Fellows-Smith 20, K Higgs 3 for 16) beat Lancashire 90 (A Wharton 52, T L Goddard 5 for 19, J P Fellows-Smith 3 for 5) and 173 (P Marner 34, G Pullar 33, D R Worsley 28, T L Goddard 5 for 60) by 5 wickets.

Thirty-Second Match vs T N Pearce's XI played at North Marine Drive, Scarborough on 7, 8 and 9 September. South Africans 304 (P R Carlstein 82, T L Goddard 52, J H B Waite 43, G M Griffin 37, D A Allen 5 for 85, P J Sainsbury 2 for 68) and 192 for 6 (J H B Waite 60, R A McLean 53, T L Goddard 25, D A Allen 2 for 19, P J Sainsbury 2 for 52) beat T N Pearce's XI 264 (E R Dexter 67, M J K Smith 54, R Swetman 47, T W Graveney 25, N A T Adcock 3 for 8, P R Carlstein 3 for 37) and 231 (M J K Smith 81, R E Marshall 67, K F Barrington 27, P J Sainsbury 26, C Wesley 4 for 51) by 4 wickets.

Test Match batting averages:

	Inns	*NO*	*Runs*	*HS*	*Ave*
J H B Waite	9	2	267	77	38.14
R A McLean	9	1	269	109	33.62
S O'Linn	8	0	261	98	32.62
J P Fellows-Smith	8	2	166	35	27.66
T L Goddard	10	1	220	99	24.44
D J McGlew	10	1	189	45	21.00
P R Carlstein	9	0	119	42	13.22
H J Tayfield	8	1	92	46*	13.14
A J Pithey	3	0	30	17	10.00
C Wesley	5	0	49	35	9.80
J E Pothecary	4	0	26	12	6.50
G M Griffin	4	0	25	14	6.25
N A T Adcock	8	4	20	8*	5.00

Test Match bowling averages:

	Overs	Mdns	Runs	Wkts	Ave
N A T Adcock	263	69	587	26	22.57
G M Griffin	72	14	192	8	24.00
T L Goddard	202	79	414	17	24.35
H J Tayfield	186.3	68	454	12	37.83
J E Pothecary	138	32	354	9	39.33
J P Fellows-Smith	19	1	61	0	-

Tour batting averages - all matches:

	Inns	NO	Runs	HS	Ave
D J McGlew	39	8	1,327	151*	42.80
R A McLean	43	3	1,516	207	37.90
T L Goddard	39	2	1,377	186*	37.21
S O'Linn	37	9	1,014	120*	36.21
J H B Waite	31	6	894	125	35.76
J P Fellows-Smith	34	7	863	109*	31.96
P R Carlstein	39	6	980	151	29.69
A J Pithey	25	3	614	96	27.90
C Wesley	31	4	595	90	22.03
C A R Duckworth	25	2	426	59	18.52
G M Griffin	22	2	353	65*	17.65
J E Pothecary	24	4	277	68	13.85
H J Tayfield	31	7	315	46*	13.12
A H McKinnon	14	6	70	22	8.75
N A T Adcock	20	5	71	11	4.73

Tour bowling averages - all matches:

	Overs	Mdns	Runs	Wkts	Ave
N A T Adcock	737	196	1,515	108	14.02
T L Goddard	752.2	308	1,439	73	19.71
A H McKinnon	436.1	136	1,107	53	20.88
H J Tayfield	1,048	333	2,664	123	21.65
G M Griffin	259.4	71	612	26	23.53
J P Fellows-Smith	319.4	69	829	32	25.90
J E Pothecary	632.5	163	1,565	53	29.52
D J McGlew	75.1	13	264	8	33.00
P R Carlstein	36.2	3	158	4	39.50

Also bowled during the tour:

	Overs	Mdns	Runs	Wkts	Ave
C Wesley	15	3	51	4	12.75
R A McLean	9.2	0	28	2	14.00
J H B Waite	1	0	1	0	-

Centuries recorded for South Africans during the tour:

T L Goddard	(4) :	186*	vs Northamptonshire (Northampton)
		146	vs Glamorgan (Cardiff)
		142	vs Middlesex (Lord's)
		116	vs Combined Services (Portsmouth)
R A McLean	(4) :	207	vs Worcestershire (Worcester)
		180	vs Northamptonshire (Northampton)
		110	vs A E R Gilligan's XI (Hastings)
		109	vs England (Old Trafford) (Fourth Test Match)
D J McGlew	(2) :	151*	vs Glamorgan (Cardiff)
		124	vs Minor Counties (Stoke-on-Trent)
P R Carlstein	(1) :	151	vs Hampshire (Southampton)
J P Fellows-Smith	(1) :	109*	vs Essex (Ilford)
S O'Linn	(1) :	120*	vs Warwickshire (Edgbaston)
J H B Waite	(1) :	125	vs Surrey (The Oval)

Fielding:

	Catches	Stumpings
J H B Waite	54	9
T L Goddard	26	
C A R Duckworth	22	2
R A McLean	22	
J P Fellows-Smith	19	
H J Tayfield	19	
S O'Linn	18	
J E Pothecary	18	
P R Carlstein	12	
D J McGlew	12	
A J Pithey	10	
C Wesley	8	
N A T Adcock	7	
G M Griffin	6	
A H McKinnon	1	

The Thirteenth South African Team in the United Kingdom, 1965

The young 1965 side led by Peter van der Merwe became the second South African team to win a Test Series in England. They won at Trent Bridge in the only game that was decided for both the Lord's and The Oval Tests ended in draws. This was of course a short tour of only three Tests (the first time since 1907) and 18 first-class games. Of the latter five were won, eleven drawn and two lost (Derbyshire and the last game of the tour at Scarborough against T. N. Pearce's XI) — the summer was of course shared with New Zealand.

All sixteen players were making their first tour of England and they proved a most attractive side with an excellent team spirit. They included the Pollock brothers, Peter and Graeme, Colin Bland, Eddie Barlow and Ali Bacher who were regrettably to make little subsequent progress in their international careers.

Significantly in their game against Gloucestershire at Bristol they came up against two young players from Natal, Barry Richards aged 19 and Mike Proctor aged 18. They shared a 116 run partnership off the tourists in just over an hour and a half (Proctor scoring 69 and Richards 59) suggesting much more to come, but not, it proved, in international cricket for they were able to play only a handful of games for their country before 1970, when international sporting relations ceased.

(*standing*) **D.Gamsy N.S.Crookes R.Dumbrill M.J.Macaulay H.R.Lance H.D.Bromfield A.H.McKinnon J.T.Botten A.Bacher Mr.M.McLennan** (Scorer)

(*sitting*) **D.T.Lindsay R.G.Pollock P.L.van der Merwe** (Captain) **Mr.J.B.Plimsoll** (Manager) **E.J.Barlow K.C.Bland P.M.Pollock**

Touring party (15):

* P L van der Merwe (*Western Province*) (Captain)
Age 28. Right-handed batsman and left-arm slow bowler.

E J Barlow (*Eastern Province*) (Vice-Captain)
Age 24. Right-handed batsman and right-arm fast-medium bowler.

R G Pollock (*Eastern Province*)
Age 21. Left-handed batsman and right-arm slow bowler.

† A Bacher (*Transvaal*)
Age 23. Right-handed batsman, right-arm slow bowler and occasional wicket-keeper.

K C Bland (*Rhodesia*)
Age 27. Right-handed batsman and right-arm fast-medium bowler and excellent cover fieldsman.

† D T Lindsay (*North-East Transvaal*)
Age 25. Right-handed batsman and wicket-keeper.

H R Lance (*Transvaal*)
Age 25. Right handed batsman and right-arm fast bowler.

P M Pollock (*Eastern Province*)
Age 24. Right-handed batsman and right-arm fast-medium bowler.

R Dumbrill (*Natal*)
Age 26. Right-handed batsman and right-arm off-spin bowler.

† D Gamsy (*Natal*)
Age 25. Right-handed batsman and wicket-keeper.

J T Botten (*North-East Transvaal*)
Age 27. Right-handed batsman and right-arm fast bowler.

A H McKinnon (*Transvaal*)
Age 32. Right-handed batsman and left-arm slow bowler.

N S Crookes (*Natal*)
Age 29. Right-handed batsman and right-arm off-spin bowler.

M J Macaulay (*Orange Free State*)
Age 26. Right-handed batsman and left-arm medium pace bowler.

H D Bromfield (*Western Province*)
Age 33. Right-handed batsman and right-arm off-spin bowler.

Manager: Mr. J B Plimsoll

Scorer: Mr. M McLennan

Summary of all matches:

Played 19   Won 5   Lost 3   Drawn 11   Abandoned 1

Summary of first-class matches:

Played 18   Won 5   Lost 2   Drawn 11

Summary of Test Matches:

Played 3   Won 1   Lost 0   Drawn 2

First Match vs Derbyshire played at Queen's Park, Chesterfield on June 26, 28 and 29. Derbyshire 143 (J R Eyre 36, I W Hall 36, R Dumbrill 4 for 32) and 126 for 3 (H L Johnson 44*) beat South Africans 149 (E J Barlow 50, R G Pollock 37, H J Rhodes 4 for 35) and 119 (I R Buxton 3 for 16, A B Jackson 3 for 35) by 7 wickets.

Second Match vs Yorkshire played at Bramall Lane, Sheffield on June 30, July 1 and 2. South Africans 266 for 7 dec (D T Lindsay 105, D Gamsy 54) and 140 for 2 (E J Barlow 69*, K C Bland 45*) drew with Yorkshire 197 (D B Close 117*, J T Botten 3 for 44) and 55 for 3 (G Boycott 22).

Third Match vs Essex played at Castle Park, Colchester on July 3, 5 and 6. South Africans 323 for 6 dec (K C Bland 94, E J Barlow 78, A Bacher 59, D T Lindsay 48, B R Knight 4 for 73) and 260 for 6 dec (R Dumbrill 54*, D T Lindsay 52, K C Bland 40, E J Barlow 31, A Bacher 28, E R Presland 1 for 24, P J Phelan 1 for 30) drew with Essex 296 (T E Bailey 77, B E A Edmeades 59, G J Smith 39, B Taylor 34, P M Pollock 5 for 67) and 222 for 9 (G J Saville 70, T E Bailey 35, M J Bear 27, A H McKinnon 5 for 75).

Fourth Match vs Surrey played at Kennington Oval, London on 7, 8 and 9 July. Surrey 270 for 8 dec (M J Stewart 60, D Gibson 48, M J Edwards 47, G G Arnold 29*, P M Pollock 5 for 50) and 193 for 4 dec (S J Storey 69*, Mohammad Younis 66, R A E Tindall 27, H D Bromfield 2 for 73) drew with South Africans 238 for 5 dec (E J Barlow 110, R G Pollock 60, D T Lindsay 34, P I Pocock 2 for 77) and 85 for 1 (E J Barlow 41*, R G Pollock 30*).

Fifth Match vs Gloucestershire played at County Cricket Ground, Nevil Road, Bristol on 10, 12 and 13 July. Gloucestershire 279 (M J Proctor 69, B A Richards 59, D A Allen 41*, A R Windows 29, H R Lance 3 for 15) drew with South Africans 39 for 0 (E J Barlow 19*, H R Lance 19*).

Sixth Match vs Minor Counties played at County Cricket Ground, Jesmond, Newcastle-upon-Tyne on 14, 15 and 16 July. South Africans 278 for 9 dec (A Bacher 121, H R Lance 56, D T Lindsay 37, P Lever 3 for 64) and 133 for 4 dec (D T Lindsay 45, R G Pollock 42*, A Bacher 34, J Smith 2 for 47) beat Minor Counties 134 (R Inglis 43, D W Hardy 29, A H McKinnon 4 for 40, J T Botten 3 for 24, N S Crookes 3 for 32) and 74 (J Smith 17, A H McKinnon 5 for 23, N S Crookes 4 for 24) by 203 runs.

Seventh Match vs Leicestershire played at County Cricket Ground, Grace Road, Leicester on 17, 19 and 20 July. Leicestershire 196 (J van Geloven 54*, P Marner 30, P M Pollock 4 for 31) and 69 for 3 (B J Booth 23, H D Bromfield 2 for 11) drew with South Africans 350 (A Bacher 119, J T Botten 90, E J Barlow 62, K C Bland 42, J S Savage 6 for 79).

Eighth Match vs England (First Test Match) played at Lord's Cricket Ground, London on 22, 23, 24, 26 and 27 July.

South Africa

E J Barlow	c Barber b Rumsey	1	c Parks b Brown		52
H R Lance	c & b Brown	28	c Titmus b Brown		9
† D T Lindsay	c Titmus b Rumsey	40	c Parks b Larter		22
R G Pollock	c Barrington b Titmus	56	b Brown		5
K C Bland	b Brown	39	c Edrich b Barber		70
A Bacher	lbw b Titmus	4	b Titmus		37
* P L van der Merwe	c Barrington b Rumsey	17	c Barrington b Rumsey		31
R Dumbrill	b Barber	3	c Cowdrey b Rumsey		2
J T Botten	b Brown	33	b Rumsey		0
P M Pollock	st Parks b Barber	34	not out		14
H D Bromfield	not out	9	run out		0
Extras	lb 14 nb 2	16	b 4 lb 2		6
Total		**280**			**248**

Fall 1st inns: 1/1 2/60 3/75 4/155 5/170 6/170 7/178 8/212 9/247 10/280
Fall 2nd inns: 1/55 2/62 3/68 4/120 5/170 6/216 7/230 8/230 9/247 10/248

Bowling	1st inns				2nd inns			
Larter	26	10	47	0	17	2	67	1
Rumsey	30	9	84	3	21	8	49	3
Brown	24	9	44	3	21	11	30	3
Titmus	29	10	59	2	26	13	36	1
Barber	10.3	3	30	2	25	5	60	1

England

G Boycott	c Barlow b Botten	31	c & b Dumbrill		28
R W Barber	b Bromfield	56	c Lindsay b P M Pollock		12
J H Edrich	lbw b P M Pollock	0	retired hurt		7
K F Barrington	run out	91	lbw b Dumbrill		18
M C Cowdrey	b Dumbrill	29	lbw b P M Pollock		37
* M J K Smith	c Lindsay b Botten	26	c Lindsay b Dumbrill		13
† J M Parks	run out	32	c van der Merwe b Dumbrill		7
F J Titmus	c P M Pollock b Bromfield	59	not out		9
D J Brown	c Bromfield b Dumbrill	1	c Barlow b R G Pollock		5
F E Rumsey	b Dumbrill	3	not out		0
J D F Larter	not out	0			
Extras	b 1 lb 4 w 1 nb 4	10	lb 7 w 1 nb 1		9
Total		**338**	**(7 wickets)**		**145**

Fall 1st inns: 1/82 2/88 3/88 4/144 5/240 6/240 7/294 8/314 9/338 10/338
Fall 2nd inns: 1/23 2/70 3/79 4/113 5/121 6/135 7/140

Bowling	1st inns				2nd inns			
P M Pollock	39	12	91	1	20	6	52	2
Botten	33	11	65	2	12	6	25	0
Barlow	19	6	31	0	9	1	25	0
Bromfield	25.2	5	71	2	5	4	4	0
Dumbrill	24	11	31	3	18	8	30	4
Lance	5	0	18	0				
R G Pollock	5	1	21	0	4	4	0	1

Umpires: J S Buller and A E G Rhodes

England drew with South Africa.

Ninth Match vs Kent at St. Lawrence Cricket Ground, Canterbury on 28 and 29 July. South Africans 365 for 3 dec (R G Pollock 203*, K C Bland 61*, A Bacher 54, D L Underwood 1 for 87) beat Kent 74 (M H Denness 30, P M Pollock 5 for 28) and 144 (A L Dixon 53, E W J Fillary 27*, M J Macaulay 4 for 22, N S Crookes 3 for 38) by an innings and 147 runs.

Tenth Match vs Glamorgan played at St. Helen's Cricket Ground, Swansea on 31 July, 2 and 3 August. Glamorgan 301 (A R Lewis 146*, B Hedges 29, P M Walker 29, A H McKinnon 4 for 54) drew with South Africans 144 (A Bacher 72, K C Bland 32, J S Pressdee 4 for 11, O S Wheatley 3 for 22) and 198 for 8 (R Dumbrill 53, H R Lance 30, J S Pressdee 3 for 70).

P. M. Pollock
South Africa

E. J. Barlow
South Africa

Eleventh Match vs England (Second Test Match) played at Trent Bridge, Nottingham on 5, 6, 7 and 9 August.

South Africa

E J Barlow	c Cowdrey b Cartwright	19	b Titmus	76
H R Lance	lbw b Cartwright	7	c Barber b Snow	0
† D T Lindsay	c Parks b Cartwright	0	c Cowdrey b Larter	9
R G Pollock	c Cowdrey b Cartwright	125	c Titmus b Larter	59
K C Bland	st Parks b Titmus	1	b Snow	10
A Bacher	b Snow	12	lbw b Larter	67
* P L van der Merwe	run out	38	c Parfitt b Larter	4
R Dumbrill	c Parfitt b Cartwright	30	b Snow	13
J T Botten	c Parks b Larter	10	b Larter	18
P M Pollock	c Larter b Cartwright	15	not out	12
A H McKinnon	not out	8	b Titmus	9
Extras	lb 4	4	b 4 lb 5 nb 3	12
Total		**269**		**289**

Fall 1st inns: 1/16 2/16 3/42 4/43 5/80 6/178 7/221 8/242 9/252 10/269
Fall 2nd inns: 1/2 2/35 3/134 4/193 5/228 6/232 7/243 8/265 9/269 10/289

Bowling	1st inns				2nd inns			
Larter	17	6	25	1	29	7	68	5
Snow	22	6	63	1	33	6	83	3
Cartwright	31.3	9	94	6				
Titmus	22	8	44	1	19.4	5	46	2
Barber	9	3	39	0	3	0	20	0
Boycott					26	10	60	0

England

G Boycott	c Lance b P M Pollock	0	b McKinnon	16
R W Barber	c Bacher b Dumbrill	41	c Lindsay b P M Pollock	1
K F Barrington	b P M Pollock	1	c Lindsay b P M Pollock	1
F J Titmus	c R G Pollock b McKinnon	20	c Lindsay b McKinnon	4
M C Cowdrey	c Lindsay b Botten	105	st Lindsay b McKinnon	20
P H Parfitt	c Dumbrill b P M Pollock	18	b P M Pollock	86
* M J K Smith	b P M Pollock	32	lbw b R G Pollock	24
† J M Parks	c & b Botten	6	not out	44
J A Snow	run out	3	b Botten	0
J D F Larter	b P M Pollock	2	c van der Merwe b P M Pollock	10
T W Cartwright	not out	1	lbw b P M Pollock	0
Extras	b 1 lb 3 w 1 nb 6	11	lb 5 w 2 nb 11	18
Total		**240**		**224**

Fall 1st inns: 1/0 2/8 3/63 4/67 5/133 6/225 7/229 8/236 9/238 10/240
Fall 2nd inns: 1/1 2/10 3/10 4/13 5/41 6/59 7/114 8/207 9/207 10/224

Bowling	1st inns				2nd inns			
P M Pollock	23.5	8	53	5	24	15	34	5
Botten	23	5	60	2	19	5	58	1
McKinnon	28	11	54	1	27	12	50	3
Dumbrill	18	3	60	1	16	4	40	0
R G Pollock	1	0	2	0	5	2	4	1
Barlow					11	1	20	0

Umpires: C S Elliott and J F Crapp

South Africa beat England by 94 runs.

D. T. Lindsay
South Africa

Twelfth Match vs Middlesex played at Lord's Cricket Ground, London on 11, 12 and 13 August. South Africans 254 (E J Barlow 41, R Dumbrill 41, K C Bland 39, P L van der Merwe 37, D T Lindsay 31, D Gamsy 28, R Herman 4 for 58, F J Titmus 3 for 22) and 207 for 5 (D T Lindsay 55, P L van der Merwe 48*, R G Pollock 45, K C Bland 27, D A Bick 3 for 40) beat Middlesex 335 for 8 dec (C T Radley 138, F J Titmus 101, J T Murray 28, E J Barlow 2 for 23) and 123 (J M Brearley 49, W E Russell 25, N S Crookes 8 for 47, R G Pollock 2 for 25) by 5 wickets.

Thirteenth Match vs Hampshire played at County Cricket Ground, Northlands Road, Southampton on 14, 16 and 17 August. Hampshire 286 for 7 dec (G L Keith 101*, B S V Timms 80, R G Caple 34, H Horton 30, N S Crookes 4 for 89) and 87 for 8 (G L Keith 21*, M J Macaulay 3 for 22) drew with South Africans 133 (A Bacher 74, P M Pollock 23, D Shackleton 6 for 29, A R Wassell 3 for 17) and 354 for 9 dec (E J Barlow 129, R G Pollock 94, D T Lindsay 32, P L van der Merwe 30, A R Wassell 5 for 135).

Fourteenth Match vs Sussex played at County Cricket Ground, Hove on 18. 19 and 20 August. South Africans 391 (R G Pollock 122, K C Bland 78, D T Lindsay 55, R Dumbrill 50, H R Lance 25, A Buss 4 for 69) and 109 for 5 dec (R G Pollock 29, A Buss 2 for 31) drew with Sussex 238 (R J Langridge 46, J M Parks 38, K G Suttle 36, A S M Oakman 32, M G Griffith 29, R Dumbrill 5 for 37, J T Botten 3 for 51) and 216 for 7 (J M Parks 106*, Nawab of Pataudi 47, M J Macaulay 2 for 20, R Dumbrill 2 for 26).

Fifteenth Match vs Warwickshire played at Edgbaston Cricket Ground, Birmingham on 21, 23 and 24 August. Warwickshire 217 for 7 dec (B A Richardson 67, R Miller 50, D L Amiss 31, A H McKinnon 3 for 50) and 170 for 9 dec (K Ibadulla 52, J A Jameson 40, D L Amiss 29, N S Crookes 4 for 76, A H McKinnon 3 for 34) drew with South Africans 208 for 4 dec (D Gamsy 79, A Bacher 70, K C Bland 38, T W Cartwright 2 for 44).

K. C. Bland
South Africa

Sixteenth Match vs England (Third Test Match) played at Kennington Oval, London on 26, 27, 28, 30 and 31 August.

South Africa

E J Barlow	lbw b Statham	18	b Statham		18
† D T Lindsay	lbw b Higgs	4	b Brown		17
A Bacher	lbw b Higgs	28	c Smith b Statham		70
R G Pollock	b Titmus	12	run out		34
K C Bland	lbw b Statham	39	c Titmus b Higgs		127
H R Lance	lbw b Statham	69	b Higgs		53
* P L van der Merwe	c Barrington b Higgs	20	b Higgs		0
R Dumbrill	c Smith b Higgs	14	c Barrington b Brown		36
J T Botten	c Cowdrey b Statham	0	b Titmus		4
P M Pollock	b Statham	3	not out		9
A H McKinnon	not out	0	b Higgs		14
Extras	nb 1	1	b 1 lb 7 nb 2		10
Total		**208**			**392**

Fall 1st inns: 1/21 2/23 3/60 4/86 5/109 6/156 7/196 8/197 9/207 10/208
Fall 2nd inns: 1/28 2/61 3/123 4/164 5/260 6/260 7/343 8/367 9/371 10/392

Bowling	1st inns				2nd inns			
Statham	24.2	11	40	5	29	1	105	2
Brown	22	4	63	0	23	3	63	2
Higgs	24	4	47	4	41.1	9	96	4
Titmus	26	12	57	1	27	3	74	1
Barber					13	1	44	0

England

R W Barber	st Lindsay b McKinnon	40	c & b P M Pollock		22
W E Russell	lbw b P M Pollock	0	c Bacher b McKinnon		70
K F Barrington	b Botten	18	lbw b P M Pollock		73
M C Cowdrey	c Barlow b P M Pollock	58	not out		78
P H Parfitt	c & b McKinnon	24	lbw b Botten		46
* M J K Smith	lbw b P M Pollock	7	not out		10
D J Brown	c Dumbrill b McKinnon	0			
† J M Parks	c Bland b Botten	42			
F J Titmus	not out	2			
K Higgs	b P M Pollock	2			
J B Statham	b P M Pollock	0			
Extras	lb 6 w 3	9	lb 6 nb 3		9
Total		**202**	**(4 wickets)**		**308**

Fall 1st inns: 1/1 2/42 3/76 4/125 5/141 6/142 7/198 8/198 9/200 10/202
Fall 2nd inns: 1/39 2/138 3/144 4/279

Bowling	1st inns				2nd inns			
P M Pollock	25.1	7	43	5	32.2	7	93	2
Botten	27	6	56	2	24	4	73	1
Barlow	11	1	27	0	6	1	22	0
Dumbrill	6	2	11	0	9	1	30	0
McKinnon	27	11	50	3	31	7	70	1
Lance	2	0	6	0	2	0	11	0

Umpires: J S Buller and W F Price

England drew with South Africa.

Seventeenth Match vs Lancashire played at Old Trafford, Manchester on 1, 2 and 3 September. South Africans 273 (R G Pollock 75, P M Pollock 51, H R Lance 39, N Crookes 34, K Higgs 4 for 46, T Greenhough 3 for 49) and 169 (R G Pollock 40, A Bacher 39, D Lloyd 3 for 44) beat Lancashire 159 (D M Green 46, H Pilling 25, N S Crookes 5 for 54, H D Bromfield 3 for 27) and 117 (D Lloyd 42, H D Bromfield 5 for 42, N S Crookes 3 for 47) by 166 runs.

Eighteenth Match vs T N Pearce's XI played at North Marine Drive, Scarborough on 4 and 6 September. T N Pearce's XI 241 (M J K Smith 65, B R Knight 45, P H Parfitt 38, T E Bailey 33*, R Dumbrill 4 for 31) and 191 for 2 (P H Parfitt 87*, M C Cowdrey 39*) beat South Africans 207 (A Bacher 60, R G Pollock 42, F E Rumsey 4 for 35) and 224 (R Dumbrill 64, D T Lindsay 48, A Bacher 26, R W Barber 4 for 50) by 8 wickets.

R. G. Pollock
South Africa

Nineteenth Match vs ‡ T N Pearce's XI played at North Marine Drive, Scarborough on 7 September. T N Pearce's XI 213 for 7 (M C Cowdrey 75, R W Barber 32, B R Knight 24, J T Botten 2 for 33) beat South Africans 200 (R Dumbrill 53, P L van der Merwe 50, A Bacher 33, B R Knight 3 for 30, T E Bailey 3 for 31) by 14 runs.

Twentieth Match vs ‡ Yorkshire (Winners of the Gillette Cup) to be played at Park Avenue, Bradford on 9 September abandoned without a ball being bowled.

Test Match batting averages:

	Inns	NO	Runs	HS	Ave
R G Pollock	6	0	291	125	48.50
K C Bland	6	0	286	127	47.66
A Bacher	6	0	218	70	36.33
E J Barlow	6	0	184	76	30.66
P M Pollock	6	3	87	34	29.00
H R Lance	6	0	166	69	27.66
P L van der Merwe	6	0	110	38	18.33
R Dumbrill	6	0	98	36	16.33
A H McKinnon	4	2	31	14	15.50
D T Lindsay	6	0	92	40	15.33
J T Botten	6	0	65	33	10.83

Also batted during Tests:

H D Bromfield 0 and 9*

Test Match bowling averages:

	Overs	Mdns	Runs	Wkts	Ave
R G Pollock	15	7	27	2	13.50
P M Pollock	164.2	55	366	20	18.30
R Dumbrill	91	29	202	8	25.25
A H Mckinnon	113	41	224	8	28.00
H D Bromfield	30.2	9	75	2	37.50
J T Botten	138	37	337	8	42.12
H R Lance	9	0	35	0	-
E J Barlow	56	10	125	0	-

Tour batting averages - all matches:

	Inns	NO	Run	HS	Ave
R G Pollock	24	4	1,147	203*	57.35
A Bacher	26	1	1,008	121	40.32
E J Barlow	28	3	971	129	38.84
K C Bland	26	2	906	127	37.75
D T Lindsay	29	1	779	105	27.82
H R Lance	21	3	475	69	26.38
P M Pollock	13	5	182	51*	22.75
R Dumbrill	22	3	429	64	22.57
D Gamsy	16	1	285	79	19.00
J T Botten	15	3	227	90	18.91
A H McKinnon	10	6	66	14*	16.50
P L van der Merwe	24	2	363	48*	16.50
N S Crookes	10	2	90	34	11.25
M J Macaulay	12	2	111	22	11.10
H D Bromfield	11	5	36	23	6.00

Tour bowling averages - all matches:

	Overs	Mdns	Runs	Wkts	Ave
P M Pollock	371.4	108	851	50	17.02
N S Crookes	318.2	75	914	47	19.44
A H McKinnon	351.1	120	759	37	20.51
R Dumbrill	287.5	75	673	31	21.70
J T Botten	340	85	818	33	24.78
M J Macaulay	329	92	739	25	29.56
H R Lance	49.3	13	120	4	30.00
H D Bromfield	266.1	88	646	20	32.30
E J Barlow	160	36	335	9	37.22
R G Pollock	123.5	31	404	8	50.50

Also bowled during the tour:

	Overs	Mdns	Runs	Wkts	Ave
A Bacher	1	0	5	0	-
K C Bland	5	0	18	1	18.00

Centuries recorded for South Africans during the tour:

R G Pollock	(3) :	203*	vs Kent (Canterbury)
		125	vs England (Nottingham) (Second Test Match)
		122	vs Sussex (Hove)
A Bacher	(2) :	121	vs Minor Counties (Jesmond)
		119	vs Leicestershire (Grace Road, Leicester)
E J Barlow	(2) :	129	vs Hampshire (Bournemouth)
		110	vs Surrey (The Oval)
K C Bland	(1) :	127	vs England (The Oval) (Third Test Match)
D T Lindsay	(1) :	105	vs Yorkshire (Sheffield)

Fielding:

	Catches	Stumpings
D Gamsy	22	3
D T Lindsay	22	2
E J Barlow	15	
A Bacher	11	
P L van der Merwe	11	
N S Crookes	10	
R Dumbrill	9	
K C Bland	6	
R G Pollock	6	
H D Bromfield	5	
M J Macaulay	5	
J T Botten	4	
P M Pollock	4	
A H McKinnon	3	

The Fourteenth South African Team in the United Kingdom, 1994

The fourteenth South African team to visit England will commence their first tour of England for 29 years with an initial non-first-class 'warm up' match at Highclere Castle just south of Newbury in Hampshire against The Earl of Carnarvon's Invitation XI on 23 June. This will be followed by a first-class three day fixture against Kent at Canterbury on 25 June. The Cornhill Test Match Series of three Test Matches against England scheduled for Lord's, Bass Headingley and The Foster's Oval - the same sequence of venues as South Africa's first Test Tour to England in 1907. Two Texaco Trophy One-Day Internationals which will be staged at Edgbaston and Old Trafford in August will also form part of the short tour. Matches will also be staged against Sussex (Hove), Hampshire (Southampton), Derbyshire or Gloucestershire (Derby or Bristol), Scotland (Titwood, Glasgow), Durham (Chester-le-Street), Northamptonshire (Northampton), Nottinghamshire or Lancashire (Trent Bridge or Old Trafford), Leicestershire (Grace Road, Leicester), Minor Counties (Torquay), Glamorgan (Pontypridd) and The President's XI for the Tesco International Trophy (Scarborough). The match against Minor Counties will be staged at the delightful Devon Riviera seaside resort ground of Torquay in August. This will be the first tourist match in Devon since 1978 when the New Zealanders visited Torquay. Fanie de Villiers has been the Torquay Club Professional during the last two summers.

Touring Party (16):

* K C Wessels (*Eastern Province/Sussex*) (Captain)
Age 37. Left-handed opening batsman and right-arm medium bowler.

W J Cronje (*Orange Free State*) (Vice-Captain)
Age 25. Right-handed middle order batsman and right-arm medium pace bowler.

D J Cullinan (*Transvaal*)
Age 27. Right-handed middle order batsman and off-break bowler.

P S de Villiers (*Northern Transvaal*)
Age 29. Right-handed late order batsman and right-arm fast-medium bowler.

A A Donald (*Orange Free State/Warwickshire*)
Age 27. Right-handed late order batsman and right-arm fast bowler.

A C Hudson (*Natal*)
Age 28. Right-handed opening batsman and right-arm medium pace bowler.

G Kirsten (*Western Province*)
Age 26. Left-handed top order batsman and off-break bowler.

P N Kirsten (*Border/Derbyshire*)
Age 39. Right-handed middle order batsman and off-break bowler.

† G J F Liebenberg (*Orange Free State*)
Age 22. Right-handed opening batsman, occasional wicket-keeper and right-arm fast-medium bowler.

A Martyn (*Western Province*)
Age 22. Left-handed late order batsman and left-arm fast-medium bowler.

C R Matthews (*Western Province*)
Age 29. Right-handed late order batsman and right-arm fast-medium bowler.

B M McMillan (*Western Province/Warwickshire*)
Age 30. Right-handed middle order batsman and right-arm fast-medium bowler.

J N Rhodes (*Natal*)
Age 25. Right-handed middle order batsman, superb fieldsman and right-arm medium pace bowler.

† D J Richardson (*Eastern Province*)
Age 34. Right-handed middle order batsman and wicket-keeper.

T G Shaw (*Eastern Province*)
Age 34. Left-handed late order batsman and slow left-arm bowler.

P L Symcox (*Natal*)
Age 34. Right-handed late order batsman and off-break bowler.

Manager: Mr. F Bing

Cricket Coach: Mr. M J Proctor

Physiotherapist: Mr. C Smith

RECORDS SECTION
FOR SOUTH AFRICA IN ENGLAND
1894-1965

Highest innings totals for South Africa

692	vs Cambridge University	Fenner's	1901
611	vs Nottinghamshire	Trent Bridge	1904
573	vs A Scotland XI	Glasgow	1907
572	vs Surrey	The Oval	1935
555/6 dec	vs Sussex	Hove	1947
543	vs Durham	Sunderland	1955
538	vs England (4th Test Match)	Headingley	1951
533	vs England (1st Test Match)	Trent Bridge	1947
521/8 dec	vs England (3rd Test Match)	Old Trafford	1955
520/7 dec	vs Warwickshire	Edgbaston	1947
512	vs Nottinghamshire	Trent Bridge	1935
510/6 dec	vs Oxford University	The Parks	1947
510/8 dec	vs South of England	Hastings	1947
507	vs Hampshire	Southampton	1960
503/4 dec	vs Essex	Colchester	1955

Highest innings totals against South Africa

579	by Yorkshire	Sheffield	1951
554/8 dec	by England (2nd Test Match)	Lord's	1947
551	by England (1st Test Match)	Trent Bridge	1947
538	by Hampshire	Southampton	1901
534/6 dec	by England (5th Test Match)	The Oval	1935
531/2 dec	by England (2nd Test Match)	Lord's	1924
505	by England (4th Test Match)	Headingley	1951

Lowest innings totals for South Africa

30	vs England (1st Test Match)	Edgbaston	1924
44	vs Lancashire	Liverpool	1912
49	vs Sussex	Brighton	1907
49	vs Gloucestershire	Bristol	1960
52	vs Surrey	The Oval	1894
56	vs Leicestershire	Grace Road, Leicester	1894
58	vs England (1st Test Match)	Lord's	1912
60	vs Lancashire	Old Trafford	1924
60	vs M.C.C. and Ground	Lord's	1894

Lowest innings totals against South Africa

32	by Derbyshire	Derby	1947
32	by Gents of Ireland	Belfast	1947
35	by Reigate Priory	Reigate	1935
36	by Scotland	Glasgow	1924
40	by Gloucestershire	Clifton	1901
45	by Durham	Sunderland	1935
46	by Derbyshire	Derby	1907
46	by Leicestershire	Grace Road, Leicester	1894
46	by Leicestershire	Aylestone Rd, Leicester	1912
49	by Kent	Canterbury	1935
49	by North Wales	Llandudno	1924
50	by Worcestershire	Worcester	1912
52	by Leicestershire	Grace Road, Leicester	1894
57	by Northamptonshire	Northampton	1907

Highest individual innings for South Africa

250	L J Tancred	vs Scotland	Edinburgh	1904
239	C M H Hathorn	vs Cambridge University	Fenner's	1901
236	E A B Rowan	vs England	Headingley	1951
229*	T A Harris	vs Club Cricket Conf.	Guildford	1947
213*	A W Nourse	vs Hampshire	Bournemouth	1912
208	A D Nourse	vs England	Trent Bridge	1951
207	R A McLean	vs Worcestershire	Worcester	1960
205*	A D Nourse	vs Warwickshire	Edgbaston	1947
203*	R G Pollock	vs Kent	Canterbury	1965
202*	E A B Rowan	vs Northamptonshire	Northampton	1951
201	K G Viljoen	vs Sussex	Hove	1947

Highest individual innings against South Africa

229	Lieut.G J Bryan	for Combined Services	Portsmouth	1924
216	C B Llewellyn	for Hampshire	Southampton	1901
211	J B Hobbs	for England	Lord's	1924
208	D C S Compton	for England	Lord's	1947
202*	P Holmes	for C I Thornton's XI	Scarborough	1924
201*	L Livingston	for Northamptonshire	Northampton	1951

Hat-tricks for South Africa

G C White	vs Kent	Canterbury	1904
S J Pegler	vs Yorkshire	Huddersfield	1912
O C Dawson	vs Northamptonshire	Northampton	1947
V I Smith	vs Derbyshire	Derby	1947
C N McCarthy	vs Sussex	Hove	1951

Hat-tricks against South Africa

T J Matthews	for Australia	Old Trafford	1912
T J Matthews	for Australia	Old Trafford	1912
J Sims	for Middlesex	Lord's	1947
J E McConnon	for Glamorgan	Swansea	1951

Most wickets in an innings for South Africa

8/18	M G Melle	vs Netherlands	Haarlem	1951
8/36	C N McCarthy	vs Sussex	Hove	1951
8/40	H J Tayfield	vs Hampshire	Southampton	1955
8/47	N S Crookes	vs Middlesex	Lord's	1965
8/50	Q McMillan	vs Somerset	Taunton	1929
8/51	H J Tayfield	vs Combined Services	Portsmouth	1960
8/52	G A Rowe	vs Lord Sheffield's XI	Sheffield Park	1894
8/54	S J Pegler	vs M.C.C. and Ground	Lord's	1924
8/60	H J Tayfield	vs Hampshire	Southampton	1955
8/67	A E E Vogler	vs M.C.C. and Ground	Lord's	1907
8/69	J H Sinclair	vs Oxford University	The Parks	1904
8/76	H J Tayfield	vs Surrey	The Oval	1955
8/90	R Graham	vs Worcestershire	Worcester	1901
8/97	J M Blanckenberg	vs Glamorgan	Arms Park, Cardiff	1924
8/99	X C Balaskas	vs Yorkshire	Sheffield	1935
8/106	A M B Rowan	vs Warwickshire	Edgbaston	1951

Most wickets in an innings against South Africa

9/28	T C Ross	for Gents of Ireland	Dublin	1904
9/56	M J Horton	for Worcestershire	Worcester	1955
9/71	W G Grace	for Gloucestershire	Bristol	1894
9/107	B J T Bosanquet	for M.C.C. and Ground	Lord's	1904
8/29	S F Barnes	for England	The Oval	1912
8/39	H Hayley	for Scarborough & Dist	Scarborough	1894
8/40	L C V Bathurst	for Oxford University	The Parks	1894
8/41	S F Barnes	for Minor Counties	Stoke-on-Trent	1929
8/45	D J Shepherd	for Glamorgan	Swansea	1960
8/51	R Tattersall	for M.C.C. and Ground	Lord's	1951
8/53	W Mead	for M.C.C. and Ground	Lord's	1901
8/59	C Blythe	for England	Headingley	1907
8/60	J Mercer	for Glamorgan	Pontypridd	1929
8/96	A E Thomas	for Northamptonshire	Northampton	1924
8/100	A Stoner	for Durham	Sunderland	1907

Most wickets in a match for South Africa

14/126	H J Tayfield	vs Hampshire	Southampton	1955
13/52	G A Rowe	vs Glasgow & District	Glasgow	1894
13/66	V I Smith	vs Derbyshire	Derby	1947
13/86	G A Rowe	vs North of Ireland	Belfast	1894
13/73	J H Sinclair	vs Gloucestershire	Bristol	1901
13/98	H J Tayfield	vs Surrey	The Oval	1955
13/153	J H Sinclair	vs Surrey	The Oval	1901
13/155	G A Rowe	vs Cambridge University	Fenner's	1901
13/227	N B F Mann	vs Kent	Canterbury	1947
13/241	C B Llewellyn	vs London County	Crystal Palace	1901

Most wickets in a match against South Africa

15/99	C Blythe	for England	Headingley	1907
14/119	J Mercer	for Glamorgan	Pontypridd	1929
13/57	S F Barnes	for England	The Oval	1912

Record partnerships for South Africa for each wicket

1st	330	B Mitchell/E A B Rowan	vs Surrey	The Oval	1935
2nd	256	H F Wade/E A B Rowan	vs Glamorgan	Arms Park, Cardiff	1935
3rd	319	A Melville/A D Nourse	vs England	Trent Bridge	1947
4th	238	E A B Rowan/J E Cheetham	vs Oxford Univ	The Parks	1951
5th	262	K G Viljoen/H B Cameron	vs Derbyshire	Ilkeston	1935
6th	187	E L Dalton/Q McMillan	vs Kent	Canterbury	1929
7th	162	P W Sherwell/A E E Vogler	vs Scotland	Edinburgh	1907
8th	156	G C White/R O Schwarz	vs Gloucs	Bristol	1907
9th	137	E L Dalton/A B C Langton	vs England	The Oval	1935
10th	103	H G O Owen-Smith/A J Bell	vs England	Headingley	1929

Record partnerships against South Africa for each wicket

1st	290	G Pullar/M C Cowdrey	for England	The Oval	1960
2nd	225	T W Hayward/J T Tyldesley	for C I Thornton's XI	Scarborough	1907
3rd	370	W J Edrich/D C S Compton	for England	Lord's	1947
4th	195	J M Parks/D S Sheppard	for Sussex	Hove	1955
5th	237	D C S Compton/N W D Yardley	for England	Trent Bridge	1947
6th	150	H P Crabtree/D R Wilcox	for Essex	Southend	1947
7th	169	A E Lawton/B S Foster	for M.C.C. & Ground	Lord's	1907
8th	125	G L Jessop/G R Cox	for South of England	Hastings	1904
9th	104	A E Lewis/B Cranfield	for Somerset	Taunton	1901
10th	131*	C Smart/W D Hughes	for Glamorgan	Arms Park, Cardiff	1935

Highest run aggregates on a tour for South Africa

	Year	M	I	NO	Runs	HS	Ave	100	50
B Mitchell	1947	23	37	4	2,014	189*	61.03	8	-
E A B Rowan	1935	28	46	2	1,948	171	44.27	6	7
A W Nourse	1924	35	54	5	1,928	147*	39.34	4	10
H W Taylor	1924	34	53	8	1,898	126	42.17	4	9
D J McGlew	1955	22	34	2	1,871	161	58.46	5	11
E A B Rowan	1951	26	41	4	1,852	236	50.05	5	9

Highest wicket aggregates on a tour for South Africa

	Year	Overs	Mdns	Runs	Wkts	Ave	5	10
S J Pegler	1912	1,286.5	352	2,885	189	15.26	17	3
G A Faulkner	1912	1,015.1	207	2,514	163	15.42	16	4
H J Tayfield	1955	1,160.5	461	2,253	143	15.75	13	3
R O Schwarz	1907	711.3	153	1,616	137	11.79	12	2

Centuries on debut in England for South Africa

103	C M H Hathorn	vs Hampshire	Southampton	1901
102	H B Cameron	vs Worcestershire	Worcester	1929

Centuries in each innings of a match for South Africa

157 & 116*	E L Dalton	vs Kent	Canterbury	1929
147 & 108*	A D Nourse	vs Surrey	The Oval	1935
189 & 104*	A Melville	vs England	Trent Bridge	1947
120 & 189*	B Mitchell	vs England	The Oval	1947

Centuries in each innings of a match against South Africa

104 & 109*	H Sutcliffe	for England	The Oval	1929

The cricketer's double '1,000 runs and 100 wickets' for South Africa

G A Faulkner in 1912 scored 1,075 runs (av. 23.88) with 2 centuries and a top score of 145* and also collected 163 wickets (av. 15.42).

Batsmen scoring three centuries for South Africa in consecutive matches

157 & 116*	E L Dalton	vs Kent	Canterbury	1929
102		vs Sussex	Hove	
147 & 108*	A D Nourse	vs Surrey	The Oval	1935
148		vs Oxford University	The Parks	
189 & 104*	A Melville	vs England	Trent Bridge	1947
117		vs England	Lord's	
131	B Mitchell	vs Lancashire	Old Trafford	1947
120 & 189*		vs England	The Oval	

Opening batsmen carrying bat through a completed innings for South Africa

L J Tancred (61* - 135)	vs M.C.C. and Ground	Lord's	1907
I J Siedle (132* - 297)	vs M.C.C. and Ground	Lord's	1935
B Mitchell (103* - 198)	vs M.C.C. and Ground	Lord's	1947
D J McGlew (114* - 251)	vs Hampshire	Southampton	1951
D J McGlew (64* - 95)	vs T N Pearce's XI	Scarborough	1951

Opening batsmen carrying bat through a completed innings against South Africa

T Langdon (78* - 151)	for Gloucestershire	Bristol	1907
J L Hopwood (73* - 128)	for Lancashire	Old Trafford	1935
E Davies (75* - 142)	for Glamorgan	Arms Park, Cardiff	1935
L G Berry (45* - 121)	for Leicestershire	Grace Road, Leicester	1947

Fastest centuries scored by batsmen in a completed innings for South Africa

103 in 75 mins	J H Sinclair	vs London County	Crystal Palace	1904
103 in 75 mins	A E E Vogler	vs Scotland	Edinburgh	1907

Fastest centuries scored by batsmen in a completed innings against South Africa

107 in 85 mins	P G H Fender	for Surrey	The Oval	1924
101 in 91 mins	P Cramner	for Warwickshire	Edgbaston	1947

Fastest scoring for South Africa in a day

574	South Africans (611) vs Nottinghamshire	Trent Bridge	1904
	(Score taken from 37 for 0 to 611 on 2nd day)		

Fastest scoring against South Africa in a day

538	Hampshire (538) vs South Africans	Southampton	1901
	(Scored on 1st day of the match)		

Most centuries in a season

For South Africa:	B Mitchell (8)	1947
For England:	D C S Compton (6)	1947

Top five South African batsmen in England
(Qualification: 40 innings)

	I	NO	Runs	HS	Ave	100	50
K G Viljoen	68	8	2,895	201	48.25	11	7
D J McGlew	102	13	4,200	161	47.19	11	17
E A B Rowan	87	6	3,800	236	46.91	11	16
B Mitchell	124	10	5,080	195	44.56	15	21
A Melville	40	2	1,547	189	40.71	6	4

Top five South African bowlers in England
(Qualification: 90 wickets)

	Overs	Mdns	Runs	Wkts	Ave	5	10
A E E Vogler	592	127	1,859	119	15.62	9	1
R O Schwarz	1,210	203	3,475	220	15.79	16	2
G A Faulkner	1,419	289	3,613	227	15.91	19	3
S J Pegler	2,328.2	641	5,437	297	18.30	24	4
C P Carter	858	198	2,220	118	18.81	8	-

South African teams' playing record tour by tour 1894 - 1965

Year	Captain	First-Class Matches						All Matches					
		P	W	D	L	T	A	P	W	D	L	T	A
1894	Castens	-	-	-	-	-	-	24	12	7	5	-	-
1901	Bisset	15	5	-	9	1	-	25	13	2	9	1	-
1904	Mitchell	22	10	9	2	1	-	26	13	9	3	1	-
1907	Sherwell	27	17	6	4	-	-	31	21	6	4	-	-
1912	Mitchell	37	13	16	8	-	-	37	13	16	8	-	-
1924	Taylor	35	8	18	9	-	-	38	8	21	9	-	-
1929	Deane	34	9	18	7	-	-	37	11	19	7	-	-
1935	Wade	31	17	12	2	-	-	41	23	16	2	-	-
1947	Melville	28	14	9	5	-	-	34	16	12	6	-	-
1951	Nourse, A.D	30	5	20	5	-	-	38	10	23	5	-	1
1955	Cheetham	28	15	9	4	-	-	31	16	11	4	-	-
1960	McGlew	30	14	11	5	-	1	31	15	11	5	-	1
1965	van der Merwe	18	5	11	2	-	-	19	5	11	3	-	1
	Total	**335**	**132**	**139**	**62**	**2**	**1**	**412**	**176**	**164**	**70**	**2**	**3**

RECORDS SECTION FOR AND AGAINST OPPONENTS

vs Derbyshire

Highest innings total for South Africans
443 at Ilkeston 1935
Highest innings total against South Africans
305 at Derby 1901
Lowest innings total for South Africans
113 at Derby 1955
Lowest innings total against South Africans
32 at Derby 1947
Highest individual innings for South Africans
184 M Bisset at Derby 1901
Highest individual innings against South Africans
93 Dr. E M Ashcroft at Derby 1904
Best bowling performance in an innings for South Africans
7 for 65 V I Smith at Derby 1947
Best bowling performance in an innings against South Africans
6 for 52 A Morton at Derby 1912
Best bowling performance in a match for South Africans
13 for 66 V I Smith at Derby 1947
Best bowling performance in a match against South Africans
10 for 96 G H Pope at Derby 1947

vs Durham

Highest innings total for South Africans
543 at Sunderland 1955
Highest innings total against South Africans
204 at Sunderland 1907
Lowest innings total for South Africans
173 at Sunderland 1924
Lowest innings total against South Africans
45 at Sunderland 1935
Highest individual innings for South Africans
151 A V C Bisset at Darlington 1901
Highest individual innings against South Africans
53 E W Elliott at Sunderland 1907
Best bowling performance in an innings for South Africans
7 for 38 A B C Langton at Sunderland 1935
Best bowling performance in an innings against South Africans
8 for 100 A Stoner at Sunderland 1907
Best bowling performance in a match for South Africans
11 for 52 A B C Langton at Sunderland 1935
Best bowling performance in a match against South Africans
8 for 100 A Stoner at Sunderland 1907

vs Essex

Highest innings total for South Africans
503 for 4 dec at Colchester 1955
Highest innings total against South Africans
380 at Southend-on-Sea 1947
Lowest innings total for South Africans
155 at Leyton 1907
Lowest innings total against South Africans
89 at Leyton 1907
Highest individual innings for South Africans
167 G M Fullerton at Ilford 1951
Highest individual innings against South Africans
147 R Smith at Ilford 1951
Best bowling performance in an innings for South Africans
7 for 47 J B Plimsoll at Southend-on-Sea 1947
Best bowling performance in an innings against South Africans
7 for 66 J W A Stephenson at Southend-on-Sea 1935
Best bowling performance in a match for South Africans
8 for 49 R O Schwarz at Leyton 1907
Best bowling performance in a match against South Africans
10 for 153 G M Louden at Colchester 1924

vs Glamorgan

Highest innings total for South Africans
497 for 8 dec at Arms Park, Cardiff 1947
Highest innings total against South Africans
301 at Swansea 1965
Lowest innings total for South Africans
83 at Swansea 1951
Lowest innings total against South Africans
64 at Swansea 1955
Highest individual innings for South Africans
153 E A B Rowan at Arms Park, Cardiff 1935
Highest individual innings against South Africans
146* A R Lewis at Swansea 1965
Best bowling performance in an innings for South Africans
8 for 97 J M Blanckenberg at Arms Park, Cardiff 1924
Best bowling performance in an innings against South Africans
8 for 45 D J Shepherd at Swansea 1960
Best bowling performance in a match for South Africans
12 for 106 G A Rowe at Arms Park, Cardiff 1894
Best bowling performance in a match against South Africans
14 for 119 J Mercer at Pontypridd 1929

vs Gloucestershire

Highest innings total for South Africans
388 for 9 dec at Bristol 1951
Highest innings total against South Africans
331 at Bristol 1929
Lowest innings total for South Africans
79 at Bristol 1912
Lowest innings total against South Africans
40 at Clifton 1901
Highest individual innings for South Africans
162* G C White at Gloucester 1907
Highest individual innings against South Africans
129 W G Grace at Bristol 1894
Best bowling performance in an innings for South Africans
7 for 20 J H Sinclair at Clifton 1901
Best bowling performance in an innings against South Africans
9 for 71 W G Grace at Bristol 1894
Best bowling performance in a match for South Africans
13 for 73 J H Sinclair at Clifton 1901
Best bowling performance in a match against South Africans
9 for 91 G H Dennett at Bristol 1912

vs Hampshire

Highest innings total for South Africans
507 at Southampton 1960
Highest innings total against South Africans
538 at Southampton 1901
Lowest innings total for South Africans
82 at Southampton 1907
Lowest innings total against South Africans
111 at Southampton 1907
Highest individual innings for South Africans
213* A W Nourse at Bournemouth 1912
Highest individual innings against South Africans
216 C B Llewellyn at Southampton 1901
Best bowling performance in an innings for South Africans
8 for 60 H J Tayfield at Southampton 1955
Best bowling performance in an innings against South Africans
7 for 35 H G Smoker at Southampton 1907
Best bowling performance in a match for South Africans
14 for 126 H J Tayfield at Southampton 1955
Best bowling performance in a match against South Africans
7 for 35 H G Smoker at Southampton 1907

vs Kent

Highest innings total for South Africans
> 491 for 7 dec at Canterbury 1929

Highest innings total against South Africans
> 436 at Canterbury 1929

Lowest innings total for South Africans
> 95 at Catford 1907

Lowest innings total against South Africans
> 49 at Canterbury 1935

Highest individual innings for South Africans
> 203* R G Pollock at Canterbury 1965

Highest individual innings against South Africans
> 176 F E Woolley at Canterbury 1924

Best bowling performance in an innings for South Africans
> 7 for 48 C L Vincent at Canterbury 1935

Best bowling performance in an innings against South Africans
> 6 for 53 C Blythe at Beckenham 1901

Best bowling performance in a match for South Africans
> 11 for 135 A H McKinnon at Canterbury 1960

Best bowling performance in a match against South Africans
> 10 for 160 C Blythe at Catford 1907

vs Lancashire

Highest innings total for South Africans
> 429 at Old Trafford 1907

Highest innings total against South Africans
> 445 for 6 dec at Liverpool 1924

Lowest innings total for South Africans
> 44 at Liverpool 1912

Lowest innings total against South Africans
> 90 at Blackpool 1960

Highest individual innings for South Africans
> 131 B Mitchell at Old Trafford 1947

Highest individual innings against South Africans
> 128 C Washbrook at Old Trafford 1947

Best bowling performance in an innings for South Africans
> 6 for 45 R O Schwarz at Old Trafford 1907

Best bowling performance in an innings against South Africans
> 7 for 28 R K Tyldesley at Old Trafford 1924

Best bowling performance in a match for South Africans
> 10 for 79 T L Goddard at Blackpool 1960

Best bowling performance in a match against South Africans
> 12 for 78 R K Tyldesley at Old Trafford 1924

vs Leicestershire

Highest innings total for South Africans
464 at Leicester (Aylestone Road) 1904
Highest innings total against South Africans
292 at Leicester (Aylestone Road) 1904
Lowest innings total for South Africans
56 at Leicester (Grace Road) 1894
Lowest innings total against South Africans
46 at Leicester (Grace Road) 1894
Highest individual innings for South Africans
169* I J Siedle at Leicester (Aylestone Road) 1929
Highest individual innings against South Africans
168 M R Hallam at Leicester (Grace Road) 1960
Best bowling performance in an innings for South Africans
6 for 21 G A Faulkner at Leicester (Aylestone Rd) 1912
Best bowling performance in an innings against South Africans
7 for 17 A D Pougher at Leicester (Grace Road) 1894
Best bowling performance in a match for South Africans
11 for 59 G A Faulkner at Leicester (Aylestone Rd) 1912
Best bowling performance in a match against South Africans
12 for 97 J H King at Leicester (Aylestone Road) 1912

vs Middlesex

Highest innings total for South Africans
424 at Lord's 1947
Highest innings total against South Africans
335 for 8 dec at Lord's 1965
Lowest innings total for South Africans
163 at Lord's 1935
Lowest innings total against South Africans
98 at Lord's 1955
Highest individual innings for South Africans
142 T L Goddard at Lord's 1960
Highest individual innings against South Africans
154 D C S Compton at Lord's 1947
Best bowling performance in an innings for South Africans
8 for 47 N S Crookes at Lord's 1965
Best bowling performance in an innings against South Africans
6 for 63 F J Titmus at Lord's 1955
Best bowling performance in a match for South Africans
11 for 112 A B C Langton at Lord's 1935
Best bowling performance in a match against South Africans
11 for 117 F J Titmus at Lord's 1955

vs Northamptonshire

Highest innings total for South Africans
461 for 3 at Northampton 1960
Highest innings total against South Africans
426 for 6 dec at Northampton 1951
Lowest innings total for South Africans
115 at Northampton 1907
Lowest innings total against South Africans
57 at Northampton 1907
Highest individual innings for South Africans
202* E A B Rowan at Northampton 1951
Highest individual innings against South Africans
201* L Livingston at Northampton 1951
Best bowling performance in an innings for South Africans
7 for 48 J J Kotze at Northampton 1901
Best bowling performance in an innings against South Africans
8 for 96 A E Thomas at Northampton 1924
Best bowling performance in a match for South Africans
11 for 130 J B Pilmsoll at Northampton 1947
Best bowling performance in a match against South Africans
10 for 83 S G Smith at Northampton 1907

vs Nottinghamshire

Highest innings total for South Africans
611 at Trent Bridge 1904
Highest innings total against South Africans
476 at Trent Bridge 1929
Lowest innings total for South Africans
165 at Trent Bridge 1901
Lowest innings total against South Africans
96 at Trent Bridge 1901
Highest individual innings for South Africans
151 H F Wade at Trent Bridge 1935
Highest individual innings against South Africans
194 A W Carr at Trent Bridge 1929
Best bowling performance in an innings for South Africans
7 for 31 J J Kotze at Trent Bridge 1901
Best bowling performance in an innings against South Africans
7 for 223 J H Pennington at Trent Bridge 1904
Best bowling performance in a match for South Africans
10 for 82 J J Kotze at Trent Bridge 1901
Best bowling performance in a match against South Africans
8 for 141 A W Hallam at Trent Bridge 1901

vs Somerset

Highest innings total for South Africans
438 at Taunton 1904
Highest innings total against South Africans
440 for 9 dec at Taunton 1901
Lowest innings total for South Africans
96 at Bath 1912
Lowest innings total against South Africans
68 at Taunton 1955
Highest individual innings for South Africans
170 C O H Sewell at Taunton 1894
Highest individual innings against South Africans
107* S S Rogers at Taunton 1951
Best bowling performance in an innings for South Africans
8 for 50 Q McMillan at Taunton 1929
Best bowling performance in an innings against South Africans
6 for 61 J J Bridges at Taunton 1924
Best bowling performance in a match for South Africans
12 for 119 A H McKinnon at Taunton 1960
Best bowling performance in a match against South Africans
8 for 77 G C Gill at Taunton 1901

vs Surrey

Highest innings total for South Africans
572 at The Oval 1935
Highest innings total against South Africans
363 for 7 dec at The Oval 1904
Lowest innings total for South Africans
52 at The Oval 1894
Lowest innings total against South Africans
112 at The Oval 1947
Highest individual innings for South Africans
195 B Mitchell at The Oval 1935
Highest individual innings against South Africans
197 T W Hayward at The Oval 1904
Best bowling performance in an innings for South Africans
8 for 76 H J Tayfield at The Oval 1955
Best bowling performance in an innings against South Africans
7 for 41 A E Street at The Oval 1894
Best bowling performance in a match for South Africans
13 for 98 H J Tayfield at The Oval 1955
Best bowling performance in a match against South Africans
11 for 125 T Richardson at The Oval 1901

vs Sussex

Highest innings total for South Africans
555 for 6 dec at Hove 1947
Highest innings total against South Africans
415 for 5 dec at Hove 1947
Lowest innings total for South Africans
49 at Brighton 1907
Lowest innings total against South Africans
76 at Brighton 1912
Highest individual innings for South Africans
201 K G Viljoen at Hove 1947
Highest individual innings against South Africans
178* K S Ranjitsinhji at Brighton 1904
Best bowling performance in an innings for South Africans
8 for 36 C N McCarthy at Hove 1951
Best bowling performance in an innings against South Africans
6 for 25 E B Dwyer at Brighton 1907
Best bowling performance in a match for South Africans
10 for 97 S J Pegler at Brighton 1912
Best bowling performance in a match against South Africans
11 for 120 W A Humphreys at Brighton 1894

vs Warwickshire

Highest innings total for South Africans
520 for 7 dec at Edgbaston 1947
Highest innings total against South Africans
440 at Edgbaston 1924
Lowest innings total for South Africans
74 at Edgbaston 1901
Lowest innings total against South Africans
76 at Edgbaston 1947
Highest individual innings for South Africans
205* A D Nourse at Edgbaston 1935
Highest individual innings against South Africans
109 A J W Croom at Edgbaston 1929
Best bowling performance in an innings for South Africans
8 for 106 A M B Rowan at Edgbaston 1951
Best bowling performance in an innings against South Africans
7 for 77 S Santall at Edgbaston 1907
Best bowling performance in a match for South Africans
10 for 67 R J Crisp at Edgbaston 1935
Best bowling performance in a match against South Africans
9 for 67 S Santall at Edgbaston 1901

vs Worcestershire

Highest innings total for South Africans
444 for 8 dec at Worcester 1929
Highest innings total against South Africans
284 at Worcester 1929
Lowest innings total for South Africans
107 at Worcester 1947
Lowest innings total against South Africans
50 at Worcester 1912
Highest individual innings for South Africans
207 R A McLean at Worcester 1960
Highest individual innings against South Africans
107 H K Foster at Worcester 1904
Best bowling performance in an innings for South Africans
8 for 90 R Graham at Worcester 1901
Best bowling performance in an innings against South Africans
9 for 56 M J Horton at Worcester 1955
Best bowling performance in a match for South Africans
10 for 93 A M B Rowan at Worcester 1947
Best bowling performance in a match against South Africans
9 for 56 M J Horton at Worcester 1955

vs Yorkshire

Highest innings total for South Africans
454 for 8 dec at Sheffield 1951
Highest innings total against South Africans
579 at Sheffield 1951
Lowest innings total for South Africans
76 at Bradford 1951
Lowest innings total against South Africans
113 at Bradford 1907
Highest individual innings for South Africans
168 I J Siedle at Sheffield 1929
Highest individual innings against South Africans
156 L Hutton at Sheffield 1951
Best bowling performance in an innings for South Africans
8 for 99 X C Balaskas at Sheffield 1935
Best bowling performance in an innings against South Africans
6 for 38 R Appleyard at Bradford 1951
Best bowling performance in a match for South Africans
11 for 187 J H Sinclair at Harrogate 1901
Best bowling performance in a match against South Africans
10 for 153 E Smith at Harrogate 1901

vs M.C.C and Ground

Highest innings total for South Africans
311 at Lord's 1929
Highest innings total against South Africans
336 at Lord's 1929
Lowest innings total for South Africans
60 at Lord's 1894
Lowest innings total against South Africans
72 at Lord's 1894
Highest individual innings for South Africans
132* I J Siedle at Lord's 1935
Highest individual innings against South Africans
147 D C S Compton at Lord's 1951
Best bowling performance in an innings for South Africans
8 for 54 S J Pegler at Lord's 1924
Best bowling performance in an innings against South Africans
9 for 107 B J T Bosanquet at Lord's 1904
Best bowling performance in a match for South Africans
12 for 83 J Middleton at Lord's 1894
Best bowling performance in a match against South Africans
12 for 93 W G Grace at Lord's 1894

vs Cambridge University

Highest innings total for South Africans
692 at Fenner's 1901
Highest innings total against South Africans
254 at Fenner's 1901
Lowest innings total for South Africans
145 at Fenner's 1960
Lowest innings total against South Africans
67 at Fenner's 1955
Highest individual innings for South Africans
239 C M H Hathorn at Fenner's 1901
Highest individual innings against South Africans
77 E T Killick at Fenner's 1929
Best bowling performance in an innings for South Africans
7 for 40 V I Smith at Fenner's 1947
Best bowling performance in an innings against South Africans
6 for 73 G G Napier at Fenner's 1907
Best bowling performance in a match for South Africans
13 for 155 G A Rowe at Fenner's 1901
Best bowling performance in a match against South Africans
9 for 204 R J O Meyer at Fenner's 1924

vs Oxford University

Highest innings total for South Africans
510 for 6 dec at The Parks 1947
Highest innings total against South Africans
429 at The Parks 1935
Lowest innings total for South Africans
145 at The Parks 1894
Lowest innings total against South Africans
90 at Christ Church Oxford 1955
Highest individual innings for South Africans
164* I J Siedle at The Parks 1935
Highest individual innings against South Africans
165 N S Mitchell-Innes at The Parks 1935
Best bowling performance in an innings for South Africans
8 for 69 J H Sinclair at The Parks 1904
Best bowling performance in an innings against South Africans
8 for 40 L C V Bathurst at The Parks 1894
Best bowling performance in a match for South Africans
9 for 119 N A Quinn at The Parks 1929
Best bowling performance in a match against South Africans
8 for 40 L C V Bathurst at The Parks 1894

vs Minor Counties

Highest innings total for South Africans
394 at Skegness 1935
Highest innings total against South Africans
272 at Norwich 1924
Lowest Innings total for South Africans
139 at Stoke-on-Trent 1929
Lowest innings total against South Africans
74 at Jesmond 1965
Highest individual innings for South Africans
168 K G Viljoen at Skegness 1935
Highest individual innings against South Africans
96 R Collins at Stoke-on-Trent 1960
Best bowling performance in an innings for South Africans
6 for 38 H G O Owen-Smith at Stoke-on-Trent 1929
Best bowling performance in an innings against South Africans
8 for 41 S F Barnes at Stoke-on-Trent 1929
Best bowling performance in a match for South Africans
10 for 68 N A T Adcock at Stoke-on-Trent 1960
Best bowling performance in a match against South Africans
8 for 41 S F Barnes at Stoke-on-Trent 1929

vs London County

Highest innings total for South Africans
332 at Crystal Palace 1904
Highest innings total against South Africans
316 at Crystal Palace 1901
Lowest innings total for South Africans
262 at Crystal Palace 1901
Lowest innings total against South Africans
167 at Crystal Palace 1904
Highest individual innings for South Africans
130 C M H Hathorn at Crystal Palace 1904
Highest individual innings against South Africans
114 L Walker at Crystal Palace 1901
Best bowling performance in an innings for South Africans
7 for 101 C B Llewellyn at Crystal Palace 1901
Best bowling performance in an innings against South Africans
5 for 117 L C Braund at Crystal Palace 1901
Best bowling performance in a match for South Africans
13 for 241 C B Llewellyn at Crystal Palace 1901
Best bowling performance in a match against South Africans
5 for 117 L C Braund at Crystal Palace 1901

vs Combined Services

Highest innings total for South Africans
499 for 5 dec at Portsmouth 1951
Highest innings total against South Africans
418 at Portsmouth 1924
Lowest innings total for South Africans
182 at Portsmouth 1924
Lowest innings total against South Africans
103 at Portsmouth 1960
Highest individual innings for South Africans
139 J H B Waite at Portsmouth 1951
Highest individual innings against South Africans
229 Lieut. G J Bryan at Portsmouth 1924
Best bowling performance in an innings for South Africans
8 for 51 H J Tayfield at Portsmouth 1960
Best bowling performance in an innings against South Africans
7 for 152 Capt. T O James at Portsmouth 1924
Best bowling performance in a match for South Africans
8 for 51 H J Tayfield at Portsmouth 1960
Best bowling performance in a match against South Africans
111 for 244 Capt. T O James at Portsmouth 1924

vs Scottish XIs

Highest innings total for South Africans
    573 vs A Scotland XI at Glasgow 1907
Highest innings total against South Africans
    258 by Scotland at Edinburgh 1907
Lowest Innings total for South Africans
    170 vs West of Scotland at Glasgow 1901
Lowest innings total against South Africans
    36 by Scotland at Glasgow 1924
Highest individual innings for South Africans
    250 L J Tancred vs Scotland at Edinburgh 1904
Highest individual innings against South Africans
    106* J Aitchison for Scotland at Paisley 1947
Best bowling performance in an innings for South Africans
    7 for 18 J H Sinclair vs West of Scotland at Glasgow 1901
Best bowling performance in an innings against South Africans
    7 for 106 H J Stevenson for East of Scotland at Edinburgh 1901
Best bowling performance in a match for South Africans
    12 for 96 J J Kotze vs A Scotland XI at Glasgow 1907
Best bowling performance in a match against South Africans
    7 for 106 H J Stevenson for East of Scotland at Edinburgh 1901

vs Named Individual XIs / Clubs

Highest innings total for South Africans
    510 for 8 dec vs South of England at Hastings 1947
Highest innings total against South Africans
    461 for 6 dec by C I Thornton's XI at Scarborough 1924
Lowest innings total for South Africans
    66 vs Lionel Robinson's XI at Attleborough 1912
Lowest innings total against South Africans
    30 by Reigate Priory at Reigate 1935
Highest individual innings for South Africans
    229* T A Harris vs Club Cricket Conference at Guildford 1947
Highest individual innings against South Africans
    202* P Holmes for C I Thornton's XI at Scarborough 1924
Best bowling performance in an innings for South Africans
    8 for 52 G A Rowe vs Lord Sheffield's XI at Sheffield Park 1894
Best bowling performance in an innings against South Africans
    7 for 52 R H Bettington for Harlequins at Eastbourne 1924
Best bowling performance in a match for South Africans
    11 for 69 G C White vs J C Bamford's XI at Uttoxeter 1907
Best bowling performance in a match against South Africans
    10 for 95 W Rhodes for H D G Leveson-Gower's XI at Reigate 1924

vs District XIs

Highest innings total for South Africans
   287 vs Liverpool & District at Liverpool 1894
Highest innings total against South Africans
   207 by Liverpool & District at Liverpool 1894
Lowest Innings total for South Africans
   87 vs Chatham & District at Chatham 1894
Lowest innings total against South Africans
   63 by Glasgow & District at Glasgow 1894
Highest individual innings for South Africans
   112 C L Johnson Liverpool & District at Liverpool 1894
Highest individual innings against South Africans
   48 D Lorrimer for Liverpool & District at Liverpool 1894
Best bowling performance in an innings for South Africans
   7 for 27 G A Rowe vs Glasgow & District at Glasgow 1894
Best bowling performance in an innings against South Africans
   8 for 39 H Hayley for Scarborough & District at Scarborough 1894
Best bowling performance in a match for South Africans
   13 for 52 G A Rowe vs Glasgow & District at Glasgow 1894
Best bowling performance in a match against South Africans
   12 for 79 H Hayley for Scarborough & District at Scarborough 1894

vs Minor County Clubs

Highest innings total for South Africans
   420 vs Norfolk at Norwich 1929
Highest innings total against South Africans
   325 by Norfolk at Norwich 1935
Lowest innings total for South Africans
   164 vs Staffordshire at Stoke-on-Trent 1901
Lowest innings total against South Africans
   60 by Staffordshire at Stoke-on-Trent 1935
Highest individual innings for South Africans
   170 H W Taylor vs Norfolk at Norwich 1929
Highest individual innings against South Africans
   111 W J Edrich for Norfolk at Norwich 1935
Best bowling performance in an innings for South Africans
   6 for 30 G A Rowe vs Staffordshire at Stoke-on-Trent 1901
Best bowling performance in an innings against South Africans
   5 for 49 E N Backhouse for Staffordshire at Stoke-on-Trent 1935
Best bowling performance in a match for South Africans
   11 for 111 J B Plimsoll vs Northumberland at Jesmond 1947
Best bowling performance in a match against South Africans
   10 for 155 Grimshaw for Staffordshire at Stoke-on-Trent 1901

vs Irish XIs

Highest innings total for South Africans
    484 vs Dublin University at Trinity College, Dublin 1904
Highest innings total against South Africans
    202 by Gentlemen of Ireland at Belfast 1947
Lowest innings total for South Africans
    64 vs Gentlemen of Ireland at Dublin 1904
Lowest innings total against South Africans
    32 by Gentlemen of Ireland at Belfast 1947
Highest individual innings for South Africans
    148 L J Tancred vs Dublin University at Trinity College, Dublin 1904
Highest individual innings against South Africans
    90 Baker for Woodbrook Club at Bray, Ireland 1912
Best bowling performance in an innings for South Africans
    7 for 10 A M B Rowan vs Gentlemen of Ireland at Belfast 1947
Best bowling performance in an innings against South Africans
    9 for 28 T C Ross for Gentlemen of Ireland at Dublin 1904
Best bowling performance in a match for South Africans
    13 for 86 G A Rowe vs North of Ireland at Belfast 1894
Best bowling performance in a match against South Africans
    11 for 64 T C Ross for Gentlemen of Ireland at Dublin 1904

vs Welsh XIs

Highest innings total for South Africans
    352 vs South Wales at Swansea 1912
Highest innings total against South Africans
    262 by Wales at Colwyn Bay 1929
Lowest innings total for South Africans
    192 vs Wales at Colwyn Bay 1929
Lowest innings total against South Africans
    49 by North Wales at Llandudno 1924
Highest individual innings for South Africans
    117 R H Catterall vs Wales at Colwyn Bay 1929
Highest individual innings against South Africans
    102 W Bates for Wales at Colwyn Bay 1929
Best bowling performance in an innings for South Africans
    6 for 12 J M Blanckenberg vs North Wales at Llandudno 1924
Best bowling performance in an innings against South Africans
    6 for 28 S F Barnes for Wales at Colwyn Bay 1929
Best bowling performance in a match for South Africans
    6 for 12 J M Blanckenberg vs North Wales at Llandudno 1924
Best bowling performance in a match against South Africans
    10 for 90 S F Barnes for Wales at Colwyn Bay 1929

TEST MATCH RECORDS FOR
SOUTH AFRICA IN ENGLAND
1907-1965

1907   1st Test   Lord's   Match Drawn
           2nd Test   Headingley   England won by 53 runs
           3rd Test   The Oval   Match Drawn

England won series 1-0

1912   1st Test   Old Trafford   Australia won by an innings and 88 runs
           2nd Test   Lord's   England won by an innings and 62 runs
           3rd Test   Headingley   England won by 174 runs
           4th Test   Lord's   Australia won by 10 wickets
           5th Test   Trent Bridge   Match Drawn
           6th Test   The Oval   England won by 10 wickets

Triangular series with Australia and England

1924   1st Test   Edgbaston   England won by an innings and 18 runs
           2nd Test   Lord's   England won by an innings and 18 runs
           3rd Test   Headingley   England won by 9 wickets
           4th Test   Old Trafford   Match Drawn
           5th Test   The Oval   Match Drawn

England won series 3-0

1929   1st Test   Edgbaston   Match Drawn
           2nd Test   Lord's   Match Drawn
           3rd Test   Headingley   England won by 5 wickets
           4th Test   Old Trafford   England won by an innings and 32 runs
           5th Test   The Oval   Match Drawn

England won series 2-0

1935   1st Test   Trent Bridge   Match Drawn
           2nd Test   Lord's   South Africa won by 154 runs
           3rd Test   Headingley   Match Drawn
           4th Test   Old Trafford   Match Drawn
           5th Test   The Oval   Match Drawn

South Africa won series 1-0 (being the First Test victory in England)

1947   1st Test   Trent Bridge   Match Drawn
           2nd Test   Lord's   England won by 10 wickets
           3rd Test   Old Trafford   England won by 7 wickets
           4th Test   Headingley   England won by 10 wickets
           5th Test   The Oval   Match Drawn

England won series 3-0

1951	1st Test	Trent Bridge	South Africa won by 71 runs
	2nd Test	Lord's	England won by 10 wickets
	3rd Test	Old Trafford	England won by 9 wickets
	4th Test	Headingley	Match Drawn
	5th Test	The Oval	England won by 4 wickets

England won series 3-1

1955	1st Test	Trent Bridge	England won by an innings and 5 runs
	2nd Test	Lord's	England won by 71 runs
	3rd Test	Old Trafford	South Africa won by 3 wickets
	4th Test	Headingley	South Africa won by 224 runs
	5th Test	The Oval	England won by 92 runs

England won series 3-2

1960	1st Test	Edgbaston	England won by 100 runs
	2nd Test	Lord's	England won by an innings and 73 runs
	3rd Test	Trent Bridge	England won by 8 wickets
	4th Test	Old Trafford	Match Drawn
	5th Test	The Oval	Match Drawn

England won series 3-0

1965	1st Test	Lord's	Match Drawn
	2nd Test	Trent Bridge	South Africa won by 94 runs
	3rd Test	The Oval	Match Drawn

South Africa won series 1-0 (Second Series win in England)

SUMMARY OF TEST SERIES

Season	*Pld*	*England Won*	*South Africa Won*	*Drawn*
1907	3	1	0	2
1912	3	3	0	0
1924	5	3	0	2
1929	5	2	0	3
1935	5	0	1	4
1947	5	3	0	2
1951	5	3	1	1
1955	5	3	2	0
1960	5	3	0	2
1965	3	0	1	2
Total	**44**	**21**	**5**	**18**

Summary of Test Matches vs Australia (1912) played in England as part of the Triangular Tournament

vs Australia in England   Played 3   Won 0   Lost 2   Drawn 1

Records at each Test venue

Lord's	England won 6	South Africa won	1	Drawn	3
Headingley	England won 5	South Africa won	1	Drawn	2
The Oval	England won 3	South Africa won	0	Drawn	7
Edgbaston	England won 2	South Africa won	0	Drawn	1
Old Trafford	England won 3	South Africa won	1	Drawn	3
Trent Bridge	England won 2	South Africa won	2	Drawn	2

Test Captains 1907-1965

	England	*South Africa*
1907	R E Foster	P W Sherwell
1912	C B Fry	F Mitchell/L J Tancred
1924	A E R Gilligan/ J W H T Douglas	H W Taylor
1929	J C White/A W Carr	H G Deane
1935	R E S Wyatt	H F Wade
1947	N W D Yardley	A Melville
1951	F R Brown	A D Nourse
1955	P B H May	J E Cheetham/D J McGlew
1960	M C Cowdrey	D J McGlew
1965	M J K Smith	P L van der Merwe

Highest individual innings in Tests

For England

211	J B Hobbs	Lord's	1924
208	D C S Compton	Lord's	1947
191	W J Edrich	Old Trafford	1947
189	W J Edrich	Lord's	1947

For South Africa

236	E A B Rowan	Headingley	1951
208	A D Nourse	Trent Bridge	1951
189	A Melville	Trent Bridge	1947
189*	B Mitchell	The Oval	1947
164*	B Mitchell	Lord's	1935

A total of 127 centuries have been scored, 77 for England and 50 for South Africa.

Leading Test century makers

7	D C S Compton	England
7	B Mitchell	South Africa
7	A D Nourse	South Africa
7	H W Taylor	South Africa
6	W R Hammond	England
6	H Sutcliffe	England

Century on debut in Tests between England and South Africa in England

104	L C Braund	Lord's	1907
119	R H Spooner	Lord's	1912
163	D C S Compton	Trent Bridge	1947
138	P B H May	Headingley	1951

No South African has recorded a century on Test debut in England. The highest innings on debut is 90 by P N F Mansell (Headingley) 1951.

Highest Test Match aggregate

1477 runs for 33 wickets at The Oval in 1947

Lowest Test Match aggregate

378 runs for 30 wickets at The Oval in 1912

Highest Test innings totals for South Africa

538	Headingley	1951
533	Trent Bridge	1947
521/8 dec	Old Trafford	1955
500	Headingley	1955

Highest Test innings totals against South Africa

554/8 dec	Lord's	1947
551	Trent Bridge	1947
534/6 dec	The Oval	1935
531/2 dec	Lord's	1924

Lowest Test innings totals for South Africa

30	Edgbaston	1924
58	Lord's	1912

Lowest Test innings totals against South Africa

76	Headingley	1907
114	Trent Bridge	1951

Test Match Ground Records

Highest innings total for England in England
554 for 8 dec at Lord's 1947
Highest innings total for South Africa in England
538 at Headingley 1951
Lowest innings total for England in England
76 at Headingley 1907
Lowest innings total for South Africa in England
30 at Edgbaston 1924
Highest individual innings for England in England
211 J B Hobbs at Lord's 1924
Highest individual innings for South Africa in England
236 E A B Rowan at Headingley 1951
Best bowling performance in an innings for England in England
8 for 29 S F Barnes at The Oval 1912
Best bowling performance in an innings for South Africa in England
7 for 65 S J Pegler at Lord's 1912
Best bowling performance in a match for England in England
15 for 99 C Blythe at Headingley 1907
Best bowling performance in a match for South Africa in England
10 for 87 P M Pollock at Trent Bridge 1965

Test Match Aggregates

Highest aggregate of runs in a series for England in England
753 (av. 94.12) D C S Compton 1947
Highest aggregate of runs in a series for South Africa in England
621 (av. 69.00) A D Nourse 1947
Highest aggregate of wickets in a series for England in England
34 (av. 8.29) S F Barnes 1912
Highest aggregate of wickets in a series for South Africa in England
26 (av. 21.84) H J Tayfield 1955
26 (av. 22.57) N A T Adcock 1960

Record Test wicket partnerships for England in England

370 W J Edrich (189)/D C S Compton (208) for 3rd Wicket at Lord's 1947
237 D C S Compton (163)/N W D Yardley (99) for 5th Wicket at Trent Bridge 1947

Record Test wicket partnerships for South Africa in England

319 A Melville (189)/A D Nourse (149) for 3rd Wicket at Trent Bridge 1947
214 H W Taylor (121)/H G Deane (93) for 4th Wicket at The Oval 1929
198 E A B Rowan (236)/C B van Ryneveld (83) for 2nd Wicket at Headingley 1951
171 J H B Waite (113)/P L Winslow (108) for 6th Wicket at Old Trafford 1955
137 E L Dalton (117)/A B C Langton (73*) for 9th Wicket at The Oval 1935
109* B Mitchell (189*)/L Tuckett (40*) for 8th Wicket at The Oval 1947
103 H G Owen-Smith (129)/A J Bell (26*) for 10th Wicket at Headingley 1929

Test Match Ground Records vs England at Lord's

Highest innings total for South Africa
327 at Lord's 1947
Highest innings total against South Africa
554 for 8 dec at Lord's 1947
Lowest innings total for South Africa
58 at Lord's 1912
Lowest innings total against South Africa
133 at Lord's 1955
Highest individual innings for South Africa
164* B Mitchell at Lord's 1935
Highest individual innings against South Africa
211 by J B Hobbs at Lord's 1924
Best bowling performance in an innings for South Africa
7 for 65 S J Pegler at Lord's 1912
Best bowling performance in an innings against South Africa
7 for 39 J B Statham at Lord's 1955
Best bowling performance in a match for South Africa
9 for 103 X C Balaskas at Lord's 1935
Best bowling performance in a match against South Africa
12 for 101 R Tattersall at Lord's 1951

Test Match Ground Records vs England at Headingley

Highest innings total for South Africa
538 at Headingley 1951
Highest innings total against South Africa
505 at Headingley 1951
Lowest innings total for South Africa
75 at Headingley 1907
Lowest innings total against South Africa
76 at Headingley 1907
Highest individual innings for South Africa
236 E A B Rowan at Headingley 1951
Highest individual innings against South Africa
138 P B H May at Headingley 1951
Best bowling performance in an innings for South Africa
6 for 17 G A Faulkner at Headingley 1907
Best bowling performance in an innings against South Africa
8 for 59 C Blythe at Headingley 1907
Best bowling performance in a match for South Africa
9 for 75 G A Faulkner at Headingley 1907
Best bowling performance in a match against South Africa
15 for 99 C Blythe at Headingley 1907

Test Match Ground Records vs England at Edgbaston

Highest innings total for South Africa
390 at Edgbaston 1924
Highest innings total against South Africa
438 at Edgbaston 1924
Lowest innings total for South Africa
30 at Edgbaston 1924
Lowest innings total against South Africa
203 at Edgbaston 1960
Highest individual innings for South Africa
120 R H Catterall at Edgbaston 1924
Highest individual innings against South Africa
138* W R Hammond at Edgbaston 1929
Best bowling performance in an innings for South Africa
6 for 152 G M Parker at Edgbaston 1924
Best bowling performance in an innings against South Africa
6 for 7 A E R Gilligan at Edgbaston 1924
Best bowling performance in a match for South Africa
8 for 119 N A T Adcock at Edgbaston 1960
Best bowling performance in a match against South Africa
11 for 90 A E R Gilligan at Edgbaston 1924

Test Match Ground Records vs England at The Oval

Highest innings total for South Africa
492 for 8 dec at The Oval 1929
Highest innings total against South Africa
534 for 6 dec at The Oval 1935
Lowest innings total for South Africa
93 at The Oval 1912
Lowest innings total against South Africa
138 at The Oval 1907
Highest individual innings for South Africa
189* B Mitchell at The Oval 1947
Highest individual innings against South Africa
161 M Leyland at The Oval 1935
Best bowling performance in an innings for South Africa
7 for 84 G A Faulkner at The Oval 1912
Best bowling performance in an innings against South Africa
8 for 29 S F Barnes at The Oval 1912
Best bowling performance in a match for South Africa
8 for 99 H J Tayfield at The Oval 1955
Best bowling performance in a match against South Africa
13 for 57 S F Barnes at The Oval 1912

Test Match Ground Records vs England at Trent Bridge

Highest innings total for South Africa
533 at Trent Bridge 1947
Highest innings total against South Africa
551 at Trent Bridge 1947
Lowest innings total for South Africa
88 at Trent Bridge 1960
Lowest innings total against South Africa
114 at Trent Bridge 1951
Highest individual innings for South Africa
208 A D Nourse at Trent Bridge 1951
Highest individual innings against South Africa
163 D C S Compton at Trent Bridge 1947
Best bowling performance in an innings for South Africa
5 for 34 P M Pollock at Trent Bridge 1965
Best bowling performance in an innings against South Africa
6 for 28 F H Tyson at Trent Bridge 1955
Best bowling performance in a match for South Africa
10 for 87 P M Pollock at Trent Bridge 1965
Best bowling performance in a match against South Africa
9 for 104 F S Trueman at Trent Bridge 1960

Test Match Ground Records vs England at Old Trafford

Highest innings total for South Africa
521 for 8 dec at Old Trafford 1955
Highest innings total against South Africa
478 at Old Trafford 1947
Lowest innings total for South Africa
130 at Old Trafford 1929
Lowest innings total against South Africa
153 for 7 dec at Old Trafford 1960
Highest individual innings for South Africa
124 K G Viljoen at Old Trafford 1935
Highest individual innings against South Africa
191 W J Edrich at Old Trafford 1947
Best bowling performance in an innings for South Africa
6 for 51 G W A Chubb at Old Trafford 1951
Best bowling performance in an innings against South Africa
7 for 58 A V Bedser at Old Trafford 1951
Best bowling performance in a match for South Africa
8 for 157 P S Heine at Old Trafford 1955
Best bowling performance in a match against South Africa
12 for 112 A V Bedser at Old Trafford 1951

SOUTH AFRICAN TEST REPRESENTATIVES IN ENGLAND 1907-1965

Player	*Year (Tests)*	*Total Tests vs England*
N A T Adcock	1955 (4) 1960 (5)	9
A Bacher	1965 (3)	3
X C Balaskas	1935 (1)	1
E J Barlow	1965 (3)	3
R Beaumont	1912 (4) * (2 Aus)	4
A J Bell	1929 (3) 1935 (3)	6
J M Blanckenberg	1924 (5)	5
K C Bland	1965 (3)	3
J T Botten	1965 (3)	3
H D Bromfield	1965 (1)	1
H B Cameron	1929 (4) 1935 (5)	9
T Campbell	1912 (1)	1
P R Carlstein	1960 (5)	5
C P Carter	1912 (2) 1924 (3)	5
R H Catterall	1924 (5) 1929 (5)	10
J E Cheetham	1951 (5) 1955 (3)	8
J A J Christy	1929 (2)	2
G W A Chubb	1951 (1)	1
J M M Commaille	1924 (5)	5
R J Crisp	1935 (5)	5
E L Dalton	1929 (1) 1935 (4)	5
O C Dawson	1947 (5)	5
H G Deane	1924 (5) 1929 (5)	10
R Dumbrill	1965 (3)	3
D V Dyer	1947 (3)	3
W R Endean	1951 (1) 1955 (5)	6
G A Faulkner	1907 (3) 1912 (6) * (3 Aus) 1924 (1)	10
J P Fellows-Smith	1960 (1)	1
E R H Fuller	1955 (2)	2
G M Fullerton	1947 (2) 1951 (3)	5
T L Goddard	1955 (5) 1960 (5)	10
G M Griffin	1960 (2)	2
P A M Hands	1924 (1)	1
T A Harris	1947 (2)	2
G P D Hartigan	1912 (2) * (1 Aus)	2
C M H Hathorn	1907 (3)	3
G A L Hearne	1924 (1)	1
P S Heine	1955 (4)	4
H J Keith	1955 (4)	4
J J Kotze	1907 (1)	1
H R Lance	1965 (3)	3
A B C Langton	1935 (5)	5
D T Lindsay	1965 (3)	3
J D Lindsay	1947 (3)	3
C B Llewellyn	1912 (5) * (2 Aus)	5
N B F Mann	1947 (5) 1951 (4)	9
P N F Mansell	1951 (2) 1955 (4)	6

C N McCarthy	1951 (5)	5
D J McGlew	1951 (2) 1955 (5) 1960 (5)	12
A H McKinnon	1960 (1) 1965 (2)	3
R A McLean	1951 (3) 1955 (5) 1960 (5)	13
Q McMillan	1929 (2)	2
M G Melle	1951 (1)	1
A Melville	1947 (5)	5
B Mitchell	1929 (5) 1935 (5) 1947 (5)	15
F Mitchell	1912 (3) * (2 Aus)	3
D P B Morkel	1929 (5)	5
A D Nourse	1935 (4) 1947 (5) 1951 (5)	14
A W Nourse	1907 (3) 1912 (6) * (3 Aus) 1924 (5)	14
E P Nupen	1924 (2)	2
A L Ochse	1929 (2)	2
S O'Linn	1960 (5)	5
H G Owen-Smith	1929 (5)	5
G M Parker	1924 (2)	2
S J Pegler	1912 (6) * (3 Aus) 1924 (5)	11
A J Pithey	1960 (2)	2
J B Plimsoll	1947 (1)	1
P M Pollock	1965 (3)	3
R G Pollock	1965 (3)	3
J E Pothecary	1960 (3)	3
N A Quinn	1929 (4)	4
A M B Rowan	1947 (5) 1951 (5)	10
E A B Rowan	1935 (5) 1951 (5)	10
R O Schwarz	1907 (3) 1912 (3) * (1 Aus)	6
W A Shalders	1907 (3)	3
P W Sherwell	1907 (3)	3
I J Siedle	1929 (3) 1935 (4)	7
J H Sinclair	1907 (3)	3
V I Smith	1947 (4) 1955 (1)	5
S D Snooke	1907 (1)	1
S J Snooke	1907 (3) 1912 (5) * (2 Aus)	8
L A Stricker	1912 (4) * (2 Aus)	4
M J Susskind	1924 (5)	5
L J Tancred	1907 (1) 1912 (4) * (2 Aus)	5
H J Tayfield	1955 (5) 1960 (5)	10
H W Taylor	1912 (6) * (3 Aus) 1924 (5) 1929 (3)	14
D S Tomlinson	1935 (1)	1
L Tuckett	1947 (5)	5
E A van der Merwe	1929 (1)	1
P L van der Merwe	1965 (3)	3
C B van Ryneveld	1951 (5)	5
K G Viljoen	1935 (4) 1947 (5)	9
C L Vincent	1929 (4) 1935 (4)	8
A E E Vogler	1907 (3)	3
H F Wade	1935 (5)	5
J H B Waite	1951 (4) 1955 (5) 1960 (5)	14
T A Ward	1912 (5) * (3 Aus) 1924 (5)	10
C Wesley	1960 (3)	3
G C White	1907 (3) 1912 (5) * (3 Aus)	8
P L Winslow	1955 (3)	3

Key:

* (Aus) = Test Matches played against Australia during 1912 Triangular Series.

Players who toured England 1894-1965 but did not appear in a Test Match for South Africa during their careers.

A V C Bisset	1901
H H Castens	1894
B C Cooley	1901
N S Crookes	1965
D C Davey	1894
S E Horwood	1904
G S Kempis	1894
J D Logan	1901
D M Ovenstone	1947
L W Payn	1947
A Reid	1901
Rev. C D Robinson	1907
C O H Sewell	1894
B Wallach	1904
R J Williams	1935

TEST MATCH AVERAGES OF SOUTH AFRICAN PLAYERS WHO HAVE PLAYED IN TESTS IN ENGLAND 1907-1965

	Tests	Batting and Fielding									Bowling						
		I	NO	HS	Runs	Ave	100	50	Ct	St	Balls	Runs	Wkts	Ave	BB	5wi	10wm
N A T Adcock	26	39	12	24	146	5.40			4		6391	2195	104	21.10	6/43	5	
A Bacher	12	22	1	73	679	32.33		6	10								
X C Balaskas	9	13	1	122*	174	14.50	1		5		1572	806	22	36.63	5/49	1	
E J Barlow	30	57	2	201	2516	45.74	6	15	35		3021	1362	40	34.05	5/85	1	
R Beaumont	5	9	0	31	70	7.77			2		6	0	0				
A J Bell	16	23	12	26*	69	6.27			6		3342	1567	48	32.64	6/99	4	
J M Blanckenberg	18	30	7	59	455	19.78		2	9		3888	1817	60	30.28	6/76	4	
K C Bland	21	39	5	144*	1669	49.08	3	9	10		394	125	2	62.50	2/16		
J T Botten	3	6	0	33	65	10.83			1		828	337	8	42.12	2/56		
H D Bromfield	9	12	7	21	59	11.80			13		1810	599	17	35.23	5/88	1	
H B Cameron	26	45	4	90	1239	30.21		10	39	12							
T Campbell	5	9	3	48	90	15.00			7	1							
P R Carlstein	8	14	1	42	190	14.61		3	3								
C P Carter	10	15	5	45	181	18.10		2			1475	694	28	24.78	6/50	2	
R H Catterall	24	43	2	120	1555	37.92	3	11	12		342	162	7	23.14	3/15		
J E Cheetham	24	43	6	89	883	23.86		5	13		6	2	0				
J A J Christy	10	18	0	103	618	34.33	1	5	3		138	92	2	46.00	1/15		
G W A Chubb	5	9	3	15*	63	10.50					1425	577	21	27.47	6/51	2	
J M M Commaille	12	22	1	47	355	16.90		1	1		1428	747	20	37.35	5/99	1	
R J Crisp	9	13	1	35	123	10.25		3	5		864	490	12	40.83	4/59		
E L Dalton	15	24	2	117	698	31.72	2	3	5		1294	578	10	57.80	2/57		
O C Dawson	9	15	1	55	293	20.92		1	10								
H G Deane	17	27	2	93	628	25.12		3	8								
R Dumbrill	5	10	0	36	153	15.30		1	3		816	336	9	37.33	4/30		
D V Dyer	3	6	0	62	96	16.00		1									
W R Endean	28	52	4	162*	1630	33.95	3	8	41	1							
G A Faulkner	25	47	4	204	1754	40.79	4	8	20		4227	2180	82	26.58	7/84	4	
J P Fellows-Smith	4	8	2	35	166	27.66		2			114	61	0				
E R H Fuller	7	9	1	17	64	8.00			3		1898	668	22	30.36	5/66	1	

TEST MATCH AVERAGES OF SOUTH AFRICAN PLAYERS WHO HAVE PLAYED IN TESTS IN ENGLAND 1907-1965

		Batting and Fielding									Bowling						
	Tests	I	NO	HS	Runs	Ave	100	50	Ct	St	Balls	Runs	Wkts	Ave	BB	5wi	10wm
G M Fullerton	7	13	0	88	325	25.00		3	10	2							
T L Goddard	41	78	5	112	2516	34.46	1	18	48		11736	3226	123	26.22	6/53	5	
G M Griffin	2	4	0	14	25	6.25					432	192	8	24.00	4/87		
P A M Hands	7	12	0	83	300	25.00		2	3		37	18	0				
T A Harris	8	5	1	60	100	25.00		1	1								
G P D Hartigan	5	10	0	51	114	11.40		1			252	141	1	141.00	1/72		
C M H Hathorn	12	20	1	102	325	17.10	1		5								
G A L Hearne	3	5	0	28	59	11.80			3								
P S Heine	14	24	3	31	209	9.95			8		3890	1455	58	25.08	6/58	4	
H J Keith	8	16	1	73	318	21.20		2	9		108	63	0				
J J Kotze	3	5	0	2	2	0.40			3		413	243	6	40.50	3/64		
H R Lance	13	22	1	70	591	28.14		5	7		948	479	12	39.91	3/30		
A B C Langton	15	23	4	73*	298	15.68		2	8		4199	1827	40	45.67	5/58	1	
D T Lindsay	19	31	1	182	1130	37.66	3	5	57	2							
J D Lindsay	3	5	2	9*	21	7.00			4	1							
C B Llewellyn	15	28	1	90	544	20.14		4	7		2292	1421	48	29.60	6/92	4	1
C N McCarthy	15	24	15	5	28	3.11			6		3499	1510	36	41.94	6/43	2	
D J McGlew	34	64	6	255*	2440	42.06	7	10	18		32	23	0				
A H McKinnon	8	13	7	27	107	17.83			1		2546	925	26	35.57	4/128		
R A McLean	40	73	3	142	2120	30.28	5	10	23		4	1	0				
Q McMillan	13	21	4	50*	306	18.00		1	8		2021	1243	36	34.52	5/66	2	
N B F Mann	19	31	1	52	400	13.33		1	3		5796	1920	58	33.10	6/59	1	
P N F Mansell	13	22	2	90	355	17.75		2	15		1506	736	11	66.90	3/58		
M G Melle	7	12	4	17	68	8.50			4		1667	851	26	32.73	6/71	2	
A Melville	11	19	2	189	894	52.58	4	3	8								
B Mitchell	42	80	9	189*	3471	48.88	8	21	56		2519	1380	27	51.11	5/87	1	
F Mitchell	3	6	0	12	28	4.66											
D P B Morkel	16	28	1	88	663	24.55		4	13		1704	821	18	45.61	4/93		
A D Nourse	34	62	7	231	2960	53.81	9	14	12		20	9	0				

TEST MATCH AVERAGES OF SOUTH AFRICAN PLAYERS WHO HAVE PLAYED IN TESTS IN ENGLAND 1907-1965

	Tests	Batting and Fielding									Bowling						
		I	NO	HS	Runs	Ave	100	50	Ct	St	Balls	Runs	Wkts	Ave	BB	5wi	10wm
A W Nourse	45	83	8	111	2234	29.78	1	15	43		3234	1553	41	37.87	4/25		
E P Nupen	17	31	7	69	348	14.50		2	9		4159	1788	50	35.76	6/46	5	1
A L Ochse	3	4	1	4*	11	3.66			1		649	362	10	36.20	4/79		
S O'Linn	7	12	1	98	297	27.00		2	4								
H G O Owen-Smith	5	8	2	129	252	42.00	1	1	4		156	113	0				
G M Parker	2	4	3	2*	3	1.50					366	273	8	34.12	6/152	1	
S J Pegler	16	28	5	35*	356	15.47			5		2989	1572	47	33.44	7/65	2	
A J Pithey	17	27	1	154	819	31.50	1	4	3		12	5	0				
J B Plimsoll	1	2	1	8*	16	16.00					237	143	3	47.66	3/128		
P M Pollock	28	41	13	75*	607	21.67		2	9		6522	2806	116	24.18	6/38	9	1
R G Pollock	23	41	4	274	2256	60.97	7	11	17		414	204	4	51.00	2/50		
J E Pothecary	3	4	0	12	26	6.50			2		828	354	9	39.33	4/58		
N A Quinn	12	18	3	28	90	6.00			1		2922	1145	35	32.71	6/92	1	
A M B Rowan	15	23	6	41	290	17.05			7		5193	2084	54	38.59	5/68	4	
E A B Rowan	26	50	5	236	1965	43.66	3	12	14		19	7	0				
R O Schwarz	20	35	8	61	374	13.85		1	18		2639	1417	55	25.76	6/47	2	
W A Shalders	12	23	1	42	355	16.13			3		48	6	1	6.00	1/6		
P W Sherwell	13	22	4	115	427	23.72	1	1	20	16							
I J Siedle	18	34	0	141	977	28.73	1	5	7		19	7	1	7.00	1/7		
J H Sinclair	25	47	1	106	1069	23.23	3	3	9		3598	1996	63	31.68	6/26	1	
V I Smith	9	16	6	11*	39	3.90			3		1655	769	12	64.08	4/143		
S D Snooke	1	1	0	0	0	0				2							
S J Snooke	26	46	1	103	1008	22.40	1	5	24		1620	702	35	20.05	8/70	1	
L A Stricker	13	24	0	48	342	14.25			3		174	105	1	105.00	1/36		
M J Susskind	5	8	0	65	268	33.50		4	1								
L J Tancred	14	26	1	97	530	21.20		2	3								
H J Tayfield	37	60	9	75	862	16.90		2	26		13568	4405	170	25.91	9/113	14	2
H W Taylor	42	76	4	176	2936	40.77	7	17	19		342	156	5	31.20	3/15		
D S Tomlinson	1	1	0	9	9	9.00					60	38	0				

TEST MATCH AVERAGES OF SOUTH AFRICAN PLAYERS WHO HAVE PLAYED IN TESTS IN ENGLAND 1907-1965

	Tests	Batting and Fielding									Bowling						
		I	NO	HS	Runs	Ave	100	50	Ct	St	Balls	Runs	Wkts	Ave	BB	5wi	10wm
L Tuckett	9	14	3	40*	131	11.90			9		2104	980	19	51.57	5/68	2	
E A van der Merwe	2	4	1	19	27	9.00			3								
P L van der Merwe	15	23	2	76	533	25.38		3	11		79	22	1	22.00	1/6		
C B van Ryneveld	19	33	6	83	724	26.81		3	14		1554	671	17	39.47	4/67		
K G Viljoen	27	50	2	124	1365	28.43	2	9	5		48	23	0				
C L Vincent	25	38	12	60	526	20.23		2	27		5851	2631	84	31.32	6/51	3	
A E E Vogler	15	26	6	65	340	17.00		2	20		2764	1455	64	22.73	7/94	5	1
H F Wade	10	18	2	40*	327	20.43			4								
J H B Waite	50	86	7	134	2405	30.44	4	16	124	17							
T A Ward	23	42	9	64	459	13.90		2	19	13							
C Wesley	3	5	0	35	49	9.80			1								
G C White	17	31	2	147	872	30.06	2	4	10		498	301	9	33.44	4/47		
P L Winslow	5	9	0	108	186	20.66	1	1	1								

SOUTH AFRICA MATCH RECORDS 1894-1965

Opponents	1894	1901	1904	1907	1912	1924	1929
MCC	SA w 11r	MCC w 53r	D / SA w 10w	SA w 3w / MCC w 19r	MCC w 108r	D	D
Scotland	SA w 9w / SA w 132r	SA w i42r / SA w 180r	SA w i188r	SA w i371r / SA w 8w	SA w i97r / SA w i97r	D / SA w i286r	SA w i5r
Minor Counties					D	MCC w 25r	D
Cambridge University		SA w i215r	SA w 70r		SA w 10w	SA w 125r	SA w i119r
Oxford University	D		SA w i97r	D		D	SA w 4w
Derbyshire	D	SA w 9w	D	SA w i108r	SA w 7w	D	D
Durham		SA w 446r		SA w i29r			SA w i60r
Essex	SA w 10w	SA w 132r		SA w i99r / SA w 104r	D	SA w 1w	SA w 327r
Glamorgan						D	SA w 170r / D
Gloucestershire	G w 5w	SA w i105r	D	SA w i38r	SA w 2w	D	G w 6w
Hampshire	D	H w i51r	SA w i19r	D	D	SA w 5w	D
Kent		K w 7w	K w 104r	SA w 2r	D	K w i89r	D
Lancashire		L w 8w	D	SA w i165r	L w 225r / D	L w 178r / D	L w 6w / L w 10w
Leicestershire	SA w 7w	L w 9w	SA w i1r	SA w 98r	SA w 60r	D	D
Middlesex				SA w 278r		SA w i136r	SA w 8w
Northamptonshire		SA w 5w		SA w 83r	D		D
Nottinghamshire		SA w 94r	SA w i49r	N w 5w	D	N w 3w	D
Somerset	S w 9w	S w 341r	SA w i86r	SA w 358r	SA w 52r	SA w 9w	SA w i34r
Surrey	S w 16r	S w 59r	D	S w 85r	SA w 52r / D	D / D	S w 125r / D
Sussex	S w 9w		D	SA w 39r	SA w 4w	D	SA w 217r
Warwickshire	D	W w i69r	SA w 10w	SA w 276 r	SA w 6w	D	D
Worcestershire		T	W w 137r		SA w i42r	SA w i28r	D
Yorkshire		Y w 151r	D / D	SA w 5w	D / D	D / D	D / D

Key: T = Match Tied | D = Drawn | A = Abandoned | SA w 9w = South Africa won by 9 wickets
SA w 11r = South Africa won by 11 runs | SA w i119r = South Africa won by an innings and 119 runs

SOUTH AFRICA MATCH RECORDS 1894-1965

Opponents	1935	1947	1951	1955	1960	1965	P	W	L	D	T	A
MCC	D	MCC w 158r	D	SA w 93r	D		14	4	4	6	0	0
Scotland	D SA w i85r	D	D				16	12	0	4	0	0
Minor Counties	SA w 8w		SA w i23r		SA w 9w	SA w 203r	8	4	1	3	0	0
Cambridge University	SA w i40r	SA w i153r	D	D	SA w 7w		11	8	0	3	0	0
Oxford University	D	D	D	SA w i137r	D		10	3	0	7	0	0
Derbyshire	SA w 209r	SA w 3w	SA w 8w	D	SA w i24r	D w 7w	13	7	1	5	0	0
Durham	SA w i45r			SA w i324r			6	5	0	1	0	0
Essex	E w 7w	SA w 8w	D	D	SA w 6w		11	6	1	4	0	0
Glamorgan	D SA w 96r	SA w i131r SA w 40r	SA w i14r G w 64r	D SA w 226r	SA w i133r SA w 9w	D	16	10	1	5	0	0
Gloucestershire	G w 87r	SA w 133r	D	D	G w 3w		12	4	4	4	0	0
Hampshire	SA w 110r	D	D	SA w 275r	SA w 9w	D	13	5	1	7	0	0
Kent	SA w i138r	SA w 88r	D	SA w 8w	SA w 160r	SA w i147r	12	6	3	3	0	0
Lancashire	D D	D	D	D	D	SA w 166r	16	2	9	5	0	0
Leicestershire	SA w 170r	SA w 10w	SA w 6w	SA w i117r	D	D	13	8	1	4	0	0
Middlesex	SA w 22r	D	D	SA w 235r	D	SA w 5w	11	5	0	5	1	0
Northamptonshire	SA w i35r	SA w i32r	D	D	N w 4w		10	5	1	4	0	0
Nottinghamshire	D	D	D	D	D		11	2	2	7	0	0
Somerset	SA w 51r	SA w i43r	SA w 24r	SA w i32r	SA w i23r		12	9	2	1	0	0
Surrey	SA w 190r SA w 205r	SA w 115r	D	S w 82r	D	D	17	5	4	8	0	0
Sussex	D	D	D	SA w 9w	A	D	11	4	1	6	0	1
Warwickshire	SA w i174r	SA w i114r	D	SA w 10w	D	D	12	6	1	5	0	0
Worcestershire	SA w i166r	W w 39r	D	W w 117r	SA w 133r		10	4	3	2	1	0
Yorkshire	SA w 128r	D	D D	SA w 193r	D	D	17	3	1	13	0	0
TOTAL							282	127	41	112	2	1

Key:

T = Match Tied	D = Drawn	A = Abandoned	SA w 9w = South Africa won by 9 wickets
SA w 11r = South Africa won by 11 runs		SA w i119r = South Africa won by an innings and 119 runs	

GROUNDS USED BY SOUTH AFRICA IN THE UK 1894-1965

Opponents	1894	1901	1904	1907	1912	1924	1929
MCC	Lord's	Lord's	Lord's (2)	Lord's (2)	Lord's	Lord's	Lord's
Scotland	Edinburgh Glasgow	Edinburgh Glasgow	Edinburgh	Glasgow Edinburgh	Glasgow Edinburgh	Edinburgh Glasgow	Perth
Minor Counties					Stoke-on-Trent	Norwich	Stoke-on-Trent
Cambridge University		Fenner's	Fenner's	Fenner's	Fenner's	Fenner's	Fenner's
Oxford University	The Parks		The Parks	The Parks	The Parks	The Parks	The Parks
Derbyshire	Derby	Derby	Derby	Derby	Derby	Derby	Derby
Durham		Darlington		Sunderland		Sunderland	Sunderland
Essex				Leyton (2)	Leyton	Colchester	Leyton
Glamorgan	Arms Park, Cardiff	Arms Park, Cardiff				Arms Park, Cardiff	Pontypridd Swansea
Gloucestershire	Bristol	Clifton	Bristol	Gloucester	Bristol	Bristol	Bristol
Hampshire	Southampton	Southampton	Alton	Southampton	Bournemouth	Southampton	Southampton
Kent		Beckenham	Canterbury	Catford	Maidstone	Canterbury	Canterbury
Lancashire		Old Trafford	Old Trafford	Old Trafford	Liverpool Old Trafford	Old Trafford Liverpool	Old Trafford Liverpool
Leicestershire	Leicester (GR)	Leicester (AR)	Leicester (AR)	Leicester (AR)	Leicester (AR)	Leicester (AR)	Leicester (AR)
Middlesex			Lord's	Lord's	Lord's	Lord's	Lord's
Northamptonshire		Northampton		Northampton	Northampton	Northampton	Northampton
Nottinghamshire		Trent Bridge	Trent Bridge	Trent Bridge	Trent Bridge	Trent Bridge	Trent Bridge
Somerset	Taunton	Taunton	Taunton	Bath	Bath	Taunton	Taunton
Surrey	The Oval	The Oval	The Oval	The Oval	The Oval (2)	The Oval (2)	The Oval (2)
Sussex	Brighton		Brighton	Brighton	Brighton	Brighton	Brighton
Warwickshire	Edgbaston	Edgbaston	Edgbaston	Edgbaston	Edgbaston	Edgbaston	Edgbaston
Worcestershire		Worcester	Worcester		Worcester	Worcester	Worcester
Yorkshire		Harrogate	Hull Scarborough	Bradford	Huddersfield Sheffield (BL)	Sheffield (BL) Bradford	Sheffield (BL) Hull

Key:	(AR) = Aylestone Road	(BL) = Bramall Lane
	(GR) = Grace Road	(2) = Two matches played on the same ground during the tour

GROUNDS USED BY SOUTH AFRICA IN THE UK 1894-1965

Opponents	1935	1947	1951	1955	1960	1965
MCC	Lord's	Lord's	Lord's	Lord's	Lord's	
Scotland	Glasgow Dundee	Paisley	Glasgow			
Minor Counties	Skegness		Norwich	Stoke-on-Trent	Stoke-on-Trent	Jesmond
Cambridge University	Fenner's	Fenner's	Fenner's	Fenner's	Fenner's	
Oxford University	The Parks	The Parks	The Parks	Christ Church, Oxford	The Parks	
Derbyshire	Ilkeston	Derby	Derby	Derby	Derby	Derby
Durham	Sunderland			Sunderland		
Essex	Southend	Southend	Ilford	Colchester	Ilford	Colchester
Glamorgan	Arms Park, Cardiff Swansea	Arms Park, Cardiff Swansea	Arms Park, Cardiff Swansea	Arms Park, Cardiff Swansea	Arms Park, Cardiff Swansea	Swansea
Gloucestershire	Cheltenham (Coll)	Cheltenham (Coll)	Bristol	Cheltenham (Coll)	Bristol	
Hampshire	Southampton	Southampton	Southampton	Southampton	Southampton	Southampton
Kent	Canterbury	Canterbury	Canterbury	Canterbury	Canterbury	Canterbury
Lancashire	Old Trafford Liverpool	Old Trafford	Old Trafford	Old Trafford	Blackpool	Old Trafford
Leicestershire	Leicester (AR)	Leicester (GR)	Leicester (GR)	Leicester (GR)	Leicester (GR)	Leicester (GR)
Middlesex	Lord's	Lord's	Lord's	Lord's	Lord's	Lord's
Northamptonshire	Northampton	Northampton	Northampton	Northampton	Northampton	
Nottinghamshire	Trent Bridge	Trent Bridge	Trent Bridge	Trent Bridge	Trent Bridge	
Somerset	Bath	Taunton	Taunton	Taunton	Taunton	
Surrey	The Oval (2)	The Oval	The Oval	The Oval	The Oval	The Oval
Sussex	Hove	Hove	Hove	Hove	Hove	Hove
Warwickshire	Edgbaston	Edgbaston	Edgbaston	Edgbaston	Edgbaston	Edgbaston
Worcestershire	Worcester	Worcester	Worcester	Worcester	Worcester	
Yorkshire	Sheffield (BL)	Sheffield (BL)	Bradford Sheffield (BL)	Sheffield (BL)	Sheffield (BL)	Sheffield (BL)

Key:

(AR) = Aylestone Road	(BL) = Bramall Lane	(Coll) = College Ground
(GR) = Grace Road	(2) = Two matches played on the same ground during the tour	

BIBLIOGRAPHY

The History of South African Cricket M.W.Luckin 1915
South African Cricket 1919-1927 M.W.Luckin 1928
South African Cricket 1927-1947 Louis Duffus 1948
Wisden Cricketers' Almanack 1895-1966
Cricket: A Weekly Record of the Game 1895-1913
Playfair Cricket Annual 1948-1966
The Protea South African Cricket Annual 1950/51-1966
The Cricketer 1921-1966
Playfair Cricket Monthly 1961-1966
Various County Annuals, Yearbooks, Tour Guides and Brochures

South African Autographs 1907

SOUTH AFRICANS

SOUTH AFRICANS

South African Autographs 1912

together with those of
England, Australia and Yorkshire

Front Row, left to right   R. A. McLean, J. H. B. Waite, R. W. Endean, J. E. Cheetham, D. J. McGlew
P. N. F. Mansell, H. J. Tayfield, A. R. A. Murray

Back Row: C. A. R. Duckworth,   V. I. Smith,   P. L. Winslow,   P. S. Heine,   N. A. T. Adcock
T. L. Goddard, H. J. Keith, E. R. H. Fuller

SOUTH AFRICA

You can obtain several of the illustrations of South African Cricketers in this book direct from the leading publishers of cricket cards in the world today, County Print Services, in a variety of cricket card sets and on postcards.

THE SOUTH AFRICAN
CRICKET TEAM 1894

C. MILLS
WESTERN PROVINCE

SOUTH AFRICAN
CRICKET TEAM, 1907.

L. J. TANCRED.

G. P. D. HARTIGAN
Border

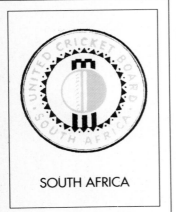

SOUTH AFRICA

South African cards are available for the entire touring teams who visited England in 1894, 1907 and 1912. Other illustrations include South African Test cricketers from the 1950's and 1960's.

For a FREE detailed colour catalogue please write direct to County Print Services, 74 Walden Way, Hainault, Essex IG6 3BJ. Payment can be made by cheque, postal order and all major credit cards.

S. J. COOK